Lawyers of the Right: Professionalizing the Conservative Coalition

CHICAGO SERIES IN LAW AND SOCIETY

Edited by John M. Conley and Lynn Mather

Lawyers of the Right

Professionalizing the Conservative Coalition

ANN SOUTHWORTH

The University of Chicago Press   *Chicago & London*

ANN SOUTHWORTH is a professor of law at the University of California, Irvine, School of Law.

The University of Chicago Press, Chicago 60637
The University of Chicago Press, Ltd., London
© 2008 by The University of Chicago
All rights reserved. Published 2008
Printed in the United States of America

17 16 15 14 13 12 11 10 09 08   1 2 3 4 5

ISBN-13: 978-0-226-76833-5 (cloth)
ISBN-13: 978-0-226-76834-2 (paper)
ISBN-10: 0-226-76833-3 (cloth)
ISBN-10: 0-226-76834-1 (paper)

Library of Congress Cataloging-in-Publication Data

Southworth, Ann.
    Lawyers of the right : professionalizing the conservative coalition / Ann Southworth.
        p. cm. — (Chicago series in law and society)
    Includes bibliographical references and index.
    ISBN-13: 978-0-226-76833-5 (cloth : alk. paper)
    ISBN-10: 0-226-76833-3 (cloth : alk. paper)
    ISBN-13: 978-0-226-76834-2 (pbk. : alk. paper)
    ISBN-10: 0-226-76834-1 (pbk. : alk. paper)   1. Cause lawyers—United States.   2. Law-
yers—United States—Political activity.   3. Conservatism—United States.   I. Title.
    KF299 .P8S66   2008
    344.73—dc22
                                                                                2008012926

To my parents, Ann and George Southworth.

Contents

Preface

Lawyers have contributed greatly to the conservative revolution in American law and politics since the 1970s. Although mistrust of lawyers and legal activism has been one of the unifying grievances of the conservative coalition, lawyers have assumed significant roles in all types of nonprofit organizations through which the conservative movement proceeds, including think tanks, trade associations, advocacy organizations, and conservative "public interest" law firms. Lawyers have founded dozens of new law-related organizations to promote conservative perspectives and to translate those views into public policy and law. They have devised arguments for reshaping law governing the family, religion, education, property, employment, race, civil justice, police power, criminal procedure, trade, and international affairs, and they have sought to implement those changes through legislation and litigation. They have filled the federal courts with conservative jurists and secured a working majority of justices on the U.S. Supreme Court. Their litigation organizations have challenged the political Left's definition of public interest law and set their own aggressive law reform agenda. Much of conservative lawyers' work occurs behind closed doors, but lawyers also are among the most recognizable public spokesmen for conservative causes.

Who *are* the lawyers who pursue the causes of the modern American conservative movement, and how much do they have in common with one another?

The research for this book revealed three broad categories of lawyers who serve conservative legal advocacy groups: social conservatives, libertarians, and business advocates. The following composite profiles capture common traits and values of the lawyers for these key constituencies of the conservative alliance—and sources of division among them.

Lawyer 1 was the first in his family to attend college. He grew up in a small town, far from any major metropolitan area. His father held a working-class job. During college he participated in university Christian fellowship and helped to establish a pro-life group. He decided to attend law school in the mid-1980s, in response to Christian leaders' call for evangelicals to confront the institutions and forces that had removed prayer from the schools and legalized abortion. Once there, however, he felt alienated from his law school classmates, who seemed primarily interested in making money. During a summer, he worked for a newly founded pro-life legal advocacy group. That experience gave him something to believe in and a purpose toward which to direct his legal training. After graduating, he worked for a variety of social conservative groups. He now plays a leading role in pro-life advocacy and other social conservative causes. He participates regularly in a Bible study group and makes most important decisions through prayer. He is active in his conservative evangelical church, and he and his wife homeschool their children.

Lawyer 2 grew up in a large city, where his parents operated a small local retail business. He has been a libertarian ever since high school, when he discovered Ayn Rand. In college, he campaigned for libertarian candidates and was active in several organizations that extol the virtues of capitalism and individual liberty. During law school, he attended a law and economics institute, which inspired him to seek a position after graduation with a newly established libertarian legal advocacy group. He later founded his own litigation organization and today is a leading advocate for libertarian causes. He belongs to a reform synagogue but is not particularly active in it.

Lawyer 3 grew up in a major city. His father was a professional, and he enjoyed a comfortable upper-middle-class upbringing. Well before graduating from college, he decided that he would attend either law or business school. He was not involved in any causes in college or law school. Today, he works in a large corporate firm, where he is a leading advocate for business interests. Although he is comfortable with the positions he takes on behalf of his clients, he views his advocacy as an occupation rather than a cause. He describes himself as fiscal conservative who leans slightly left on social issues. Some of his best friends are Democrats. He is loosely affiliated with a mainstream Protestant church, but he rarely attends services.

When and how might these lawyers cooperate with one another or induce their clients to do so? In what ways, if any, do such lawyers and their organizations influence the fortunes of the conservative movement? These are the central questions of this book.

Acknowledgments

I am indebted to the seventy-two lawyers and other "informants" who allowed me to interview them. They sacrificed valuable time—in some cases, much more than the hour I requested—to help me understand their work, backgrounds, values, careers, and networks.

Dozens of scholars gave me useful advice on pieces of the manuscript. I would particularly like to thank Nomi Stolzenberg, Rebecca Sandefur, Scott Cummings, David Wilkins, Andrew Kaufman, Ernest Young, Jonathan Adler, Gary Simson, and Malcolm Feeley, and participants in workshops at Case Western Reserve Law School, Northwestern University's Institute for Policy Research, Harvard Law School, UCLA Law School, Southwestern Law School, Loyola Law School, University of California, Berkeley's Center for the Study of Law and Society, University of Southern California School of Law, Chapman University School of Law, and annual meetings of the American Society for Legal History and the Law and Society Association.

Case Western Reserve University School of Law, the American Bar Foundation, and Harvard Law School gave me essential research support. Carol Tyler Fox, Ronald Page, Jefferson Bell, Lynda Vaughn, John Weber, Deborah Dennison, Andrew Dorchak, and Marcia Lehr provided invaluable research assistance. Catherine Zaccarine created the figures.

Several people played especially large roles in helping me complete the book. John Tryneski, the editorial director for Social Sciences and Paperback Publishing, University of Chicago Press, first advised me about the project when we met in a taxicab line in 2005, and he provided steady direction throughout the review and publication process. Series coeditor

Lynn Mather patiently reviewed an extremely ragged early draft and thereafter read and commented on two more versions. Jack Heinz offered regular doses of wisdom and encouragement. Series coeditor John Conley, outside reviewers for the University of Chicago Press, and four immensely generous colleagues—Richard Abel, Bryant Garth, Jack Heinz, and Anthony Paik—gave me comments on the entire manuscript. Sharon Brinkman was my superb copyeditor.

Above all, I am grateful to my husband, John Weissenbach, and my children, Amy and Ben, who gave me the time and space I needed to write the book while also keeping me enmeshed in important worlds beyond it.

The manuscript includes some material adapted from previously published work. Chapter 2 draws from "Conservative Lawyers and the Contest over the Meaning of 'Public Interest Law'" (2005). Chapter 4 draws from an essay in *The Worlds Cause Lawyers Make.* Chapter 3 devotes several pages to findings from Heinz, Paik, and Southworth (2003). Figures 6.1–6.3 and their analyses come from Paik, Southworth, and Heinz (2007).

1

Introduction

This book provides a window into the world of lawyers for conservative causes and probes the little discussed cultural conflict among them. It shows how lawyers for the various constituencies of the conservative alliance established highly specialized legal advocacy organizations to challenge the Left's vision of lawyers' proper roles and to reshape public policy. It analyzes their characteristics, values, professional identities, and strategies and the extent to which they, and the organizations they serve, operate as a coordinated whole.

Lawyers are generally understood to hold privileged and especially influential positions in American public policy formation. They play dominant roles in courts, agencies, and legislatures, and they shape other aspects of the policy landscape through service to organizational clients. Scholars have produced a large store of research about lawyers who devote themselves to causes of the political left, but lawyers who serve causes of the Right have drawn relatively little attention. Lee Epstein and Karen O'Connor examined conservative interest groups' use of the courts in the early 1980s (Epstein 1985; O'Connor and Epstein 1983), and Oliver Houck addressed the propriety of charitable status for public interest law firms that served business interests (Houck 1984). Several more recent studies have analyzed litigation campaigns by the Christian Right (Brown 2002; den Dulk 2001, 2006; Hacker 2005; Krishnan and den Dulk 2002); the commitments of property rights advocates (Bisharat 1998; Hatcher 2005); the organizational history of the conservative law movement (Teles 2008); and the structure of conservative legal advocacy (Heinz, Paik, and Southworth 2003; Southworth 2005; cf. Nielsen and Albiston 2006). But causes of the political left continue to receive the lion's share of scholarly attention. This book is intended to help right the balance.

The lawyers examined here serve several strands of the conservative alliance that has coalesced behind the Republican Party during the past few decades. Most prominent among those elements are social conservatives, libertarians, and business interests. These constituencies pursue competing and sometimes contradictory goals (Himmelstein 1990, 14; Hodgson 1996, 158–59; Nash 1998, xv–xvi). Religious conservatives seek to overturn *Roe v. Wade,* to defend traditional social arrangements, and to reshape the balance between religious and secular values in public life. They are prepared to use federal governmental power to advance these goals, and they insist on judicial nominees who publicly commit to them. Other conservatives seek to stem immigration and protect the culture of America's middle class. Libertarians try to bolster property rights and personal liberty and generally resist government regulation, especially controls designed to enforce personal virtue. Business leaders pursue favorable trade policies, tort reform, tax cuts, and restrictions on union activity, and they sometimes pursue federal fixes to promote uniformity and predictability. The diversity of policy positions encompassed within today's conservative coalition reflects the fundamental challenge of winning American elections in a two-party system. Gary Miller and Norman Schofield (2003, 249) have observed that "successful American parties must be coalitions of enemies" and that "maintaining such diverse majority coalitions is necessarily an enormous struggle against strong centrifugal forces." Despite their differences, these diverse constituencies have formed a successful and enduring coalition in American politics since the late 1960s. Throughout the book, I refer to these constituencies collectively as the "conservative coalition" or the "conservative alliance."

One might expect lawyers to influence the likelihood of cooperation among the different parts of the conservative alliance. Indeed, lawyers may be among a relatively small set of occupational groups—along with politicians, public intellectuals, political patrons, and perhaps religious leaders and journalists—who are well positioned to play such an integrative role. Lawyers' common characteristics and experiences—membership in one profession, shared educational backgrounds and professional socialization, common understanding about the relationship between law and politics, and shared occupational interests (Halliday 1987, 47–51; Heinz et al. 2003)—might draw them together and link the constituencies they serve. They might tend to steer their client organizations toward litigation and other mainstream political strategies at the expense of radical tactics, and they might use their dominance in those policy arenas to help control and coordinate the conservative movement. Alternatively, lawyers for conservative causes could be sharply divided along the lines of the interests they represent and thus contribute little to the movement's integration. One of this book's purposes is to assess the likelihood of these competing possibilities. Are the alliances and divisions of American electoral politics also reflected in the social structure of conservative and libertarian legal advocacy? Are the lawyers for the various constituencies similar in social background, educational experience, outlook, and roles with respect to the causes they serve? If not, do they nevertheless see themselves as part of a larger conservative movement, or as coventurers in a common professional enterprise? Do they even *like* one another?

This book will show that there are striking differences among the lawyers who serve the primary constituencies of the conservative coalition. Lawyers who work for social conservative groups have little in common with lawyers for large business interests. They work on different issues for different clients in different practice settings, and they are divided by social characteristics, educational background, values, geography, and professional identity. Lawyers for libertarian causes form a distinct block but share attributes and commitments with lawyers for the other primary constituencies. The divisions are not only among different constituencies but also between different strata of lawyers—lawyers whose elite status links them to the establishment and true believers who generally lack those ties.

If lawyers for the core constituencies come from different social backgrounds and hold different political commitments and professional identities, what social forces and institutions, if any, bring them together? This book considers experiences, interests, and organizations that may help forge common ground among lawyers who are divided by ideology, geography, and class. It focuses particularly on lawyers' shared interest in promoting strategies in which they play leading roles and on the function of "mediator" organizations, which seek to appeal to all constituencies of the conservative alliance and to promote communication and cooperation among them.

This book draws primarily from semistructured interviews conducted in 2001 and 2002 with seventy-two lawyers for conservative and libertarian nonprofit organizations. The interviews grew out of a project that I have pursued jointly with John P. Heinz of the American Bar Foundation and Northwestern University and Anthony Paik of the University of Iowa. To define the set of lawyers to study, we drew a sample of conservative nongovernmental organizations, using several complementary methods. I requested interviews with ninety-eight prominent lawyers for these organizations and interviewed seventy-two of them. The appendix describes the research design.

The interviewed lawyers included many of the best-known lawyers of the conservative movement, representing all of the major constituencies. They worked for conservative religious groups, abortion opponents, libertarian organizations, groups devoted primarily to business interests, affirmative action opponents, "order-maintenance" groups (that is, organizations concerned with crime and/or preserving the established social and cultural order), and mediator organizations. The lawyers served these organizations in various roles: as organizers, officers, litigators, scholars, and consultants. The largest number were located in Washington, D.C., but others practiced in Virginia, New York, California, Arizona, Illinois, and several other Midwestern states. Eighteen of the interviewed lawyers had previously served in Republican administrations, and several of them accepted government positions after the interviews were completed. The overwhelming majority of the lawyers were committed Republicans, but, as explored in chapter 5, some expressed considerable ambivalence about the GOP. I assured the interviewed lawyers that I would not reveal their identities. Therefore, this book uses the contents of the interviews without attributing them to specific individuals.

My purpose in writing this book was to portray lawyers of the conservative coalition rather than to evaluate their causes. Therefore, I have presented these lawyers' accounts without critiquing them or taking sides in the public policy battles in which the lawyers participate. Lawyers' self-reports may be unreliable sources of information about the lawyers' conduct and the events in which they participate, but they provide telling evidence of lawyers' values, attitudes, and perceptions of role.

Throughout the book, I use the term "conservative" as it is commonly used in American political discourse to describe the various strands of the uneasy coalition that has united behind the Republican Party in the past few decades (Gottfried 1993; Nash 1996). The label applies to the causes pursued by the organizations for which these lawyers worked rather than the views or positions of the lawyers themselves, and it refers to policy positions associated with the conservative movement, without assessing whether those positions are really "conservative" in intellectual or philosophical terms. Most of the interviewed lawyers embraced the "conservative" designation, but a few of them rejected any association with conservative ideals. Several libertarians urged me to describe this as a study of lawyers for conservative and *libertarian* causes and to distinguish carefully between them. Several business lawyers emphasized that they did not view themselves or their purposes as conservative; they stressed their commitment to clients rather than causes and their self-image as political moderates rather than hard-liners. A few religious lawyers also sought to distance themselves from conservatism. A Catholic pro-life advocate, for example, emphasized that his organization took liberal positions on most economic issues, and a lawyer who worked for a group that sought to promote religious expression in the public sphere asserted that his organization was arguably "more pro-liberty and pro-human rights" than the American Civil Liberties Union. Taking these objections into account, I nevertheless use the term "conservative" advisedly throughout the book to refer to the diverse constituencies that have coalesced behind the Republican Party, while recognizing—indeed, dwelling upon—their differences and disagreements.

This book focuses on lawyers for conservative causes, not the smaller set of "cause lawyers" within the coalition. By definition, cause lawyers pursue causes they believe in; they do not select work in order to burnish their reputations or to serve their financial goals (Sarat and Scheingold 2005). This analytical category, then, turns on motivation, which is notoriously difficult to assess. Much of the literature on cause lawyers simply assumes that lawyers who serve particular causes and work in certain types of practices must be cause lawyers. But lawyers' motivations sometimes may be mixed; they may pursue work for reasons that include both ideological elements and more crass and mundane concerns. Moreover, lawyers with impure purposes sometimes contribute substantially to social movements (Shamir and Chinsky 1998). Therefore, this book treats professional identity as an issue to be explored (see chapter 4) and not one that can be assumed from lawyers' practice settings, types of clients served, causes pursued, or strategies employed.

The following chapters describe how conservative lawyers have tried to "right the profession and professionalize the right"—to make the legal profession more conservative while also giving lawyers more significant roles in the conservative movement—and how differences among lawyers of the conservative coalition threaten that common objective. Chapter 2 traces how conservative and libertarian lawyers have created dozens of legal advocacy organizations in the image of public interest organizations of the political left and how these groups have strengthened, sharpened, and institutionalized ideas that had not previously succeeded in shaping law and public policy. It shows how elite lawyers have lent respectability to the conservative movement as they have assumed leading roles, but it also suggests that they have jeopardized the standing of the rank and file and exacerbated tensions within the movement. Chapter 3 explores how lawyers for the two core constituencies of the conservative alliance—social conservatives and business lawyers—come from different backgrounds and places. It offers portraits of leading lawyers for the different constituencies, identifying what they have in common but also considering sources of disagreement and mistrust. Chapter 4 examines the major differences in the professional identities of lawyers for business interests and other types of conservative and libertarian constituencies, showing that the former are more likely than the latter to view their roles in conventional professional terms. Chapter 5 addresses possible sources of ties among lawyers of the conservative coalition, considering whether those elements of common ground are likely to overcome the substantial differences identified in chapters 3 and 4. It concludes that those factors, even in combination, may be less powerful than forces of professional stratification. Chapter 6 investigates the substantial investment made by conservative foundations and individual philanthropists in "mediator" organizations, which seek to hold this unlikely alliance together and to tame its more radical elements. It focuses on two particularly prominent and influential groups that attempt to integrate lawyers—the Federalist Society for Law and Public Policy and the Heritage Foundation. Chapter 7 considers what types of work lawyers of the conservative coalition perform and how they view the relationship between law and the causes they serve. It shows that while these lawyers mix strategies in different proportions, they all share a broad view of policy formation in which litigation and legislation are significant but not exclusive elements. These lawyers also appear to share the confidence that they play—and should play—important roles in the causes they serve. In the arena in which lawyers exercise greatest control—the courts—their constituencies generally have avoided open conflict. Finally, chapter 8 considers the present status of conservative lawyers' campaign to push the legal profession rightward and to translate conservative impulses into law and policy. It concludes that lawyers for conservative causes have succeeded in many respects but that tensions between the movement's elite and populist elements may contain the seeds of the conservative law movement's undoing. It identifies several recent major brawls within the Republican coalition—over Harriet Miers's Supreme Court nomination, the firing of U.S. Attorneys, the Department of Justice's hiring and promotion practices, and the Bush Administration's treatment of detainees in the War on Terror—and considers how each reflects not only deep policy disagreements among the strands of the conservative alliance but also conflict among its lawyers over professional values.

2

The Creation of an Infrastructure for Conservative Legal Advocacy

This book is primarily about lawyers who serve the conservative coalition and what brings them together and drives them apart. But it is difficult to understand these lawyers and their influence within the conservative coalition without some background about the movement they are a part of and the organizations they serve. This chapter, therefore, sets the stage. It considers how lawyers responded to the challenge posed by the liberal "public interest law" movement, not only by trying to weaken and discredit it, but also by establishing a vibrant and diverse set of parallel institutions—a "support structure" (Epp 1998) for conservative legal advocacy. It explores how "institutional entrepreneurs" (Nownes and Neeley 1996; Rao 1998; Salisbury 1969) competed for resources, sparred among themselves and with their liberal opponents over the meaning of public interest law, and established a specialized set of institutions serving all constituencies of the conservative coalition. Conservative lawyers adopted not only the institutional form of public interest law but also the notion that idealistic young lawyers should play leading roles in a social movement. They would serve as the advocates for conservative causes in the courts but also as chief strategists and spokesmen. As the movement matured, an elaborate set of connections among foundations, advocacy organizations, law schools, and Republican administrations gave ambitious lawyers opportunities to build successful careers around service to conservative ideals.

The creation of a field of conservative legal advocacy organizations during the past three decades was just part of a larger phenomenon of conservative institution building that began around the time of Barry

Goldwater's failed 1964 presidential bid. That campaign was "the first political expression of a rising conservative movement" whose intellectual roots lay in the work of traditionalists, classical liberal economists, and anticommunists (Smith 1991, 167–89). Despite substantial contradictions among these currents, they came together in opposition to the liberal establishment, which conservatives blamed for Goldwater's overwhelming defeat. This powerful coalition united behind the task of building a conservative "counter-establishment" to win hearts and minds for conservative ideas, just as the Brookings Institution and other intellectual centers supported by the Ford and Rockefeller Foundations had won support for the view that an activist federal government would promote national progress (Blumenthal 1986). Conservatives invested in existing organizations, such as the Hoover Institution and the American Enterprise Institute, as well as new ones, such as the Heritage Foundation, the Institute for Contemporary Studies, the Cato Institute, and dozens of other think tanks, policy institutions, and media outlets (Smith 1991; Stefancic and Delgado 1996). This trend accelerated in the mid to late 1970s, as a weak economy and corporate resistance to regulation and government deficits prompted business to increase its support for conservative policy organizations (Ferguson and Rogers 1986, 78–113; Morgan 1981). The law and economics movement, with substantial funding from the Olin Foundation, brought Chicago-style economic analysis to law graduates and judges and promoted research that generally favored markets and opposed government intervention (Duxbury 1995, 330–419; Dezalay and Garth 2002, 276–77). Southern opponents of desegregation and Northern opponents of school busing marshaled resources to fight court-mandated racial integration. Catholic advocacy organizations mobilized to oppose abortion and to support state aid to parochial schools (Byrnes and Segers 1992; den Dulk 2001). Evangelical Protestants organized around a variety of social issues, including family, education, and the relationship between church and state, through a network of fundamentalist churches, television preachers, and private Christian schools (Himmelstein 1990, 97–128; Soper 1994; Liebman and Wuthnow 1983). Together, these strands of conservatives built an organizational infrastructure to challenge what they perceived as the liberal consensus (Hodgson 1996; Nash 1998).

This chapter focuses on one aspect of that larger effort—the evolution of "conservative public interest law." It considers how conservative law organizations articulated and institutionalized ideas about law and policy that had not previously prevailed and gave lawyers prominent roles in framing, promoting, and implementing those positions. That process did not unfold smoothly. It began with a set of organizations that were parochial, unsophisticated, and largely ineffectual—no match for the liberal public interest groups they sought to check. Since then, however, lawyers have established a more professional and effective set of institutions targeting all policy-making arenas. They have developed a dynamic and influential network of advocates committed to moving law and policy to the right. These lawyer organizations and networks play powerful roles in setting and implementing American public policy.

A NEW ORGANIZATIONAL FORM:
PUBLIC INTEREST LAW FIRMS

Conservatives have a long history of organized advocacy in the U.S. courts—for example,, to oppose union activity, immigration, women's suffrage, federal aid, and the New Deal (Epstein 1985, 16–44; Lipset 1986). But the conservative public interest law movement, which began to coalesce in the 1970s, was primarily a response to liberal public interest law organizations and the legal and social changes these groups fostered. A small band of lawyers, dubbed "the new public interest lawyers" in a 1970 *Yale Law Journal* article, created intense interest in an alternative model of legal practice through which lawyers would speak for constituencies whose interests were not adequately protected through the market for legal services. These public interest organizations and their lawyers, in turn, drew from earlier models (Houck 1984; Rabin 1976), including the American Civil Liberties Union (ACLU), which represented political and religious dissenters, and the National Association for the Advancement of Colored People Legal Defense Fund (LDF), which campaigned to dismantle racial segregation (Walker 1990; Tushnet 1987). They distinguished themselves from their predecessors, however, by pursuing broader issue agendas and expanding the range of strategies beyond constitutional litigation to other types of law reform litigation and administrative and legislative advocacy. While the ACLU and LDF pursued the interests of relatively powerless minorities, the new public interest law groups would vindicate the interests of diffuse majorities (Heineman 1974). And unlike the ACLU and LDF, which in their early years relied heavily on volunteers to supplement their small professional staffs, the new public interest law groups would use foundation grants to support full-time employed counsel. This change allowed public interest lawyers to develop highly specialized expertise, develop ongoing monitoring relationships with agencies, and compete effectively with opponents represented by large private law firms (Rabin 1976, 232–33).

Public interest lawyers maintained that new types of organizations were needed to respond to pluralism's deficiencies (Halpern and Cunningham 1971, 1098). Consumer advocate Ralph Nader and his comrades claimed to speak for ordinary citizens with a stake in the decisions of unresponsive corporate and government bureaucracies (Buckhorn 1972, 154–55; Nader 1978). Charles Halpern, cofounder of the Center for Law and Social Policy (CLASP), argued that corporations were concerned primarily with "production, profit and the maintenance of power," while regulatory agencies charged with holding corporations accountable to other social values had "proven too limited in resources, too remote from grassroots concerns, and too amenable to political influence to accomplish their task adequately" (Halpern and Cunningham 1971, 1097). Public interest law groups would open administrative processes to the citizens they were supposed to benefit. They would give citizen activists "direct and significant participation in the central decision making process of the corporations and bureaucracies," with recourse to administrative hearings and the courts where such access was denied (Halpern and Cunningham, 1097–98).

The public interest law movement was based in a strong critique of the legal profession—the view that lawyers' conceptions of professionalism aligned their duties with their economic self-interest (Halpern and Cunningham 1971, 1102–3; Nader 1969b; Wexler 1970). The very label "public interest lawyer" asserted moral superiority over attorneys who represented private clients in conventional practices. Indeed, Nader baldly claimed that most lawyers, in most of their work, undermined the public interest (Nader 1969b). Halpern argued that government lawyers could not be trusted to promote citizen participation in agency proceedings and that "private practice, committed as it was almost exclusively to corporate interests, provided little hope for administrative reform" (Halpern and Cunningham 1971, 1103). This challenge to traditional practice norms briefly appeared to threaten the stream of top law school graduates into large law firms (Reinhold 1969; Smith 1971). One observer described it as part of a "modern legal revolution"—a "potentially . . . devastating" challenge to "lawyers' concepts of who they are and thus to the plush and prestigious world many of them inhabit" (Riley 1970). It contradicted the professional elite's position that lawyers advanced the public interest through their work for clients (Auerbach 1976, 277–81), their efforts to reconcile clients' objectives with the purposes of the legal framework (Gordon 1988, 23–24), and their direct engagement in public service (Smigel 1964, 8–9; Gordon 1990, 267–75).

Liberals established dozens of public interest law organizations in the late 1960s and early 1970s (Borosage 1970, 1112; Epstein 1985, 119–20; O'Connor and Epstein 1989, 37–39). Some legal services programs, departing from the model provided by legal aid organizations of the late nineteenth and early twentieth centuries, adopted a mission of law reform (Johnson 1974; Katz 1982, 136–59). By 1976, there were over ninety public interest law organizations employing more than six hundred attorneys (Council for Public Interest Law 1976, 2–3), many of them supported by the Ford Foundation (Dezalay and Garth 2001, 360). Law schools forged ties to these organizations, and public interest groups recruited large numbers of elite law school graduates (Kalman 1996, 43–59; Komesar and Weisbrod 1978, 80, 83). Benefiting from a receptive judiciary and from looser standards regarding standing, ripeness, sovereign immunity, and private rights of action, public interest law groups achieved highly publicized successes in the courts, administrative agencies, and legislatures. These organizations, lawyers, and patrons provided an essential "support structure" for America's "rights revolution" (Epp 1998).

Galvanized by the achievements of this new breed of lawyers and their organizations, conservatives mobilized to respond. Some attacked the premises of the movement, arguing that public interest law undermined democratic processes by replacing the decisions of elected officials with edicts from "activist judges" (e.g., Glazer 1975). Indeed, the primary justification for public interest groups of the Left—that they provided access to interests that were not adequately represented in the judicial and administrative systems (Rabin 1976, 230; Stewart 1975, 1764)—drew criticism from across the political spectrum (e.g., Rabkin 1985, 342; Stewart 1975, 1764; cf. Hegland 1971, 807–8). Some critics, including many religious conservatives (den Dulk 2001; Glendon 1991), also rejected the rights discourse of public interest law. Conservatives launched a long-term campaign to discredit the movement, to eliminate or reduce funding for its organizations, and to restrict the range of strategies available to its lawyers.

But conservatives also jumped into the public interest law game by creating a new set of institutions to represent competing interests. They created their own organizations with similar form and opposing mission—to "support a conservative or right-wing agenda" (Hueter 1986, 64). One of the interviewed lawyers remarked that "all these liberal litigating organizations are out there bringing citizen suits . . . and the idea was to take a leaf from their book and start conservative litigating organizations that would bring lawsuits from their side of the spectrum." The founder of one conservative group explained, "[W]e decided not to become an enemy of the public interest law movement, but to become a part of [it] . . . ," and another observed that liberal public interest law firms were "extremely successful" and that "conservatives tried to replicate that." The new conservative groups would be "public interest's alternate form" and would complement the work of "traditional" public interest law organizations by completing the ideological continuum (Popeo 1981). Not incidentally, this "representation" rationale was essential to claims by the new conservative law groups that they qualified as public charities to which contributions were tax deductible.[1]

The proliferation of conservative public interest law groups over the past three decades is consistent with a recent literature on "institutional isomorphism," which analyzes how institutional forms persist over time (DiMaggio and Powell 1983; Rao et al. 2000) and how organizational entrepreneurs in one field adopt models from others (Armstrong 2002; Clemens 1993). It also demonstrates the political significance of the social meanings attached to organizational forms. As Elisabeth Clemens observed in her study of women's adaptation of voluntary associations for political ends between 1890 and 1920, "models of organizations are not only conventions for coordinating action but also statements of what it means for certain people to organize in certain ways for certain purposes" (Clemens 1993, 775). By embracing the organizational form and rhetoric of the public interest movement, conservatives engaged in a form of "legitimacy politics" (Stryker 1994). Public interest law carried an association with lawyer idealism and devotion to the public good, qualities not generally associated with the conservative movement. The investment in conservative public interest law groups reflected a critical strategic decision to enlist lawyers—especially idealistic and ambitious young lawyers—to help articulate the conservative agenda and lend it credibility.

Lawyers were the principal founders and leaders of conservative public interest law organizations, but they received critical support from business leaders, who organized in the 1970s to respond to a spate of new regulatory legislation (Silk and Vogel 1976; Walker 1983); clergy, who reacted to civil liberties groups' success in relaxing abortion laws and imposing stricter boundaries between church and state (Blanchard 1994, 22–36; den Dulk 2001); and other conservative activists, who resisted liberalized criminal laws, busing, the Equal Rights Amendment, and affirmative action (Diamond 1995, 66–91). Crucial resources came from foundations committed to supporting conservative causes and from an emerging policy research network capable of translating conservative and libertarian ideas into legislative and litigation campaigns (Allen 1992; Jenkins 1987). Individual conservative patrons also provided substantial financial backing—men such as Joseph Coors, John Olin, Charles Keating, and Richard Mellon Scaife. Public figures, such as Irving Kristol, Nathan Glazer, and Francis Schaeffer, and magazines, such as *The Public Interest, Commentary,* and *Christianity Today,* challenged the connection between liberalism and the public interest and helped to legitimate the positions that conservative law groups advocated.

Thus, various leaders and patrons supplied resources that were essential for the success of the new conservative public interest law groups. But lawyers were critical to the effort. They were the primary organizers of these groups; they initiated the enterprises, sold their ideas to members and/or patrons, and built programs around these organizational missions.[2] They also had a distinctive stake in their success. The moral activism that liberal public interest lawyers posed as the alternative to standard practice norms supported causes that many conservative lawyers rejected. Some conservative lawyers were outraged that liberal elites had managed to equate lawyer idealism with social change on behalf of groups favored by the Democratic Party. Conservative public interest law groups would vindicate the notion that conservatives, like liberals, could field a cadre of principled crusaders. They would also enhance lawyers' status and influence within the conservative movement.

THE EARLY CONSERVATIVE PUBLIC INTEREST GROUPS

The mobilization of conservatives to counter the influence of left legal activists began with several groups that claimed to speak for diffuse constituencies associated primarily with populist elements. In 1957, for example, Charles Keating founded Citizens for Decency through Law to pressure law enforcement officials to enforce obscenity laws (Epstein 1985, 80). Americans for Effective Law Enforcement (AELE) was established in 1966, the year of the U.S. Supreme Court's decision in *Miranda v. Arizona,* which held that criminal suspects must be informed of their right to counsel and their right against self-incrimination before questioning by police. The organization sought to provide an "'organized voice' for law-abiding citizens" (AELE 2004) and to respond to the ACLU's success in liberalizing criminal laws during the Warren Court years (Epstein

1985, 89). The National Right to Work Committee founded a Legal Defense Foundation in 1968 to handle legal work tied to its opposition to compulsory unionism (Epstein 1985, 48–49). Catholic organizations began sponsoring right-to-life advocacy around the same time (den Dulk 2001, 45–47).

The first groups to call themselves conservative public interest law organizations appeared in the mid-1970s. The counterattack began with business-oriented firms soon after the release of the Powell memorandum, which warned that "the American economic system is under broad attack" (Powell 1971). Delivered to the U.S. Chamber of Commerce by Lewis Powell shortly before his appointment to the U.S. Supreme Court, the memo identified Ralph Nader as "[p]erhaps the single most effective antagonist of American business." It argued that "the time has come—indeed, it is long overdue—for the wisdom, ingenuity and resources of American business to be marshaled against those who would destroy it." Powell claimed that American business had paid too little attention to litigation, where "the most active exploiters . . . have been groups ranging in political orientation from 'liberal' to the far left." He urged business to take a more aggressive stance "in all political arenas," but especially the courts: "[t]he judiciary may be the most important instrument for social, economic and political change" (Powell 1971, 8).

The Powell memorandum contemplated that the U.S. Chamber of Commerce would become the primary representative of American business in the courts and agencies, and his proposal eventually led to the creation of the National Chamber Litigation Center in 1977 (Epstein 1985, 59–60). Several years earlier, however, groups that styled themselves as conservative public interest law organizations began to emerge with support from a few foundations and businesses (Houck 1984, 1456). In 1973, Ronald Zumbrun, an attorney who had participated in a task force convened by Edwin Meese III to implement welfare reform under then California Governor Ronald Reagan (Bisharat 1998a, 13–14), worked with the California Chamber of Commerce and other government lawyers to establish the Pacific Legal Foundation (Edwards 2004; Weinstein 1975, 39). By 1978, six more firms had been created under the auspices of an umbrella group, the National Legal Center for the Public Interest: Southeastern Legal Foundation, in Atlanta; Mid-America Legal Foundation, in Chicago; Gulf and Great Plains Legal Foundation (renamed Landmark Legal Foundation in the mid-1980s) in Kansas City; Mountain States Legal Foundation, in Denver; the Mid-Atlantic Legal Foundation (now the Atlantic Legal Foundation), in Philadelphia; and the Capital Legal Foundation, in Washington,

D.C. (Singer 1979, 2056). Several independent conservative public interest law groups also appeared around this time, including the New England Legal Foundation and the Washington Legal Foundation (O'Connor and Epstein 1989, 163).

In the 1970s, religious conservatives began to produce their own public interest law firms. The Catholic League for Religious and Civil Rights was founded in 1973 to protect the rights of Catholics to participate in public life. In 1976, Americans United for Life, a nonsectarian educational organization, established its own Legal Defense Foundation to serve as the legal arm of the pro-life movement (Epstein 1985, 94–99). The first Protestant evangelical group to litigate was the Center for Law and Religious Freedom, founded in 1975 to address First Amendment issues and promote state accommodation of religious beliefs (O'Connor and Epstein 1989, 51). Evangelical groups initially focused primarily on defending private religious schools from government interference (Krishnan and den Dulk 2002, 251). But, in the mid-1980s, they launched litigation to fight abortion and promote greater religious expression in the public sphere, especially in the public schools (Brown 2002; den Dulk 2001, 249–51).

The new conservative organizations claimed to defend and advance the interests of their own favorite underrepresented constituencies. Raymond Momboisse, a founder of the Pacific Legal Foundation, said that his organization represented "the free enterprise system and the little guy" (Singer 1979, 2054). Daniel Popeo, who created the Washington Legal Foundation, described his group's constituents as "consumers, workers, unions, property owners as well as property seekers, the victims of crime, and the victims of unfair labor practices" (Popeo 1981). A lawyer who helped establish another of the first conservative public interest law firms said, "Some groups . . . in the established movements chose the environmental field. Others chose welfare as a field. Others chose poverty law as a field, and so forth. So we staked out a claim initially to taxpayers and small businessmen and jobs creation and things like this as our field of public interest law." John Whitehead, the founder of the Rutherford Institute, one of the first evangelical law organizations, explained that "Christians and other religious people need an advoca[cy] group that will fight for their causes, just like [sic] the ACLU fights for their[s]" (Whitehead 1999, 147–48).

Conservatives also challenged the suggestion sometimes made by liberal public interest law groups that the *positions* they took reflected the public interest. One lawyer interviewed for this project said, "That was

[Charles Halpern's] arrogance—to think that the liberal [perspective represented] the public interest." The founder of another conservative lawyer group claimed that liberal public interest firms represented "extreme viewpoints." Dan Burt, the president and director of the Capital Legal Foundation asserted, "Despite their 'public interest' motto, ... most of these groups have a particular political ideology, a set agenda for economic, political and social change, and limited constituencies. They are, in fact, *special interest* groups and no different from any other group that attempts to lobby public opinion and garner governmental support for a particular cause. Their use of the 'public interest' label is a ruse and a disguise" (Burt 1982, 133). Daniel Popeo said of his reasons for establishing the Washington Legal Foundation, "For too long, the Ralph Naders and the Jane Fondas of this world have had unlimited license to say what the public interest is" (*Forbes* 1980, 86).

The new conservative groups mimicked the conventions and tactics of the "traditional" public interest firms, but their purposes and approaches differed in important respects. Like their liberal counterparts, they emphasized litigation and administrative advocacy. But liberal public interest law organizations resorted to the courts to redress their constituencies' political disadvantage in other arenas (Vose 1959; Sorauf 1976), while conservative firms were primarily a response to liberals' successes in courts and administrative agencies (Epstein 1985, 656). One conservative founder said that his organization sought to "change the psychology" of government regulators who otherwise might be tempted to adopt positions advocated by left activists to avoid lawsuits. Groups such as his, he said, would show regulators that "whichever way I rule, I'm going to be sued." In contrast to liberal firms, which frequently initiated lawsuits in the 1960s and 1970s, conservatives participated primarily as amicus curiae (O'Connor and Epstein 1983, 480–82). Like the liberal organizations, which relied heavily on the Ford and Rockefeller Foundations (Handler 1978, 42, 47; Rabin 1976, 210–29), the first conservative public interest law firms drew financial support from a few foundations, including the John M. Olin and Sarah Scaife Foundations and the J. Howard Pew Freedom Trust (Aron 1989, 77). Unlike their liberal counterparts, however, they also received money directly from American businesses (Houck 1984), and their projects often were determined by their donors' interests rather than by coherent and well-defined ideological commitments.[3] While many liberal public interest law firms developed highly specialized expertise, which enabled them to monitor important developments and compete with adversaries in private practice, the first conservative groups generally did not do so. In contrast to their liberal opponents, which were concentrated in Washington, D.C., most of the earliest conservative groups were located outside Washington, D.C.—for example, in Sacramento, Atlanta, Kansas City, Denver, Philadelphia, and Chicago—far removed from the site of most federal policy making.[4] And while liberal public interest law groups attracted brilliant lawyers from top law schools, conservative public interest law groups generally relied on lawyers with less impressive credentials.

CRITIQUES FROM THE LEFT

Public interest lawyers enjoyed exalted status in law schools and elite law firms in the 1970s (Dezalay and Garth 2001, 357), and conservative groups attempted to turn the luster of this new practice model to their advantage. They banked on the expectation that their own groups were sufficiently similar to their counterparts on the Left to give them similar rhetorical high ground. Conservatives sought to show that the argument that was gathering steam in American electoral politics—that government was the problem rather than the solution—was a proposition around which idealistic young lawyers could rally. They hoped that the "frames" of public interest law—theories about how it would correct the failings of pluralism—would shape public perception of the new groups as appropriate and valid.

In the first few years of the conservative public interest law firms' existence, conservative and liberal groups exchanged fire about each other's claims to serve the public interest. Leaders of some conservative groups asserted that their claim to the public interest mantle was superior to that of their liberal counterparts because they represented broader constituencies. One founder said that his group's reliance on corporate funding and individual donations was actually a virtue: "We . . . put ourselves in the position of being able to say, if you can't sell your program to the public, you probably aren't truly a public interest organization." But critics from the Left argued that conservative public interest law groups represented the interests of constituencies that already dominated American politics. Ralph Nader claimed that conservative public interest law groups were "agents of corporations and not public interest law firms" (Blodgett 1984, 71). An attorney for Public Advocates quipped that "[t]he Pacific Legal Foundation is a public-interest law firm in the same way that catsup is a vegetable under Reagan's new school lunch guidelines" (Gerber 1981, 28).

THE "HOROWITZ REPORT"

Conservative groups also faced attacks from within the conservative movement. Several influential critics suggested that organizations established in the 1970s had adopted the form of liberal public interest law firms without grasping why those groups succeeded. By far the most influential of those critics was Michael Horowitz, a Yale Law School graduate who was general counsel for the Office of Management and Budget in the Reagan Administration and now serves as a senior fellow at the Hudson Institute. In the late 1970s, Horowitz persuaded the Scaife Foundation to finance a study of conservative public interest groups. His scathing report, submitted in 1980, found that most of the existing organizations had failed to meet "the great need for vibrant, intellectually respectable conservative law/action centers." Instead, he argued, "traditional" public interest lawyers had largely succeeded in "isolat[ing] their conservative counterparts as hyphenated 'public-interest' pretenders"—as organizations "largely oriented to and indeed dominated by business interests, a description which is unhappily not wide of the mark for many such firms." Horowitz predicted that the conservative public interest movement would "make no substantial mark on the American legal profession or American life as long as it is seen as and is in fact the adjunct of a business community possessed of sufficient resources to afford its own legal representation" (Horowitz 1980, 1–2).

Horowitz asserted that recruiting elite lawyers into conservative public interest law and giving them leading roles was critical for the movement's long-term success. The business leaders who led and controlled early conservative public interest law firms had "little feel for the longer range potential of the movement on the legal process and as an instrument to . . . redefine what is moral in law" (Horowitz 1980, 5). "[W]hat is at stake in public interest law," he wrote, "is not so much a battle over cases won and lost as of ideas and ideologies." [5] The focus, therefore, should shift from "courts and legislatures to law schools and bar associations," where lawyers could be enlisted in the effort to "alter the prevailing wisdom of what constitutes the more moral and compassionate principles of law" (3–4):

> [T]he principal objective of any conservative public interest law movement, and the only means by which it can achieve a significant "multiplier" effect from its necessarily limited day-to-day work, is to help establish as an accepted proposition that the real interests of America's poor and vulnerable inhere in such goals as abatement of inflation, enhanced economic produc-

tivity, restraint on the power of government and the courts, and growth of such "middle class" values as the work ethic, education, effective criminal prosecution, etc. Such "conservative" ideas can and must generate idealism and enthusiasm on the part of large numbers of young, able and motivated attorneys and can and must effectively challenge the moral monopoly still largely enjoyed by traditional public interest lawyers and their allies (3).

Without a transformation of lawyers' professional ideals, Horowitz argued, conservative public interest law would "at best achieve episodic tactical victories which will be dwarfed by social change in the infinite number of areas beyond reach of its case agendas" (3).

The Horowitz report also recommended that conservative public interest law groups move beyond litigation to engage with other policy arenas. Horowitz observed that the traditional public interest law movement had achieved "enormous impact" by influencing legislation and legislative appropriations and oversight processes. He marveled at the traditional public interest law movement's success in moving its alumni into senior executive branch appointments and other high-level government posts— "positions whose incumbents are the true initiators and implementers of federal policy" (21). The personal and ideological ties that emerged from those networks, he argued, greatly increased the odds that the public interest law movement's "statist" views would prevail (23). Horowitz also noted that the traditional movement had been "alive to its interests" in building a judiciary that would sympathize with its agenda (19), and he urged conservatives law groups to do the same.

Horowitz concluded that the existing conservative public interest law groups were parochial, beholden to business patrons, and excessively focused on litigation—especially amicus filings. More troubling still, these organizations were staffed by "appallingly mediocre" lawyers. Horowitz viewed the inability of these groups to attract top-flight young lawyers as strong evidence of their failure to alter "still-prevailing notions of law students and young attorneys that their career options are largely restricted to serving the public interest (i.e., enhancing governmental power) or 'selling out' (i.e., working for a private law firm and its private sector clients)" (6).

Horowitz urged conservative foundations to withdraw support from most of the existing groups and to invest in organizations that would replicate the strategic choices of liberal public interest law firms—groups that made intellectually coherent and morally plausible claims to speak for unrepresented interests, built relationships with elite law schools and bar associations, worked in administrative agencies and Congress as well as the courts, and recruited first-rate lawyers. The latter goal, he argued, was particularly important: "Only when the staffs at conservative public interest law firms are comprised of law review editors, former law clerks and, in no small part, of alumni of national law schools, will the movement be in a position to initiate and participate in a real dialogue and in a truly national competition as to which legal policies and ideologies are truly 'in the public interest'" (Horowitz 2–6, 54–64).

OTHER CRITIQUES FROM WITHIN

Several activists interviewed for this research echoed the Horowitz report's claim that the earliest conservative public interest law organizations had misunderstood the reasons for liberal groups' success. One respondent observed that the first organizations had "made a number of really big mistakes" that rested "on a really basic misunderstanding about how these firms on the liberal side actually worked":

> One of the fundamental mistakes was to think that Ralph Nader was successful because he was a gas-bag and had an opinion about everything. And that's, of course, not true. If you look at the Naderite institutions or at the environmental law firms, they know exactly what they're doing. So, it's much better to have a very highly specialized center for auto safety that does nothing but auto safety than to have sort of Liberalism Incorporated or Liberal Lawyers Incorporated. And what the conservative firms had all done at the outset was not to specialize but to sort of agitate for conservative nostrums.

The same person asserted that conservatives were also wrong to have viewed liberal public interest lawyers as "mavericks who were somewhat isolated from American politics and . . . got in court what they couldn't get in Congress." Liberals had succeeded, in part, because public interest law groups and Congress worked in tandem: "these groups in effect act as the monitors and deputies of the congressional committees that run this stuff, and vice versa." Conservative groups should change their approach, he said, to "look around for niches in the legal system where you can in fact operate, where the legal environment is relatively favorable for you, and where you don't depend on the good graces of Ed Muskie and Henry Waxman to make your gains."[6] Another person interviewed for this project argued that conservatives had overlooked the value of playing insider politics. He said of Charles Halpern of the Center on Law and Social Policy, "[His] brilliant insight was—he had been working for Arnold and Porter and he saw lawyers there every day reading the Federal Register on behalf of private interests—and he wanted guys to do the same on behalf of the public interest. . . . Here were all these conservative public interest law firms that didn't want Washington to be the source and center of all power and decision making. So they were setting up public interest law firms around the country." He called this approach "insane":

> You've got to come to Washington. That's where decisions are made. The real thing that makes things happen is not the lawsuit you file, not the formal meeting you schedule when you fly in from Kansas City, but the brown bag lunches that the Environmental Defense Fund was having with the head of EPA, the informal calls, the personal links . . . , being known to and feeling free to call and being a source for newspaper reporters. . . . If you're way the hell out there in Sacramento, it's meaningless. The liberal groups never made that mistake.

Although the first conservative public interest law organizations failed to replicate the most successful liberal public interest law firms, they initially met little competition from within the conservative movement. A lawyer for one of these groups observed, "[W]e were the only public interest law firm that was philosophically other than liberal to radical, which left us all the room we needed." As the field became more specialized, however, newer groups disputed older organizations' commitment to principle and criticized their failure to adopt specialized and proactive strategies.

Newer organizations benefited from the interest of conservative foundations in building a more substantial and respectable set of institutions to sustain the conservative movement. One former foundation officer observed, "One of the things that had been learned from the early Reagan years was how important it would be to have an institutional conservative infrastructure, which then didn't exist, with few exceptions . . . You want to create an infrastructure that the media can go to, that people on the Hill can go to, that an Administration can go to and come here and empty all our offices." In the 1980s, conservative philanthropists withdrew support for many conservative antiregulatory groups established in the mid-1970s (Aron 1989, 78). As one respondent observed, "There was this sort of sense of crisis . . . The donors thought they hadn't gotten their money's worth, and a lot of these conservative firms hit the skids."

THE REAGAN/BUSH I ERA

Republican electoral victories in the 1980s, reflecting broader trends, such as the civil rights movement and Democrats' loss of the South, generated opportunities for conservative lawyers and spurred the growth of conservative legal organizations. Ronald Reagan's presidential victory launched a twelve-year period of Republican control over the White House. The GOP also held the Senate during six of those years, facilitating the appointment of conservative judges and other government officials. Presidents Reagan and George H. W. Bush named 545 federal judges (Reagan 358, and Bush 187)—including five Supreme Court Justices—and welcomed myriad conservative lawyers into their administrations.[7] Those Republican appointments, in turn, created more receptive targets for the advocacy of conservative public interest law groups. They also produced abundant incentives for young lawyers to join the movement and eventually partake of the plums available to those who distinguished themselves. In short, Republicans' electoral successes created highly favorable conditions for mobilizing conservative lawyers and their organizations.

In the early 1980s, conservative foundations began investing in organizations that more closely resembled their most successful liberal opponents.[8] Just as the Ford Foundation in the 1960s tried to professionalize social and civil rights activism (Dezalay and Garth 2002, 68–69), so did some conservative philanthropists seek to create a more professional field of conservative advocacy organizations. They supported long-term strategies, including large intellectual projects designed to articulate conservative ideals and their relationship to law. The newer conservative public interest law groups sought to distinguish themselves from their predecessors by showing that they had better developed agendas and more plausible claims to represent underrepresented constituencies. While most of the first conservative public interest law groups focused primarily on filing amicus briefs, many of the newer groups sponsored cases and thereby acquired greater control over fundamental strategic concerns, such as selecting clients, developing the factual record, and framing issues on appeal (Ivers 1998, 294).

Many founders interviewed for this research recounted how patrons had supported conservative intellectuals and lawyers to write articles and books that would eventually contribute to ambitious law reform campaigns. One observed, "[T]he success of conservative movement politics has depended in very large measure on intellectuals and importantly on the donors' ability to comprehend that point. And not immediately look for . . . 'What's the payoff two years down the road?' but 'Is this an important thing?' The Manhattan Institute is the best example of that. All it did, initially, at least, was find Wally Olson, find Peter Huber and [Charles Murray]. Just let them write." A libertarian recounted how, with substantial support from conservative patrons, a speech he delivered in the early 1980s had generated a conference, a book, an ABA [American Bar Association] program, a Federalist Society panel, and eventually the influential institution he now runs: "[Y]ou see from these little seeds you get trees eventually, and you get to change the terms of the debate."

Conservative foundations focused on organizations they expected to succeed, rather than distributing grants more broadly (Miller 2006, 115), and they coordinated their philanthropy to maximize its impact (Miller 2006, 115).[9] One long-time lawyer activist said,

> There were some visionaries on the philanthropic side. . . . They knew what the other groups were doing and they were not isolated mosaic tiles . . . They pulled back to see the big picture. If you only have five philanthropies and you know that each one is giving $50,000 to one group, then you expect more from that group and so on and so forth. So they were . . . farsighted in trying to pick winners and losers and trying to give money where they thought it would do some good.

Several particularly influential directors—Michael Joyce for the Olin Foundation (later director of the Bradley Foundation), Richard Larry for the Sarah Scaife Foundation, and Leslie Lenkowsky for the Smith Richardson Foundation—were the principal architects of this cooperation (Easterbrook 1986, 277).

During the Reagan/Bush years, ambitious young lawyers found plentiful opportunities to participate in redefining public interest law and advancing a vision of limited government associated with the Reagan revolution. One remembered that during his first few years in practice with a fledgling legal advocacy organization he "had very little supervision" and so "was really able to do things that a second year lawyer probably should not have been doing." Many of the interviewed lawyers found positions in the Reagan Justice Department shortly after graduating from law school. One remembered that "they were looking for conservative young attorneys to work there." Another, who landed an important political appointment less than five years out of law school, recalled that "there were very few conservative lawyers at that time who had any civil rights experience whatsoever." A lawyer who had begun working for a conservative advocacy organization soon after graduating from law school marveled that his boss had asked him to decline the solicitor general's request to divide time for oral argument in the Supreme Court: "And I got Charles Fried on the phone, and here I am this little peon guy talking to the Solicitor General . . . So there I am participating in cases at US Supreme Court!" Young conservatives who were thrust into major roles in the early years of the conservative law movement later assumed leading positions in the emerging infrastructure for conservative public interest law. One of those lawyers observed that "[t]he credentialing of lawyers during the Reagan [years] is probably the single biggest factor, along with the selection of conservative judges, in . . . really launching the [conservative law] movement into a more prominent and successful role."

CHRISTIAN EVANGELICAL GROUPS

The ambivalence of Christian evangelicals about engaging with secular law delayed their participation in legal rights advocacy (den Dulk 2001). In the mid-1970s, however, evangelical leaders began urging lawyers to confront the forces that had removed prayer and Bible reading from the schools and that had led to the Supreme Court's ruling in *Roe v. Wade*. Televangelist Jerry Falwell campaigned to persuade fundamentalists to overcome their distaste for politics and to engage with secular legal institutions (Jeffries and Ryan 2001, 342). Editorials in *Christianity Today* asserted that evangelicals had been "apathetic" in the face of the abortion rulings. "For all practical purposes, the Supreme Court has unwittingly legalized murder," one stated, and "Christians must stand up, speak out, and be counted" (*Christianity Today* 1979). Another editorial urged evangelical Christians to begin considering law as an "alternative field[] for Christian mission" (*Christianity Today* 1981). Francis Schaeffer published *A Christian Manifesto,* in which he decried the "shift from the Judeo-Christian basis for law" toward a "new sociological law" (1981, 42–43). He asked, "[W]here were the Christian lawyers during the crucial shift from forty years ago to just a few years ago? . . . [S]urely the Christian lawyers should have seen the change taking place and stood on the wall and blown the trumpets loud and clear" (47). In a conference that launched the Federalist Society for Law and Public Policy Studies in 1982, John T. Noonan, then a Berkeley law professor (and later a federal appellate judge appointed by President Reagan), noted that the pro-life movement was impaired by "an amateur, predominantly nonlegal leadership" that was "in great need of expert advice." He urged law students to enlist in an effort to "reverse what by every standard is the most serious invasion of state power in our century" (Noonan 1982). Collectively, these calls to action encouraged aspiring lawyers to view legal advocacy as a means for obeying spiritual obligations (den Dulk 2006, 207). The Christian Right began to field its own organizations to translate dismay about the Supreme Court's rulings on religion and abortion into a new brand of conservative public interest law.

Like the libertarians, social conservatives initially produced shoestring operations, led mostly by lawyers with modest credentials. But these organizations later yielded to more professional groups. Christian evangelicals started with several small, poorly funded groups served by volunteers and a few staff attorneys who worked "sacrificially" (in the words of one lawyer)—without dependable salaries and in conditions that made high-quality legal work difficult. The Rutherford Institute, founded by John Whitehead in 1982, and Free Speech Advocates/New Hope Life Center, established in New Hope, Kentucky, in 1984, occupied the field. One lawyer said of Rutherford's "model":

> [B]asically . . . you motivate Christians, Christian lawyers around the country, to volunteer their time to do religious liberty work. Now that was revolutionary for Christian lawyers, because there wasn't anything like that before. The Achilles heel to that is that most often you have guys doing wills and estates and suddenly the religious liberty case walks in, and they fumble the case. They don't really know what they're doing, and you really can't do it from the center. . . . You can't do it from the inside out successfully. You might win a case here or there. But to do major litigation, you have to do it with people who do nothing but that kind of work—do it full time.

By the early 1990s, evangelicals had launched several strategic organizations supported by major figures of the Christian conservative movement. The American Family Association Center for Law and Policy, founded by Don Wildman, and the American Center for Law and Justice (ACLJ), founded by Pat Robertson, enjoyed budgets sufficient to elevate the quality of the legal work. One lawyer observed, "ACLJ provided an infusion of cash to move the work to a much higher level. Suddenly you could travel and cover a case in Spokane, Washington or California. You could stop everything and spend two weeks writing up the perfect Supreme Court brief instead of having to do private cases in order to put bread on the table. So this was a revolutionary change. . . . " The "genius" of these groups, he said, "was that suddenly you had enough money to be able to put competent full-time litigators on religious liberty cases, and to do nothing but those cases."

THE FEDERALIST SOCIETY FOR LAW
AND PUBLIC POLICY STUDIES

In terms of professionalizing the movement and implementing the Horowitz report's call for cultivating "large numbers of young, able and motivated attorneys," no organization has contributed more than the Federalist Society for Law and Public Policy Studies. It began in 1982 as a small debating society launched by Steven Calabresi, Lee Liberman, and David McIntosh, who were friends as undergraduates at Yale and active members of the Yale Political Union.[10] They entered law school the year following Ronald Reagan's successful presidential campaign—Calabresi at Yale and Liberman and McIntosh at the University of Chicago. Frustrated that conservatives were losing in the legal academy even as they were winning in electoral politics, these students sought to help build a conservative counterelite. Calabresi and his friends established an organization at Yale, with support from Yale Law professors Ralph Winter and Robert Bork (Abramson 1986, 99–100). Liberman and McIntosh founded a chapter at the University of Chicago Law School, where Antonin Scalia, then a member of the faculty, served as their adviser, and professors Richard Epstein, Richard Posner, and Frank Easterbrook provided encouragement (Abramson 1986, 101).

The two chapters convened a symposium on federalism in April 1982, with money supplied by the Institute for Educational Affairs, the Olin Foundation, and the Intercollegiate Studies Institute (Acknowledgements 1982). The conference proposal asserted that "[l]aw schools and the legal profession are currently strongly dominated by a form of orthodox liberal ideology which advocates a centralized and uniform society" and that "[w]hile some members of the legal community have dissented from these views, no comprehensive conservative critique or agenda has been formulated in this field" (Miller 2006, 89). The conference would provide an opportunity "for such a response to begin to be articulated" (Miller 2006, 89).[11]

The national organization grew out of the conference, with the Olin Foundation funding a Federalist Society speakers' bureau and helping the organization establish chapters at other law schools. The *Harvard Journal of Law and Public Policy,* launched in 1978 by Steven J. Eberhard and Spencer Abraham (who later served as a U.S. Senator and then as energy secretary during President George W. Bush's first term), became the Federalist Society's official publication (Schlesinger 2001; Ginsburg 2002). The preface to the first symposium issue signaled that the journal and its organizational sponsor would take conservatives' fight to the law schools and the bar: "At a time when the nation's law schools are staffed largely by professors who dream of regulating from their cloistered offices every minute detail of our lives, at a time when the legal profession's largest lobbying group pushes on with its statist agenda, the Federalists met—and proclaimed the virtues of individual freedom and of limited government" (Preface 1983, iii–iv). Although the Federalist Society began as a student organization, its planning memos indicated that it would eventually include lawyers and law faculty (Teles 2008, 140). It would present itself as an alternative to the ABA—not only a forum for conservative ideas but also a vehicle for increasing conservative lawyers' voice within the profession and in public policy formation (Teles 2008, 167–73). With help from Michael Horowitz and other senior lawyers who recognized the Federalist Society's potential to create a cadre of young elite conservative lawyers, the organization began building connections between young Federalist Society members and prominent conservative lawyers in Washington.

The organization also sought from the start to create a large tent. The Federalist Society's first and only executive director, Eugene Meyer, is the son of Frank Meyer, who in the 1950s tried to unite libertarians and traditionalists around "fusionism," a synthesis of ideas about freedom and moral authority (Nash 1996, 321–22; Gottfried 1993, 16–17). Under Eugene Meyer's leadership, the Federalist Society has tried to reach law students and lawyers from all constituencies of the conservative movement.

INCREASED SPECIALIZATION AND COMPETITION

Lawyers founded dozens of new legal advocacy organizations during the 1980s and 1990s. Those organizations included libertarian groups, such as the Competitive Enterprise Institute Free-Market Legal Program, Cato Institute's Center for Constitutional Studies,[12] the Center for Individual Rights, the Institute for Justice, and American Civil Rights Union, as well as social conservative organizations, such as the Home School Legal Defense Association, Liberty Counsel, American Center for Law and Justice, American Family Association Center for Law and Policy, and the Alliance Defense Fund.[13] As the conservative law movement gained momentum, the pace of the creation of these groups also increased. Table 2.1 lists some of those organizations and their founding dates.

This proliferation of legal advocacy organizations in the 1980s and 1990s reflected aggressive institutional entrepreneurship by conservative lawyers during those years.[14] Lawyers who founded and maintained the

TABLE 2.1: Founding Dates of Selected Conservative and Libertarian Law Organizations

Goldwater Era Precursors

1957	Citizens for Decency through Law
1962	Morality in Media
1966	Americans for Effective Law Enforcement
1968	National Right to Work Legal Defense Foundation

First Wave

1973	Catholic League for Religious and Civil Rights
	Pacific Legal Foundation
1975	Center for Law and Religious Freedom, Christian Legal Society
	National Legal Center for the Public Interest
1976	Americans United for Life Legal Defense Foundation
	Gulf and Great Plains Legal Foundation
	Southeastern Legal Foundation
	Mid-America Legal Foundation
	Atlantic Legal Foundation
	Landmark Legal Foundation
	Washington Legal Foundation
1977	Mountain States Legal Foundation
	Capital Legal Foundation
	New England Legal Foundation
1979	Pacific Research Institute

The Reagan/Bush Era

1981	Concerned Women for America Education and Legal Defense Foundation
	Oregonians in Action Legal Center
	Eagle Forum Education and Legal Defense Fund
1982	Federalist Society for Law and Public Policy Studies
	Rutherford Institute
	Criminal Justice Legal Foundation
1983	Home School Legal Defense Association
1984	Free Speech Advocates/New Hope Life Center
1985	National Legal Foundation
1986	Competitive Enterprise Institute Free Market Legal Program
	Manhattan Institute, Center for Legal Policy
1987	Northwest Legal Foundation
1989	Center for Individual Rights
	Cato Institute, Center for Constitutional Studies
	Liberty Counsel
	Lincoln Legal Foundation
1989	American Center for Law and Justice
	National Family Legal Foundation (now Community Defense Counsel)
	American Family Association Center for Law and Policy
1991	Institute for Justice
1992	Stewards of the Range
	Defenders of Property Rights
1993	Alliance Defense Fund
	Center for the Study of Popular Culture, Individual Rights Foundation

TABLE 2.1 (*continued*)

	National Law Center for Children and Families
1994	Judicial Watch
	Becket Fund
	Texas Justice Foundation (now Justice Foundation)
	Northstar Legal Center
1995	Western Center for Law and Religious Freedom
	Center for Equal Opportunity
1997	James Madison Center for Free Speech
	Pacific Justice Institute
	Liberty Legal Institute
	Thomas More Society, Inc.
1998	American Civil Rights Union
	Center for Individual Freedom
	European Centre for Law and Justice
	Slavic Centre for Law and Justice
1999	Claremont Institute Center for Constitutional Jurisprudence
	Foundation for Individual Rights in Education
	Thomas More Law Center
	Center for the Original Intent of the Constitution
2000	National Federation of Independent Business Legal Foundation
2001	American Unity Legal Defense Fund
2002	Foundation for Moral Law
2005	Advocates for Faith and Freedom

newer, more specialized groups often came from older organizations, striking out on their own as they sought to build their careers. Established groups frequently served as "training grounds" (Salisbury 1969) and sources of inspiration for newer organizations. One Christian advocate likened this process of founding and staffing breakaway organizations to rock bands' disintegration and regeneration with new combinations of musicians: "Graham Nash was with the Hollies, and then he goes to Crosby, Stills, Nash . . . You almost need a chart." [15]

As the field of conservative public interest organizations expanded, groups and their leaders struggled to compete in the market for patrons, credit, and influence. Lawyers interviewed for this research generally were keenly aware of their organizations' positions in the constellation of conservative advocacy groups and able to describe their own distinctive strengths. One lawyer observed that it is no longer possible to raise money with a general fund-raising pitch:

> In . . . the early days of direct mail and in the early days of going to foundations, we could get general operations grants for a broad program statement.

I think it is harder and harder to do that these days. . . . You really have to have a pretty well-defined product to sell, and I think that is what has driven the formation of a lot of these new groups. They have to have a pretty clearly defined product so that they can find their niche in the market. . . .

Other lawyers described intense competition among groups serving the same constituency. One referred to "antagonism" generated by "economics"; because they perceive themselves all to have fishing lines in a small pond. Maybe when somebody else drops a line in there, everybody's got to move over and . . . everybody gets fewer fish." Another lawyer said of the property rights groups, "we like to compete. We all want to be out there getting the biggest cases, the most important cases, the cases where we think we can do the most good"; and another described disputes among libertarian groups about funding and credit for litigation successes: "There's not a lot of incentive for them to work together." Several lawyers also recounted struggles among groups for control over the creation of precedent in their issue areas.

The competition among conservative law groups has provoked infighting. One lawyer interviewed for this project said that in the 1970s, anti-regulatory public interest law groups were "at war" with each other until the Heritage Foundation intervened to insist on cooperation. Several lawyers for religious liberties organizations spoke of hot disputes among Christian groups (one described it as "internecine warfare" and another called it "the dark side of the right-wing evangelical movement"). That rivalry eventually led national religious leaders, including James Dobson of Focus on the Family, D. James Kennedy of Coral Ridge Ministries, and Bill Bright of Campus Crusade for Christ, to create the Alliance Defense Fund (ADF)—an organization designed to suppress factional fighting by channeling foundation money to cooperating groups. A lawyer involved in religious liberties work said that he thought that ADF's efforts to serve as a neutral umbrella funding agency to coordinate the work of religious liberties groups had "only been partially successful": "Every now and then someone tries to do a summit of a sort and get everybody to agree, but there are colossal egos in each of these organizations and everyone wants their fiefdom to be the dominant and most important one." Thus, despite efforts to cajole and pressure leaders of rival groups to cooperate, competition for resources, recognition, and control continues.

The field of conservative public interest law is now highly specialized, with distinct constituencies of conservatives represented by different organizations and lawyers. An attorney who has participated in conservative public interest law since the mid-1970s said, "We've seen a lot more groups form ... around much narrower interests." A movement that began with a few regional organizations representing the business perspective on regulatory matters now supports dozens of groups, including some libertarian organizations that attempt to distance themselves from large business interests. The views of Christian evangelicals, which in the 1980s found expression primarily through the Christian Legal Society and the Rutherford Institute, are now advocated by many more groups representing much more particular interests, differentiated along theological lines and by issue. In addition to firms that were established in the 1970s, there now are specialized organizations focusing on affirmative action, home-schooling, pornography, property rights, school vouchers, tort reform, and gun ownership. Organizations also distinguish themselves from one another according to the types of strategies pursued—direct representation versus amicus participation; grassroots activism versus insider networking; and research targeted at Congress and the media versus scholarly publications directed primarily at professors and judges.

THE CONTEST OVER THE MEANING OF "PUBLIC INTEREST LAW"

As conservatives have deployed an organizational model born of liberal legal activism, they have unsettled conventions and assumptions about public interest practice, increased competition in the courts and agencies, and gained the upper hand in public policy debates. The creation of conservative legal advocacy groups to compete with liberal public interest law groups has eliminated the equation between public interest law and liberal politics and dramatically increased the number and diversity of nonprofit organizations that seek to influence public policy making.

In the late 1960s, the public interest law movement was almost synonymous with left legal activism, but today dozens of conservative and libertarian organizations claim the public interest mantle.[16] As liberal groups have chosen other words to describe their missions—"progressive," "critical," and more specific tags associated with their constituencies' concerns—conservative groups have aggressively applied the public interest label to themselves. The Institute for Justice, for example, describes itself as "the nation's premier libertarian public interest law firm," whose mission is to "preserv[e] freedom of opportunity and challeng[e] government's control over individuals[ ]. . . . " The Washington Legal Foundation claims to be "the nation's preeminent center for public interest law, advocating free-enterprise principles, responsible government, property rights, a strong national security and defense, and balanced civil and criminal justice system." Pat Robertson's American Center for Law and Justice asserts that it is "this nation's preeminent public interest law firm and educational organization dedicated to defending and advancing religious liberty, the sanctity of human life, and the two-parent, marriage-bound family." The Criminal Justice Legal Foundation calls itself "a nonprofit public interest law organization dedicated to restoring a balance between the rights of crime victims and the criminally accused." Defenders of Property Rights claims to be "the nation's only national public interest legal foundation dedicated exclusively to property rights protection."[17] Of the ninety-eight organizations that described themselves using the words "public interest" in briefs filed in the U.S. Supreme Court from January 2000 through July 2007, twenty-nine were organizations listed in table 2.1.[18] Moreover, those twenty-nine organizations were especially active: they filed or signed onto 210 of 283 Supreme Court briefs filed during that same period by groups that described themselves as public interest organizations. In a recent book on "the freedom-based public interest law movement" published by the Heritage Foundation, Edwin Meese describes lawyers of the traditional movement as "so-called public interest lawyers" (Meese 2004, ii).

In accordance with the Horowitz report's recommendations, conservative legal advocacy organizations and foundations are establishing ties with law schools and aggressively recruiting law students and recent law school graduates to their causes. ADF, for example, offers a nine-week Blackstone Fellowship annually to approximately sixty "highly motivated Christian law students" between their first and second years of law school. The program's purpose is "to train a new generation of lawyers who will rise to positions of influence and leadership as legal scholars, litigators, judges, and perhaps even Supreme Court justices." Several libertarian groups also offer paid summer internships and promote them as highly competitive opportunities.[19] Some conservative groups now are able to attract students from top law schools, although most social conservative groups continue to draw primarily from less elite schools and from several new schools that were created to challenge established, secular norms of legal education. The latter include Ave Maria Law School, founded by billionaire Tom Monaghan of the Domino's pizza "empire" (Hansen 2006) to provide "legal education in fidelity to the Catholic faith"; the University of St. Thomas School of Law, opened in 1999 with a "faith-based mission of service and leadership" (Mengler 2003); and Regent University School of Law, established in 1986, "to bring to bear the will of our Creator, Almighty God, upon legal education and the legal profession." (Regent Law 2008).

Some methods used by conservative public interest law groups to identify and recruit clients and to shape public opinion make liberal groups' outreach and public education strategies look narrow and modest. Jay Sekulow, for example, finds new cases for the American Center for Law and Justice through his radio show *Jay Sekulow Live!,* which airs on nearly 850 radio stations, and his television show, *ACLJ This Week* (American Center for Law and Justice 2008). Mathew Staver, founder of Liberty Counsel and dean of Liberty University School of Law, hosts two radio programs and a television show called *Law and Justice* (Crampton 2004). Michael Farris, chairman of the Home School Legal Defense Association, teaches an online high school–level constitutional law course, whose required text is his own *Constitutional Law for Christian Students* (*Constitutional Law for Enlightened Citizens* 2008). Several conservative public interest law groups, including the Rutherford Institute, Institute for Justice, and Liberty Counsel, encourage prospective clients to submit information about their claims through the organizations' Web sites.

Conservative and libertarian public interest law groups also have expanded the cooperating attorney model pioneered by the ACLU. The Institute for Justice holds seminars on public interest litigation for hundreds of students, policy activists, and lawyers, and it invites graduates of these programs to join its "Human Action Network." ADF runs week-long training programs—"National Litigation Academies"— to "train a generation of attorneys" to "restore America's legal system. . . . " Each lawyer who attends the academy commits to provide 450 hours of pro bono legal work "on behalf of the Body of Christ" (ADF 2007b). As of August 2007, one thousand lawyers had graduated from twenty-eight of these training sessions and contributed $70 million worth of pro bono legal services (ADF 2007b).

The rise of conservative public interest law groups has coincided with a substantial decline in the fortunes of liberal public interest law. The more conservative composition of the federal judiciary resulting from appointments by presidents Reagan and Bush I and II, legislative restrictions on lawyers' activities, and cutbacks in funding for legal services programs have encouraged the retreat of many progressive lawyers from a bold vision of their roles in social change through law reform to a more modest and circumscribed part in community-based political action. But the same conditions that have discouraged progressive lawyers have emboldened conservative activists. Conservative and libertarian groups now frequently initiate litigation, while "traditional" public interest law firms play largely defensive roles. Lawyers for conservative and libertarian causes have sought to eliminate or diminish rights forged by liberal public interest law groups and to establish and revitalize "counter-rights" (Burke 2001, 1267–69). Some of their litigation initiatives have focused on rolling back constitutional doctrines recognized by the Warren and Burger courts—for example, the right to abortion under *Roe v. Wade,* constitutional protections for criminal defendants, especially ones affecting search and seizure, and Establishment Clause restrictions on school voucher programs. They also have campaigned to broaden some constitutional guarantees—for example, to invalidate affirmative action and desegregation programs as violations of the Equal Protection Clause, revitalize the privileges and immunities and due process clauses of the Fourteenth Amendment to overturn economic regulation, bolster property rights, enforce "enumerated powers" constraints on federal government authority, expand constitutional protection for religious expression, strike down campaign finance laws under the First Amendment, and overturn gun control laws under the Second Amendment. This interest in pursuing law reform through the courts, explored in more detail in chapter 7, is partly captured in numbers. In the six years from 2000 through 2006, fifty-three of the conservative and libertarian public legal advocacy organizations listed in the table 2.1 filed briefs in 204 Supreme Court cases.

As shown in table 2.2, some conservative and libertarian legal advocacy organizations now rival their liberal counterparts in size and resources. ADF, which awards grants to other social conservative advocacy groups, had $22 million in revenue in fiscal year 2005, and the American Center for Law and Justice had almost $14.5 million.[20] Other well-funded groups include the Cato Institute ($22.4 million) and Concerned Women for America ($8.5 million). None of these groups rivals the Natural Resources Defense Council ($76.3 million) or the ACLU ($58.4 million), but their resources compare favorably with other major "liberal" public interest law organizations, such as the NAACP Legal Defense and Educational Fund ($12.8 million), Public Citizen ($8.8 million), Alliance for Justice ($5.2 million), NOW Legal Defense and Education Fund (now called "Legal Momentum"; $4.6 million), Center for Law and Social Policy ($3.4 million), and Public Advocates ($1.7 million).

The mobilization of public interest law groups on the Right to match such groups on the Left has dramatically diminished the advantage that

TABLE 2.2: Budgets of Selected Conservative, Libertarian, and Liberal Organizations, 1985 and 2005

Organization Name	FY 1985 budget ($millions)[a]	Annual revenue FY 2005 ($millions)
Conservative and libertarian groups:		
Heritage Foundation	11.0	53.0
Alliance Defense Fund	—	22.0
Cato Institute	1.4	22.4
American Center for Law and Justice	—	14.5
Pacific Legal Foundation	3.0	7.7
Institute for Justice	—	7.5
Federalist Society	0.3	6.8
National Right to Work Legal Defense and Education Foundation	4.0	6.5
Reason Foundation	1.5	5.2
Washington Legal Foundation	1.8	4.1
Mountain States Legal Foundation	1.2	3.3
Competitive Enterprise Institute	0.1	3.2
Eagle Forum Education and Legal Defense Fund	0.6	2.3
Center for Individual Rights	—	2.0
Foundation for Individual Rights in Education	—	1.6
Southeastern Legal Foundation	0.3	0.9
Liberal groups:		
Natural Resources Defense Council	7.0	76.3
Environmental Defense Incorporated (formerly Environmental Defense Fund)	3.4	67.9
ACLU	11.4	58.4
Earthjustice (formerly Sierra Club Legal Defense Fund)	21.4	21.1
NAACP Legal Defense and Education Fund	10.1	12.8
Lambda Legal Defense and Education Fund	0.6	9.7
Public Citizen	0.5	8.8
Mexican American Legal Defense and Educational Fund	3.0	7.9
NARAL Pro-Choice America Foundation (formerly National Abortion Rights Action League)	2.6	5.6
Alliance for Justice	0.1	5.2
Americans United for Separation of Church and State	1.3	5.1
Legal Momentum (formerly NOW Legal Defense and Education Fund)	1.7	4.6
Center for Law and Social Policy	0.4	3.4
Public Advocates	0.7	1.7

A dash (—) indicates that organization had not yet been founded. FY = fiscal year.

[a]All but two of the 1985 budget figures come from *Public Interest Profiles* 1986–87. Lambda Legal and Legal Momentum provided 1985 budget figures directly to me.

progressive groups may once have enjoyed in the courts during the heyday of left liberal activism. During the 1960s and 1970s, various disadvantaged groups and broad public constituencies represented by liberal organizations won significant litigation victories—successes that would have been unlikely in other policy-making arenas. As Schlozman and Tierney have noted, however, "there was nothing institutionally inevitable about this" (1985, 378). The proliferation of conservative advocacy organizations and the appointment of conservative jurists have transformed the courts into sites of intense interest group competition. Today, courts may be no more receptive to underdogs than other policy-making forums (Epstein 1985, 148).

Public law litigation now attracts substantial participation from conservative law groups. *Lawrence v. Texas,* the challenge to Texas's antisodomy statute, for example, drew amicus curiae briefs not only from gay rights groups, the ACLU, NOW Legal Defense Fund, and other civil rights and human rights organizations but also from more than a dozen conservative and libertarian organizations.[21] In *Grutter v. Bollinger* and *Gratz v. Bollinger,* a pair of cases brought by the Center for Individual Rights challenging the University of Michigan's affirmative action programs, the Supreme Court received briefs in support of the plaintiffs from the Cato Institute, Claremont Institute Center for Constitutional Jurisprudence, Center for Equal Opportunity, Independent Women's Forum, American Civil Rights Institute, Center for Individual Freedom, Reason Foundation, Pacific Legal Foundation, Criminal Justice Legal Foundation, and the Center for New Black Leadership. In *Elk Grove Unified School District v. Newdow,* a challenge to the use of the pledge of allegiance in public schools, liberal groups met opposition from over a dozen conservative organizations,[22] and in *Gonzales v. Carhart,* which upheld the Partial-Birth Abortion Ban Act of 2003, the eight briefs filed in support of finding the statute unconstitutional were matched by nineteen briefs on the other side.

This increased competition among public interest law groups of the Left and Right has made public policy formation in the courts highly complex and antagonistic (see O'Connor and Epstein 1989, 482; Epstein 1985, 655; Hassler and O'Connor 1985–1986), and it has laid bare an essential truth about public interest law—that advocates for 501(c)(3) law reform organizations, all viewing themselves as public interest lawyers, may disagree fundamentally about what the public interest requires.[23] These battles also have highlighted the relationship between judicial philosophy and litigation outcomes. If disadvantaged groups once found allies in judges who believed it was their role to intervene in economic and social affairs (Schlozman and Tierney 1986, 380), conservatives have benefited similarly from the appointment of judges who share their political sympathies. The rise of conservative public interest group activity has coincided with a campaign to appoint conservative judges. Indeed, many of the groups examined in this chapter have played important roles in teeing up candidates and supporting judicial nominees drawn from their ranks.

Lawyers' aggressive building of law-related institutions has placed them in the center of the conservative movement. One lawyer interviewed for this project observed,

> If you look at the conservative movement generally since World War II, in the 1940s and 1950s it was primarily an intellectual movement. . . . In the 1960s particularly with the Goldwater nomination , . . . a political dimension was added. . . . And then with Ronald Reagan . . . , it became a governing movement as well. Starting roughly in the 70s, the resources of the conservative movement expanded considerably. . . . [T]he whole conservative legal movement, which started in the 70s. . . . the combination of the public interest legal groups and the Federalist Society, has given a much more prominent position to lawyers in the conservative movement.

As lawyers championed the idea that public interest law organizations could be created and mobilized on behalf of conservative causes, they ensured a large role for themselves in implementing that strategy.

The growth and success of conservative public interest law is closely tied with the conservative movement's improved record of recruiting elite lawyers and creating attractive career paths for them. A *Wall Street Journal* editorial in 1981, reporting on the findings of the Horowitz report, observed that conservative public interest groups, unlike "[t]he Naderite public interest law firms," had failed to "tap[ ] into the national legal community" (*Wall Street Journal* 1981). Twenty-five years later, however, as Republicans' electoral success has created abundant opportunities for lawyers with conservative credentials, conservative public interest organizations and Republican administrations draw from a more elite pool (cf. Heinz, Paik, and Southworth 2003). Lawyers associated with today's conservative law groups include partners in major law firms, senior government officials, and judges. Many of the lawyer founders identified in this chapter served in high levels in the Reagan and Bush I administrations—some of them while they were very young.[24] One lawyer associated with religious law groups asserted that the conservatives' constitutional litigators now match the Left's most able lawyers: "Fifteen years ago our best people were not as good as their best people, but now I think they really are." Twenty-five years ago, one might have been hard-pressed to name a handful of well-known conservative lawyer activists. But today's most prominent lawyers associated with the conservative movement—for example, Edwin Meese, Theodore Olson, James Bopp, Jay Sekulow, Robert Bork, C. Boyden Gray, Charles Cooper, Clint Bolick, and Kenneth Starr—are better known even if they are not household names, and all of them participate in organizations that groom younger conservative lawyers.

Conservative lawyer networks also have flourished during the past few decades. The Christian Legal Society, established by lawyers who met to pray together at an ABA convention in 1959, now has 3,800 members, with 165 student chapters and ninety-four attorney chapters. The Federalist Society boasts 40,000 members, chapters in every accredited law school, sixty-five metropolitan attorney chapters, and a law faculty division. One long-time observer of the conservative movement asserted that conservatives had cultivated "the next generation of Lloyd Cutlers and Joe Califanos who are prepared to run law firms and to assume major government positions." A libertarian said of the availability of qualified and credentialed conservative lawyers, "this administration, unlike earlier Republican administrations, has actually a monstrous infrastructure to draw on." Another said of the difference between conservative lawyers' influence in the 1970s and today, "[It] is like day and night."

In short, the field of conservative public interest law has grown considerably in size, diversity, and influence since the mid-1970s. One of the interviewed lawyers observed of today's conservative public interest law groups, "I don't think it is any longer debatable whether they have a meaningful presence on the scene."

CONCLUSION

This chapter has examined how lawyers have created dozens of conservative and libertarian public interest law organizations during the past few decades and how those organizations have channeled energy and resources into law-related strategies, altered the dynamics of public law litigation, and moved lawyers into key positions in the conservative movement. The lawyers who have built and served these institutions have advanced visions of the public interest sharply at odds with the ones set forth by liberal law reformers of the 1960s and 1970s and more consistent with the values of the various strands of the conservative alliance they serve. They have copied the organizational form and rhetoric of liberal public interest law and used them with great success in their confrontation with legal liberalism. But the process of differentiation described in this chapter produced not one, but many alternative visions of the public good. For libertarians and business interests, law should better reflect the teaching of economics and markets. For social conservatives, law should more consistently conform to conservative religious beliefs. As shown in the next two chapters, these fundamental differences in views about what values law should embody correspond with deep social divisions among the lawyers of the conservative coalition and the constituencies they serve.

3

Divided Constituencies
and Their Lawyers

Maintaining cooperation among the diverse constituencies that have coalesced behind the Republican Party has been difficult (Nash 1996). The coalition is divided on both of the primary principles that organize party competition in the United States (Miller and Schofield 2003). On the social dimension—the more salient axis in American politics today—social conservatives are at odds with business elites, who are generally uncomfortable with the Republican Party's association with Protestant fundamentalism, pro-life advocacy, prayer in the schools, and traditional "family values." The submerged economic dimension also generates significant tension. Social conservatives tend to dislike big business and tax policies that favor the wealthy. Blending the social and economic elements of the Republican alliance into an integrated political force has been one of the central challenges for the American conservative movement since the 1950s (Himmelstein 1990, 31; Hodgson 1996, 158–59).

Some of the conservative movement's heroes are men who have partially succeeded in forging consensus. They include William F. Buckley, who in 1955 launched the *National Review,* not only to give intellectual respectability to conservative ideas, but also to "consolidate the Right" (Nash 1996, 135). He helped build the coalition by giving audience to the views of traditionalists, libertarians, anti-Communists and neoconservatives (Hart 2005; Nash 1996, 134–40). In the early 1960s, Frank Meyer sought to unite the factions around "fusionism"—a synthesis of ideas about freedom and moral authority (Meyer 1964, 229–32). Although this enterprise did not yield a coherent philosophical framework, it did produce agreement around a set of intermediate principles that would temporarily sustain the alliance. In the 1980s, Ronald Reagan managed to personify all strands of the American Right, and he remains a unifying figure, reminding conservatives of the coalition's capacity to translate its shared rejection of twentieth-century liberalism into political success.

Various types of actors have attributes that might enable them to help integrate the conservative coalition. Public intellectuals such as Buckley and Meyer promoted consensus by articulating a shared agenda. Reagan *embodied* the diverse impulses of the conservative alliance (Nash 1996, 332) and gave them governing power. As noted in chapter 2, patrons and foundations encouraged harmony by linking financial support to cooperation among competing groups. Lawyers too might play some role in bridging the constituencies. Their similar educational experience, common professional language, shared understanding of the relationship between law and politics, and mutual occupational interests might promote respect and trust (Halliday 1987, 47–51; Heinz et al. 2003). Moreover, if lawyers operate as a professional community, or several professional communities, with established social networks (Mather, McEwen, and Maiman 2001), ties among them might help maintain the coalition.[1]

But whether lawyers actually play such an integrative role will depend on whether their common characteristics and interests are overcome by their differences and disagreements. Sources of division include social background, values, geography, professional orientation, and specialization (see generally Heinz et al. 2005). The next three chapters consider whether lawyers of the conservative coalition are likely to contribute to mutual understanding and cooperation within the alliance or whether disagreements and dissimilarities among them make them unlikely to build consensus.

This chapter shows that rifts within the American conservative coalition are present among the lawyers who serve the alliance. Lawyers for the different constituencies are divided by social background, geography, and values. Lawyers for social conservative causes come primarily from religious and nonelite backgrounds, while business lawyers come from more secular and privileged environments. Moreover, the organizations served by these lawyers receive support from different sets of philanthropists, who are themselves socially divided. Lawyers for mediator organizations are especially elite and have strong ties to the legal establishment. The organizations that these lawyers serve command far and away the largest amount of public foundation money, suggesting that conservative philanthropists expect those groups to promote cooperation and suppress conflict.

PREVIOUS RESEARCH ON A SET OF 1300 LAWYERS FOR CONSERVATIVE CAUSES

The backdrop for this chapter is previous research on the characteristics of, and relationships among, a set of 1300 lawyers who served eighty-one organizations that were active on seventeen legislative events important to the various constituencies of the conservative coalition in the late 1990s (Heinz, Paik, and Southworth 2003). To compare the lawyers, we divided the organizations into categories defined by their principal issue interests: religious conservative, libertarian and business organizations, abortion opponents, affirmative action opponents, "order-maintenance" groups, and "mediators."[2]

Table 3.1 shows the gender, type of law school attended, and practice location of the lawyers affiliated with one or more of the organizations.[3] There was little variation in the percentages of male and female lawyers; the lawyers in all categories were overwhelmingly male. However, there were pronounced differences in the law school backgrounds of these lawyers. Almost three-quarters of the lawyers for mediator organizations had attended "elite" or "prestige" law schools—schools ranked in the top twenty in the 2000 *U.S. News & World Report* rankings—and 70 percent of lawyers for affirmative action opponents had done so.[4] But only 20 percent of the lawyers for the abortion opponents and 34 percent of lawyers for the religious conservative organizations had attended those schools. More than half (57 percent) of the lawyers for groups that opposed abortion and 42 percent of lawyers for religious conservative groups attended local law schools, defined as schools ranked below 50, while only 13 percent of lawyers for mediator groups and 21 percent of lawyers for groups that opposed affirmative action had attended those schools. The educational credentials of lawyers for business and libertarian groups were less elite than those of lawyers working for mediator and anti-affirmative action organizations but more elite than those of advocates for religious conservative and anti-abortion groups.

There were also significant differences in the location of the lawyers' offices. Lawyers for business organizations and affirmative action opponents tended to be located in the Washington, D.C., area and other major cities. Lawyers for religious conservative, abortion, order-maintenance, and libertarian groups generally did not work in major urban centers.

The sources of philanthropy for social conservative legal advocacy organizations also differed from those supporting business and libertarian advocacy organizations. Using information compiled by the *Foundation*

TABLE 3.1: Characteristics of 1300 Lawyers, by Organizational Categories (Column Percentages)[a]

Characteristic	Religious	Abortion	Order maintenance	Libertarian	Affirmative action	Business	Mediator	Total
Gender:								
% Male	87	88	82	88	90	83	90	84
% Female	13	12	18	13	10	17	10	16
Law school:	**	***	*		***		***	
% Elite	15	8	10	20	39	24	48	22
% Prestige	19	12	19	28	31	26	24	25
% Regional	24	24	21	16	8	19	15	19
% Local	42	57	49	36	21	31	13	34
Location:	***	**	*			***		
% D.C.	14	12	22	26	40	41	38	32
% D.C. suburbs	4	2	12	3	0	5	4	5
% Major cities	13	18	10	16	21	15	15	15
% Elsewhere	69	69	56	55	40	38	43	47

[a]Significant χ^2-tests are indicated for each category.

*$P < .05$.

**$P < .01$.

***$P < .001$.

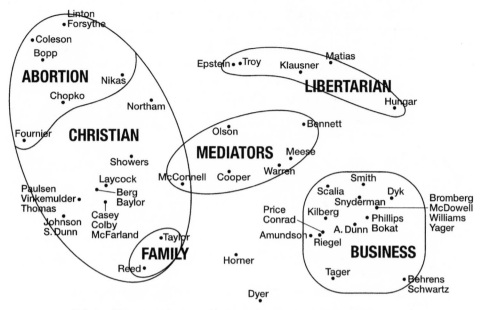

3.1: Relationships among lawyers with ties to three or more organizations

Grants Index, we identified the five largest foundation funders for each category.[5] Three foundations, the Lynde and Harry Bradley Foundation, the Sarah Scaife Foundation, and the Olin Foundation, appeared among the top five funders in three categories—mediator, libertarian, and affirmative action. Two of these three foundations, Bradley and Olin, also appeared in the top five in the business category. But these foundations were not among the top supporters of religious conservatives and abortion opponents.

We also analyzed the relationships among the lawyers for these constituencies, using social network analysis to "map" in spatial terms similarities and differences in their patterns of affiliation with conservative and libertarian nonprofit organizations.[6] Using multidimensional scaling,[7] figure 3.1 shows the similarities in the patterns of organizational affiliation of the fifty-four lawyers who were active in three or more of these organizations. Similarity in the organizational constituencies of each pair of lawyers is represented as distance; the closer the pair of lawyers, the more similar are sets of organizations they serve. Only distance counts; direction is insignificant.[8]

Figure 3.1 shows two primary clusters of lawyers. At the lower right is a group composed entirely of lawyers working for business organizations.

At the lower left is a large cluster of lawyers who serve religious conservative groups. Above and to the right, libertarians make up a smaller set with their own distinct affiliations. The structure is clearly divided between business conservatives on one side and religious conservatives on the other. Of the fifty-four lawyers included in figure 3.1, only two served both a business organization and a religious conservative group.[9]

In the center of figure 3.1 are several lawyers whose patterns of affiliation might enable them to transmit information from one side of the network to the other and/or to mediate disputes among the constituencies.[10] All five lawyers in the core of figure 3.1 were associated with one or more mediator organizations—the Ethics and Public Policy Center, the Heritage Foundation, and the Federalist Society—whose missions placed them between the two factions, with ties to both.[11]

The concentration of lawyers in two largely separate clusters—a business group and a religious conservative group—appears to reflect a fundamental divide within the American conservative coalition. Lawyers and organizations in the core of this network are well positioned to promote cooperation within the conservative alliance.

THE INTERVIEWED LAWYERS: CLASS AND CULTURAL CONFLICT AMONG LAWYERS OF THE CONSERVATIVE COALITION

What do the statistics and figures generated by these analyses *mean?* Do the divergent characteristics of the 1300 lawyers reflect deeper social and cultural divisions within the conservative alliance? Are there also differences among the prominent lawyers interviewed for this book, or are those lawyers similar in ways that the larger set of 1300 lawyers are not? What, if anything, distinguishes lawyers associated with mediator organizations, who seem to hold particularly important and powerful positions in the conservative network by virtue of their place between the two primary competing constituencies?

Data from my interviews help to explain and give texture to the findings of the earlier research. They show that lawyers for the core constituencies of the American conservative coalition inhabit different social worlds. Lawyers for social conservative and libertarian causes were generally more focused on the goals of the constituencies they served than on the fate of the conservative alliance. Only the lawyers for mediator groups appeared particularly interested in finding common ground.

Table 3.2 identifies basic characteristics of the interviewed lawyers. Like those in the larger set examined in the prior research (Heinz, Paik, and Southworth 2003), the interviewed lawyers were overwhelmingly male:

TABLE 3.2: Characteristics of Interviewed Lawyers

Characteristic	n	%
Gender:		
Male	67	93
Female	5	7
Constituency:		
Religious	16	22
Abortion	9	12
Order maintenance	4	6
Libertarian	19	26
Affirmative action	4	6
Business	11	15
Mediator	9	12
Religion:		
Catholic	15	21
Protestant II	16	22
Protestant I	19	26
Jewish	16	22
Not religious	4	6
Other	2	3
Practice setting:		
Advocacy organizations	35	48
Think tanks	5	7
Universities	8	11
Trade associations	4	6
Large firms	7	10
Small firms and solo	13	18
Age group:		
30s	6	8
40s	27	38
50s	24	33
60s	10	14
70s	4	6
80s	1	1
Law school:		
Elite	21	29
Prestige	12	17
Regional	14	19
Local	25	35
Federal clerkship:		
Yes	13	19
No	59	81
Location:		
D.C.	30	41
D.C. suburb	4	6
Other major city	22	31
Elsewhere	16	22

only five were women. The proportion of women in the interviewed set (five of seventy-two, or roughly 7 percent) is somewhat smaller than their proportion of the larger pool (16 percent), but it reflects women's scant representation among leading lawyers in the organizations selected for this research. Women's political values may help to explain their relative absence. Although women certainly have been among the core activists in conservative politics (see Klatch 1987; McGirr 2001), voting patterns indicate that they are less supportive of the conservative agenda—in all its variety—than men are (Edsall 2006). The under-representation of women at the top of the conservative law movement is also consistent with their failure to break into the highest ranks of other sectors of the legal profession. Women are now about 27 percent of American lawyers (Carson 2004) but a much smaller proportion of the profession's most prominent and financially successful members. A recent study of the Chicago bar found that the predicted probability that women would earn salaries in the top quartile for American lawyers in 1995 was 7 percent (Heinz et al. 2005, 68) and that the likelihood that they would be partners in a firm with a hundred or more lawyers by age 43 (the mean age in the survey) was only 6 percent (Heinz et al. 2005, 67).[12]

The interviewed lawyers represented all constituencies of the conservative coalition. They came from varied religious backgrounds; Protestants were most numerous, but Catholics and Jews also were well represented. Roughly half worked in advocacy organizations, and the remaining lawyers held jobs in think tanks, universities, trade associations, and firms. Most were in their forties, fifties, and sixties. Almost half of the interviewed lawyers attended schools in the elite and prestige categories. Two-fifths of them worked in Washington, D.C. Roughly one-third worked in other major cities, and one-fifth worked "elsewhere."

The remainder of this section compares the characteristics, backgrounds, and values of the lawyers for the various constituencies. It demonstrates a strong correspondence between lawyers' social backgrounds and their present commitments and attitudes, a finding consistent with research showing that people tend not to repudiate the worlds from which they come (e.g., Klatch 1999; Mattei and Niemi 1991; Niemi and Jennings 1991). Religious conservatives usually come from rural and less economically privileged environments, and many of them openly invoke God as a source of inspiration and guidance. Lawyers for libertarian groups also generally come from modest backgrounds, but they are less religious and more enamored with markets and personal liberty. Most of the business representatives come from economically secure circumstances and describe their advocacy for business-oriented causes as work rather than activism. Lawyers for mediator groups differ from lawyers for the other constituencies in their especially elite educational credentials, prominence, ties to the legal establishment, and commitment to identifying common ground.

Religious Conservatives

Nineteen of the twenty-five religious conservatives and abortion opponents I interviewed were Catholics and "type II" Protestants—a category including the more conservative Protestant denominations and excluding only the "mainstream" denominations: Episcopalian, Methodist, Lutheran, Presbyterian, and Congregationalist (Laumann et al. 2000, 60). Ten worked outside of major cities, and all but six of the twenty-five worked in the Southeast, Midwest, and West. They came primarily from working-class backgrounds, although several had fathers in higher status occupations: the ministry, the military, business, and medicine. Eight of them had graduated from Protestant or Catholic colleges, and four had attended divinity school. Three had graduated from religiously affiliated law schools, and two-thirds of them held degrees from local or regional law schools. Only one of twenty-five had clerked for a federal judge.

Some of these lawyers expressed considerable ambivalence about lawyers and other economic elites. A leading advocate for Christian causes reported that his father had been dismayed that his son planned to attend law school because he believed that lawyers were "pond scum and parasites." An abortion opponent reported that his family thought that lawyers were "all politicians and crooks." A religious liberty advocate recalled that several interviews with law firms during law school had made him "feel creepy." Another noted that he had disliked most of his law school classmates, many of whom already had tried to do something idealistic with their lives but had returned to law school to prepare to make money. Several of these lawyers indicated that they continued to identify with ordinary Americans after becoming lawyers. An advocate for an antipornography organization, for example, said that he "grew up not having a lot of money" and that he "still felt like one of the little guys, one of the little people." Another lawyer, whose organization sponsors Christian legal services programs, said that he strongly believed that the system was "stacked" against the poor.

Several social conservatives indicated that their parents' backgrounds and views had strongly influenced their own. An abortion opponent explained that his father was a doctor who "was absolutely convinced that it was unethical to do abortions": "All of his textbooks were arrayed above my bed in my room . . . , and one textbook was embryology. And I can still remember the pictures. . . . and what science said about the unborn."[13] Another abortion opponent reported that his mother was an obstetrical nurse who "[came] home with stories all the time, so that I was highly sensitized to prenatal life." A lawyer whose parents were active in his state's right-to-life organization said that he "probably got interested in this issue through them originally."

Other mentors and sources of inspiration for these lawyers included priests and ministers, teachers, and prominent leaders of the religious populist wing of the movement, including Stanton Evans, Richard John Neuhaus (author of *The Naked Public Square* [1984]), and Francis Schaeffer.

Lawyers for social conservative groups generally indicated that they were active in their churches and highly committed, and many discussed the role of prayer and calling in their lives. One had served as the dean of a Christian law school. Another had founded several churches himself, and yet another was a part-time minister. An abortion opponent and religious liberty advocate said of his decision to become a lawyer, "A lot of prayer went into it. As a Christian person it was important to me . . . that I do things that seem to me to be in the service of God." Another religious conservative explained that his decision to pursue law reflected his belief that he had been "called by the highest power to do justice and serve our fellow men and women." A religious liberties advocate said that his transition from journalism to law was God's will: "I don't think God wanted me to be a journalist; He wanted me to be a lawyer." Another said of his choices, "I think God sort of had His hand on me, sort of pushing in a certain direction." A lawyer who left practice for the seminary, expecting to become a pastor, thereafter concluded that God had called him to serve as general counsel for a religious group: "I've thought a lot about God's calling in my life. . . . It's a calling that says, 'I've gifted you in these different ways. You have this kind of experience. You figure out how best to serve the kingdom. . . . '" Recounting his decision to pursue work for a Christian organization, another lawyer said, "I was being drawn to God by the Spirit."

Like many of their counterparts on the political left (Granfield 1992, 37–40; Zemans and Rosenblum 1981), some religious conservatives indicated that they had been motivated to attend law school out of a vague sense that doing so would prepare them to serve people. A lawyer who eventually became a pornography opponent said that he went to law school without any particular social or political agenda, but "buried in my soul was a desire to do something good with my life." Another said that his decision to attend law school "was stimulated in my mind by a concept that, as an attorney, you can do more good than one can as a layperson." An abortion opponent reported that his decision to pursue law came "primarily from my study of the prophets in the Old Testament and their concern with social justice," and another said that "the idea of helping people, particularly the poor . . . representing their rights in court was quite appealing to me." An advocate for a Catholic group became interested in doing legal services work for the poor and spent much of his second and third years of law school working in a legal aid program. A religious liberties advocate reported that he had believed that law school would give him the tools necessary "to help people in their own personal crisis situations."

Several religious conservatives described epiphanies that had led them to leave private practice for jobs that would better fulfill their religious commitments. One recounted driving down the highway as he was thinking about how to reconcile his Christian beliefs with his career—"whether I want[ed] my life to be about prestige and money and whether those things were really what my life was supposed to be about"—when "the radio . . . all of a sudden lock[ed] into this . . . Christian station and . . . one of Jim Dobson's *Focus on the Family* shows had started and the topic of the show was "Where are the Christian lawyers?.'" The same lawyer recalled that becoming a born-again Christian led him to conclude that "this change in my life, acknowledging, recognizing that I'm a Christian, should have something to do with how I spend the better part of my day, what my job is, what my career is, what my vocation is, what my calling is." Another lawyer, who was then a partner in a large firm, remembered kneeling down in prayer, saying, "God, I have no idea what to do with my life" and later concluding that God had answered his prayers by placing him "in the vortex of the Christian law movement." Another said, "I was really good at my job [as a prosecutor of obscenity] but I didn't really connect with the spiritual side of things" until one day when he received a message in church: "I felt like the hair on the back of my neck stood up." Thereafter, he said, "God became much more relevant to my life . . . —a constant presence . . . , every moment, every day—and had direct input in what I did for a living."

Several lawyers described other aspects of their home lives that distinguished them from other categories of interviewed lawyers. Two of them homeschooled their children for religious reasons, and one said that he regularly participated in "an accountability group" consisting of several friends who "meet once a week to pray and talk about, Are we being accountable to God, to our church, to our families?"

Religious devotion appeared to strongly influence the goals to which these lawyers devoted their work and the processes through which they charted careers. As explored in chapter 4, most of these lawyers emphatically rejected conventional professional norms, according to which lawyers are not morally accountable for the ends and means they pursue on behalf of clients as long as those ends and means are legal.

Libertarians and Affirmative Action Opponents

Many of the libertarians and affirmative action opponents also came from modest backgrounds; eight reported that their fathers had held working-class jobs, and another five said that their parents had owned or run very small businesses. They were disproportionately Jewish (nine of twenty-three), but their ranks also included five type I Protestants, four type II Protestants, three Catholics,[14] and two lawyers who said that they were not religious. Ten of the twenty-three libertarians and affirmative action opponents had attended law schools in the elite and prestige categories, and four had clerked for federal judges. Many of those who indicated that they were associated with a church or synagogue said that they were not particularly active. One described himself as "ethnically Jewish but religiously . . . secular," and another said that he was an atheist. The only libertarian who described himself as a "very conservative Christian" said that he did not "talk much about that in public" because that information might hurt him in libertarian circles. The libertarians and affirmative action opponents were heavily concentrated in Washington, D.C., and the West.

Many libertarians attributed their beliefs to their upbringing and other early formative experiences. A child of immigrants who had fled communism explained that his parents had liked Reagan's confrontational approach to the Soviet Union and that he shared his parents' political views: "The apple doesn't fall far from the tree." A property rights advocate said, "I've always had a basic distrust of government agencies," and he attributed to his father his own view that land development generally should be allowed: "I know how personally proud he felt when he saw development going on [in the suburb where they lived]. . . . I have no idea why, but I'm sure that some of that came through. It was sort of in the blood. It was just a feeling that that sort of thing was *good,* and that people are able to do things like that, and that's probably what makes this country what it is."

A libertarian recalled having to pay taxes in his first job as a commission salesman and being audited that year on a salary of $3000; "That experience gathered the mind . . . [and] my anti-government leanings, which were already fairly well-rooted, started to flourish." An affirmative action opponent said that both of his grandfathers were conservatives who had taken a strong interest in politics, and he remembered "very early on understanding and appreciating the distinction between de facto and de jure discrimination or segregation": "It seemed to me to make perfect sense to say that you couldn't have de jure segregation—that it was wrong to segregate people on the basis of color. And also that it made no sense at all to say that people were going to be bused in order to reach a particular racial balance. I mean that was something that I didn't have to struggle with at all. I mean, yeah, well of course that's right."

Several of the libertarians ascribed importance to reading Ayn Rand's books during their teenage years. One said of Ayn Rand's influence, "That got me started in certainly in a more libertarian direction, and not only got me thinking about these issues but also instilled in me a great passion for them and a desire to really want to go out and change the world." He asserted that the same was true of many of his libertarian colleagues: "It usually begins with Ayn Rand—I think that is true of a lot of people who get involved in libertarian-type issues. . . . " Another lawyer said of his increasingly libertarian perspective during his teenage years in the 1970s, "I saw what was going on around me, and started to read some of Ayn Rand, which is probably a familiar story." A third libertarian noted that he had been "dating a girl who listened to me talk about government and gave me a copy of Barry Goldwater's *Conscience of a Conservative.* . . . She then gave me a copy of Ayn Rand's, *Atlas Shrugged.* . . . " A fourth said, "I've been . . . a libertarian since my last year of high school after watching *The Fountainhead* on the late night movie showing on television."

Mentors and sources of inspiration for these lawyers included Bernard Siegan, a University of San Diego professor and strong property rights proponent, Henry Manne, a founder of the law and economics movement who ran institutes and seminars for students and faculty during the 1980s, and University of Chicago economist, Milton Friedman. Some of the older libertarians had been members of the Mont Pelerin Society, an organization established after World War II to consider the "state and . . . fate" of liberalism. Many of these lawyers reported that they had been influenced by law and economics programs, libertarian law organization meetings, and Federalist Society events in college and law school.

Business Representatives

Most of the lawyers for business advocacy groups came from middle- or upper-middle-class backgrounds. Their fathers included a lawyer, two accountants, several business executives, one commercial real estate developer, a dentist, a scientist, and a small business owner. One recalled that he had been familiar since he was a young boy "with business and what lawyers do" because his father had owned several businesses and "from time to time there would be meetings at home and lawyers would be there." Another recalled that he had liked what he saw of the lives of large-firm lawyers when he was young: "[T]he people I knew that were close to me, parents of friends, . . . There's something about senior partners in law firms—there's just a way that they carry themselves. . . . Their lives are interesting." Six of eleven had attended top 20 law schools, and three had clerked for federal judges. They worked in nicely appointed office buildings, primarily in Washington, D.C. Some were partners in well-known national law firms, and others were leaders of national trade associations and business advocacy organizations.

Several of the business lawyers attributed their decision to pursue law to pressure imposed by their parents or their own concerns about financial security. One said, "My dad died when I was ten. . . . There was very little money left. My mother worked at night and on the weekends. . . . And I realized there was no business to go into, there [were] no family heirlooms, and I had to start something on my own. And my mom said, after my dad died, that I was the man of the house, and I realized that I had to build my own castle, so to speak." Another business lawyer remembered that he had hoped to enter academia, but his parents told him that he "was a lunatic and that that was no way to earn a living." He then "went out one night, and got drunk, and came back and applied to take the LSATs." Another business lawyer recalled, "My parents were very flexible and gave me two options when I went to college. I could either go to get an MBA afterwards or get a law degree. . . . " A business litigator in a private firm said that he "sometimes regretted" his decision to practice law because he could have "made a lot more money" using his quantitative aptitude in another field.

Lawyers for business nonprofit advocacy organizations appeared to be comfortable in the business world and to believe in their clients' broad goals, a finding consistent with Robert Nelson's conclusion about large-firm lawyers: "[O]n questions of law and policy related to their own practice [they] strongly identify with positions favorable to clients" (Nelson

1988, 12). But these lawyers did not view the largely defensive posture of their work as a type of political advocacy. One, for example, denied that he was "any kind of activist": "There isn't anything in my back-ground . . . that said I was going to law school to be the next . . . Ralph Nader or . . . anything like that. . . . I didn't get into it to push an agenda." Another business lawyer said of his decision to attend law school, "I wasn't like . . . Ralph Nader. . . . I didn't go there to change the world." A lawyer for a trade association claimed that he "was not a politically active type," and another said of his decision to study law, "I was not out on a cause. I just thought it was important in how people were guarded. Law was fundamentally our protection." Another business lawyer recalled that pursuing social change through law "was the last thing on [his] mind" when he decided to attend law school. These lawyers viewed law as an occupation rather than a politi-cal activity or calling, and they were happy to be part of the establishment. Chapter 4 explores these essential differences in the professional identities of lawyers who worked primarily for large commercial interests and advo-cates for other conservative and libertarian causes.

Although all of them identified some religious affiliation—mostly mainstream Protestant and Jewish—most of the business lawyers claimed only loose ties, if any, to organized religion. One (who likes yoga) said, "I was raised a Lutheran, but . . . I'm not particularly enamored of organized religion . . . because I think it only likes those who are like them. There isn't really much respect for other religions." Another reported, "I am not an atheist and I'm not an agnostic, but I am not a member of a church." An advocate for a trade group said that he was involved in "a very loose-knit Jewish group" made up of Jews and non-Jews "who don't feel terribly comfortable in a traditional religious synagogue." Another secular Jew in a large firm said, "I do attend on the high holy days by purchasing a ticket from a local synagogue, but I have not joined it." A litigator who represented business groups on regulatory matters said, "We're Episcopa-lians. . . . But I'm not deeply involved, I must say," and another described himself as "Lutheran, when I go [to church] on Christmas Eve." Another business advocate said of his religious views, "I play golf on Sunday."

Mediators

Lawyers for mediator organizations were the children of professionals and other high-status occupational groups. Many said that they were active in their churches and synagogues, but none was associated with an evangeli-cal Protestant denomination. They were among the best-known lawyers of the conservative movement, and all had participated in constructing and/or maintaining the organizational infrastructure for conservative public interest law described in chapter 2. Their mentors included major conservative figures—such as leading economists and prominent conservative judges (including U.S. Supreme Court Justices Scalia, Thomas and Rehnquist), well-known conservative lawyers (such as William Bradford Reynolds and Kenneth Starr), public intellectuals (including William F. Buckley and Walter Olson), and professors (Yale's Ralph Winter [later chief judge of the U.S. Court of Appeals, Second Circuit]; Cornell's Jeremy Rabkin; the University of Chicago's Richard Epstein and Richard Posner [later U.S. Court of Appeals judge for the Seventh Circuit]; Michael McConnell [now U.S. Court of Appeals judge for the Tenth Circuit]; and Philip Kurland). Eight of the nine lawyers for mediator groups had attended top twenty law schools, and six had served on law review. Five of them had clerked for federal judges, and three had clerked for U.S. Supreme Court justices. Seven of the nine had served at very senior levels in Republican administrations. All but one lived and worked in major metropolitan areas.

Just as the backgrounds and values of lawyers for social conservative and libertarian causes may have led them to become involved in the causes they serve, so too did the backgrounds of the lawyers for mediator groups seem to predispose them to serve as brokers within the conservative movement. These lawyers' more elite social and educational credentials gave them a sense of themselves as natural leaders—as people of ideas and influence. Three of the nine had once been Democrats. Many of them had strong ties to selective institutions that spanned party lines. One was a member of the American Law Institute, an elite society of lawyers, judges, and legal scholars, and another had chaired an ABA section. Another, who had graduated from an elite law school class that had produced many major public figures of the Left, emphasized that he continued to share with those classmates a commitment to "making a difference." An experienced appellate advocate noted proudly that he was on everyone's short list to judge moot courts for lawyers preparing for Supreme Court arguments: "I would do a moot court for almost anybody on the right or the left. My most recent moot court was for a Georgetown law professor. . . . I even mooted a public defender who was representing some accused criminal on a Fourth Amendment evidentiary matter!"

Lawyers for mediator organizations spoke optimistically about maintaining the conservative coalition, and they tended to downplay divisions. One said that he "personally believe[d] in fusionism"—a position associated with Frank Meyer, who asserted in the 1960s that traditionalists and classical liberals shared a faith in "an objective moral order" and a commitment to limits on the power of the state (Meyer 1964). This lawyer observed that conservative and libertarian public interest law groups were part of a "loose community" who "all view each other as allies and fellow members of a movement," with a common pledge "to pursue traditional values" through means that do not impinge on liberty. Another lawyer said that conservatives and libertarians agree on several "general principles." Yet another lawyer said of disagreements among lawyers of the conservative movement, "with any group of strong-minded individuals you're going to have differences," but "the tensions are often more apparent than real" and "there's usually an exaggeration of the differences in the news media."

The mediators' optimistic assessments of relationships within the conservative alliance contrasted with the views of lawyers for other types of organizations, some of whom identified substantial conflicts in policy objectives and values. Several libertarians insinuated or stated directly that business advocates were unprincipled. An affirmative action opponent described as "a general problem, from my perspective, with corporate America" that "[t]hey don't really like controversy [because] controversy is bad for business. . . . " A property rights advocate said that business people tend to be hypocritical; they oppose regulation that interferes with their business objectives but support regulation that serves their class interests:

> It is a curious phenomenon that captains of industry, who take out full-page ads in the *Wall Street Journal* opposing intrusive government regulation, are the fiercest defenders and promoters of government regulation when it comes to their suburban homes and their tree-shaded lawns. . . . [T]hey are not interested in limiting government power to regulate in that context, because it serves their purposes. It makes their suburbs more exclusive, more expensive, and in recent decades it also meant that their equities have appreciated in spectacular fashion. And also on the dark side, it keeps out people they consider undesirable. . . .

This lawyer argued that such hypocrisy explains why the "property side" of the conservative movement has "historically taken such a beating"— because businessmen "are a bunch of idiots" who "do not see the connection."

Libertarians also emphasized their differences with social conservatives. One noted that he and his libertarian friends and family "were never . . . part of the social conservatives—we never had much . . . in common." Another said that, although "the libertarians and conservatives have some overlap, it's also important not to lose sight of" what divides libertarians and social conservatives: "[I]n the area of . . . government enforcing virtue, the area of so-called victimless crimes or crimes without complainants, as I call them, consensual adult conduct, it's hard for libertarians to understand the legitimate role for government to make in deciding what people are free to choose to read or not read, what substances people choose to ingest or not ingest for medical reasons or for recreational reasons." Another noted that while libertarians were consistent regarding the role of government, conservatives were not: "there is a great murky area with conservatives . . . where you wonder, What is your position on this? Are you in favor of less government of more government? Well, in some areas less, some areas more."

Social conservatives similarly stressed their differences with libertarians and business advocates. One said of "economic libertarian types" that "we don't run in the same circles." Libertarians, he explained, "need moral ballast to [their] worldview or it just becomes empty." A religious liberties advocate declared that he was not an advocate of federalism. He noted that social conservatives "don't have a dogmatic position that the role of the federal government should decrease and the role of the states increase" because they sometimes value the federal government's power to enforce moral imperatives: "I don't believe that the federal government should play an ever decreasing role in significant civil rights issues. . . . We are not ideologues in the jurisprudential sense or in the political sense. We use the tools that are available and sometimes those tools have to be very large hammers delivered by the Congress." Social conservatives disparaged business lawyers' focus on money and prestige. One said that he had disliked most of his law school classmates, whose "big ambition was to work for a large, smelly corporate 'big dog' law firm." A lawyer who had left a large firm to lead a Christian organization said that he had become increasingly uncomfortable in an environment that worshiped "two false gods—personal autonomy and wealth," and he concluded that his partners were equally uncomfortable with him; they had begun to view him as "one of those wild-eyed evangelicals." A lawyer who represents religious organizations on liability matters said that most business people simply do not understand religious people.

Business lawyers also emphasized their differences with social conservatives. A business lawyer who described himself as "an economic, fiscal conservative" said that his conservatism did not "spill over into social issues." Another volunteered that "the religious right . . . makes my skin crawl."

SOURCES OF PUBLIC FOUNDATION SUPPORT
FOR THE ORGANIZATIONS REPRESENTED
BY THE INTERVIEWED LAWYERS

Is there any relationship between the cultural differences among lawyers described above and foundation funding for the organizations they serve? The research summarized at the beginning of this chapter showed that the categories of organizations represented by the larger set of 1300 lawyers drew systematically from different sources of foundation funding, suggesting that the institutional patrons of conservative organizations were divided by constituency, just as the lawyers themselves were. An analysis of the categories of organizations represented by the *interviewed* lawyers tells a similar story.[15] I took the list of sixty-nine organizations for which the interviewed lawyers worked and broke them into categories by type of constituency served.[16] I then compiled a table of the five largest public foundation supporters for each organizational category for the years 2003–5—the latest year for which complete foundation funding data were available. Table 3.3 shows that there was no overlap among the top five foundation funders of religious and pro-life groups on the one hand and business and libertarian groups on the other.

Differences in the foundations' causes, in turn, reflect pronounced differences in the commitments of their founders and/or current administrators. The Edgar and Elsa Prince Foundation, the largest contributor to religious conservative causes, was founded by a Michigan auto parts manufacturer (*National Journal* 2004). His widow, Elsa Prince, sits on the board of the Family Research Council, one of the strongest proponents of the constitutional amendment to ban gay marriage (*National Journal* 2004).[17] The second largest funder of religious conservative causes, the Aimee and Frank Batten, Jr. Foundation, supports primarily Christian missionary and charitable organizations. Its founder, Frank Batten, Jr., is the chairman and chief executive officer of Landmark Communications, Inc. The third largest funder in this category, the Richard and Helen DeVos Foundation, was founded by Rich DeVos, cofounder of the Amway Corporation. It is a major patron of churches, ministries, Christian schools, and Christian advocacy groups (*Chronicle of Philanthropy* 2006). Richard DeVos, Jr., is married to the daughter of Edgar and Elsa Prince

TABLE 3.3 : Five Largest Foundation Supporters for Categories of Organizations
Represented by Interviewed Lawyers, 2003–2005

Foundation	Amount, $
Religious:	
Edgar and Elsa Prince	2,267,000
Aimee and Frank Batten, Jr. Foundation	2,000,000
Richard and Helen DeVos Foundation	1,575,000
Arthur DeMoss Foundation	1,136,275
God's Gift	1,050,000
Abortion:	
Arthur S. DeMoss Foundation	470,000
Thomas and Dorothy Leavey Foundation	100,000
Leptas Foundation	50,000
Stewardship Foundation	30,000
Ochylski Family Foundation	25,000
Libertarian:	
Walton Family Foundation, Inc.	3,085,623
Lynde and Harry Bradley Foundation	2,232,500
Sarah Scaife Foundation	1,615,000
Lilly Endowment	1,125,000
ExxonMobil Foundation	1,000,000
M. J. Murdoch Charitable Trust	1,000,000
Affirmative action:	
Lynde and Harry Bradley Foundation	615,000
F. M. Kirby Foundation	350,000
Sarah Scaife Foundation	275,000
W. K. Kellogg Foundation	200,000
Carthage Foundation	150,000
Business:	
Marcus Foundation, Inc.	500,000
ExxonMobil Foundation	457,000
Lynde and Harry Bradley Foundation	312,500
F. M. Kirby Foundation	280,000
General Motors Foundation	165,000
Mediators:	
Lynde and Harry Bradley Foundation	6,257,700
Sarah Scaife Foundation	5,925,000
Brady Education Foundation	5,712,500
Samuel Roberts Noble Foundation	5,000,000
Kovner Foundation	4,257,035
Order maintenance:	
Sarah Scaife Foundation	725,000
Lynde and Harry Bradley Foundation	451,000
Carthage Foundation	425,000
F. M. Kirby Foundation	240,000
Arthur S. DeMoss Foundation	150,000

(Risen 2007). The Arthur DeMoss Foundation, the fourth largest contributor to the religious conservative category and the largest contributor to abortion opponents, draws on the fortune of Arthur S. DeMoss, who sold insurance to conservative Christians (Van Biema 1999). He began his life as a bookie but, after a religious conversion in his midtwenties, decided to devote his life to Christian causes (Van Biema 1999). When he died in 1979, his wife took control of the foundation, whose projects have included a $9 million TV campaign for youth abstinence and a $20 million per year campaign of anti-abortion TV spots featuring the phrase "Life. What a beautiful choice" (Van Biema 1999). A 1986 book published by the foundation and edited by DeMoss's daughter calls on Christians to "reclaim a dying America":

> We must go back to the cross, where the incarnate Son of God was cursed, condemned, crucified for man—the creature's sin. The crisis is acute. The danger is imminent. Time is running out. Something miraculous must happen in the heart and soul of America . . . now, before it is too late. The choice is clear. It is repent or perish, revival or ruin, Christ or chaos. The question of the hour is: Which Way America?" (DeMoss 1986, 16, 229).

God's Gift, ranked fifth in this category, was established in 1998 by Helen Lovaas in Temecula, California, to support human services and religious organizations (Foundation Directory 2006, 683). The Bolthouse Foundation, the sixth largest contributor to the religious groups, makes grants only to evangelical Christian organizations. All grantees must, by board resolution, affirm the Bolthouse Foundation's Statement of Faith, which includes a declaration that the Bible is "inerrant in the original writing" and that "man was created by a direct act of God in His image, not from previously existing creatures" (Bolthouse 2006). The Thomas and Dorothy Leavey Foundation, a major supporter of Catholic causes, is the second largest funder of pro-life organizations. Third is the Leptas Foundation Trust, a small private foundation in Littleton, Colorado, that supports a variety of Christian missionary and service organizations. Ranked fourth in this category is Milwaukee's Stewardship Foundation, established by the grandson of Frederick Weyerhaeuser, founder of the timber company, Weyerhaeuser Co. It "provides resources to Christ-centered organizations whose mission is to share their faith in Jesus Christ" (Postman 2006).[18] The Ochylski Family Foundation, the next largest contributor in this category, is based on the fortune of Edward Ochylski, Jr., who began working as a butcher at the age of fourteen and eventually built several large meatpacking businesses. He attends Mass daily and has contributed millions to the Catholic Church (Madden 2004).

The foundation supporters of the libertarian, anti-affirmative action, and business groups articulate missions to advance markets and entrepreneurial activity. The Walton Family Foundation, the largest contributor to libertarian causes, was created in 1987 by Sam Walton, the founder of Wal-Mart, with assets in 2005 worth nearly $1.329 billion. The foundation initially gave away relatively small amounts of money to many organizations, but it has since targeted its efforts on vouchers and charter schools (Serwer 2004). The Lynde and Harry Bradley Foundation, the second largest contributor to the libertarian category and the largest funder of the affirmative action and mediator categories, became a significant force in conservative politics in 1985, when Allen-Bradley was sold to Rockwell International for over $1.5 billion and the existing foundation received $290 million.[19] The foundation seeks to promote "democratic capitalism and the institutions, principles and values that sustain and nurture it" (Bradley 2006). Its 2005 Form 990 stated that its assets were worth $706 million. The Sarah Scaife Foundation, the third largest supporter of the libertarian category and one of the largest supporters of the anti-affirmative action and mediator categories, was created by the granddaughter of Andrew Mellon. Her son, Richard Mellon Scaife, began promoting conservative causes through his family's foundations in 1973 (Himmelstein 1990, 147–48). Scaife also controls the Carthage Foundation, the fifth largest contributor to the affirmative action organizations and the third largest contributor to the order-maintenance groups. As briefly described in chapter 2, the Scaife foundations, along with Bradley, Olin, and Smith Richardson—sometimes called "the four sisters" (Gottfried 1993, 128)—have played major roles in bankrolling the development of the libertarian conservative counterestablishment.[20] The Lilly Endowment, based in Indianapolis and founded by three Lilly family members through contributions of stock in their pharmaceutical business, focuses primarily on state and local community development projects in Indiana and Indianapolis. The ExxonMobil Foundation and the M. J. Murdoch Charitable Trust tied for fifth place, each contributing $1 million to the libertarian groups during 2003–2005. ExxonMobil focuses on the communities in which it has operations and on national issues of interest to the oil industry, and the M. J. Murdoch Charitable Trust emphasizes science and technology. The F. M. Kirby Foundation, one of the largest supporters in the affirmative action and business categories, was founded in 1931 by Fred

Morgan Kirby, cofounder of the F. W. Woolworth store chain (Medeiros 2006). The foundation has distributed over $150 million since 1985 and $345 million in the past 40 years (Medeiros 2006) toward projects it deems likely to "encourage [ ] self-reliance and diminish[] government's role." The Kellogg Foundation, the fourth largest contributor to affirmative action organizations, focuses its philanthropy on "young people, ethnic groups, creators of wealth, social entrepreneurs and corporate innovators," with an emphasis on "helping people help themselves."[21] The Marcus Foundation, the largest contributor to the business category, is the personal foundation of Bernard Marcus, cofounder of Home Depot.

The top foundation supporters of the mediator groups are more ideologically diverse, reflecting the breadth of the issues pursued by these organizations. The third largest contributor to mediator groups, the Brady Education Foundation, is based on the fortune of William H. Brady, who was a prominent Milwaukee industrialist and one of the founding supporters of the *National Review*, the Heritage Foundation, and the Ethics and Public Policy Center. The Brady Education Foundation focuses on "the institutional foundations of a free society: morality and public life, family and community, and competitive educational structures. . . . " The fourth largest supporter of the mediator category, the Samuel Roberts Noble Foundation, was founded by an Oklahoma oilman. It emphasizes agricultural research but also has given major support to the Heritage Foundation—at least $9 million since 1998.[22] The Kovner Foundation, which distributed almost $3 million to the mediator groups in 2003–2005, was founded by Bruce Kovner, the founder and chairman of Caxton Associates, a hedge fund.[23] Kovner serves as chairman of the Board of Trustees of the American Enterprise Institute.

There is, then, a clear divide in the institutional sources of financial support for the two major constituencies served by the interviewed lawyers. That is not to say that there is no common ground among the foundations that support the religious and pro-life groups on the one hand and the libertarian, affirmative action, and business groups on the other. Below the top five supporters, in the lower ranks of contributors, there is some overlap. For example, the Edgar and Elsa Prince Foundation, the biggest supporter of religious conservative groups, gave very small gifts to libertarian organizations. The Bradley Foundation focuses overwhelmingly on libertarian and mediator organizations,[24] but it also made grants to several social conservative groups represented by the interviewed lawyers during the 2003–2005 period. Generally, however, the separation in

TABLE 3.4 : Total and Mean Foundation Funding for Categories of Organizations Represented by Interviewed Lawyers, 2003–2005

Organizational category	Total foundation funding, $	Mean, $
Mediators	48,650,643	6,081,330
Libertarian	21,784,926	1,815,410
Religious	11,523,543	576,177
Business	3,110,750	222,196
Order maintenance	2,365,800	473,160
Affirmative action	1,875,000	625,000
Abortion	710,000	177,500

the sources of foundation support by organizational category is consistent and striking.

As shown in Table 3.4, by far the largest amount of foundation funding—$48,650,653—went to the mediator organizations. Libertarian groups were in second place, with $21,784,926, and religious groups were third, with $11,523,543. Business-oriented groups received relatively little foundation funding, probably because foundations expected businesses themselves to provide financial support for these groups. Order-maintenance groups, affirmative action opponents (who suffered a major blow in 2003 when the U.S. Supreme Court upheld the University of Michigan Law School's affirmative action policy in *Grutter*), and groups that focus exclusively on abortion received relatively modest amounts of foundation support.

The disproportionate amount of foundation money invested in mediator organizations, and the especially elite and prominent lawyers they attract, provide some evidence that these organizations may play an important role in integrating the conservative movement. They are, in some sense, the conservative movement's institutional response to the dissensus described in this chapter. Conservative patrons may also believe that these organizations tend to enhance the legitimacy of conservative ideas and tame the movement's more radical elements. Mediator institutions and their roles in the conservative movement are examined more closely in chapter 6.

CONCLUSION

The data presented in this chapter suggest that lawyers for the constituencies that compose the conservative movement are fundamentally divided.

Lawyers' accounts of their backgrounds and values suggest that they do not see themselves as a single professional community, and the diverse sources of foundation support for these organizations support the view that the organizations serve distinct strands of the conservative coalition. As one interviewed lawyer said, "We are seeing now more an emphasis on cooperation, but we come together for a like interest on a case or on a project, or something like this, but there is no real established interconnectivity that means we're all functioning as part of a whole or anything." Although the success of the conservative movement may depend in part on promoting a shared sense of purpose among these lawyers, fundamental class and cultural differences tend to separate these lawyers and their organizations along the lines of the constituencies they represent.

4

Professional Identity

Do lawyers who serve conservative and libertarian causes feel personally committed to the causes they serve, or do they view their work simply as client service in the conventional sense? Are there differences in professional identities by types of causes pursued? This chapter considers whether the interviewed lawyers identified with the goals and constituencies they served and how differences in their personal backgrounds shaped their understanding of professional role. It draws primarily from lawyers' own accounts of their career histories and service to causes rather than any objective assessment of their motivations, commitments, and behavior. Although individual accounts are notoriously unreliable sources for objective factual reports (Snow and Machalek 1984, 175), they provide compelling evidence of how individuals perceive their roles and explain their actions (Hunt and Benford 1994, 489; Engel and Munger 1996). What, then, do lawyers for conservative causes say about why they do what they do?

Two extreme possibilities mark the theoretical ends of a continuum of lawyers' personal identification with the causes they serve. On one end is the "hired gun," who denies moral accountability for the ends and means pursued on behalf of clients. However loathsome his clients and their goals might be, he serves them unapologetically, without regard for the work's moral or political implications.[1] On the other end of the spectrum is the cause lawyer, who accepts work only for clients and causes he believes in. The quintessential cause lawyer serves selflessly, without regard for his own career prospects or financial well-being (Scheingold and Sarat 2004).[2] He is more interested in the causes he serves than the particular clients involved, and he may sacrifice clients' interests and professional standing to serve the cause (Luban 1988; 319–40; Scheingold and Sarat 2004, 16–17).

Most real lawyers, of course, fall somewhere between these boundaries, as do all of the lawyers interviewed for this research. Even lawyers who espouse conventional understandings of their professional roles tend to identify with the interests and views of their clients (Nelson 1988), and even the most ideologically driven lawyers care about developing their careers and paying their bills. This chapter analyzes whether and to what extent the interviewed lawyers identified with the causes they represented. It shows that none of them fits either of the extreme models—the hired gun or the pure cause lawyer. However, many exemplify less radical versions of those competing conceptions of professionalism. Some emphasize service to clients delivered through markets, and others stress personal accountability and commitment to a cause. Those differences in professional orientation are, in turn, tied to professional hierarchies within the conservative movement. The more conventional conception of role draws together business lawyers and their moneyed clients and promotes ties among elite lawyers across sectors and political lines. The cause lawyer model, on the other hand, insists on worthiness rather than financial reward or career development as the primary criterion for selecting clients. True believers tend to come from less elite backgrounds, to hold less fancy credentials, and to have fewer connections to the professional establishment.

PROFESSIONAL IDENTITY BY TYPES OF CAUSES SERVED

While chapter 3 addressed striking differences in the social backgrounds and values of lawyers for the various constituencies, this chapter considers how lawyers are divided by professional identity. In line with other research about the relationship between lawyers' professional norms and "the arenas" that produce them (Nelson and Trubek 1992), including bar associations (Schneyer 1992), the workplace (Nelson and Trubek 1992; Southworth 1996), and "communities of practice" (Mather, McEwen, and Maiman 2001), this chapter explores how lawyers' views about professional role vary by types of causes served. The starkest difference on this dimension was between the lawyers for business interests, on the one hand, and advocates for social conservative and libertarian interests, on the other. Lawyers who worked in large firms and trade associations on behalf of business interests appeared to agree with the positions they advocated on behalf of clients, but they did not view the work as an expression of personal political commitment. Lawyers for social conservative and libertarian groups, on the other hand, generally seemed more personally committed to the causes and constituencies they served. In this respect, then, lawyers for social conservative and libertarian groups were similar to one another and quite unlike the business advocates.

Business Lawyers

Business lawyers in large firms and trade associations generally did not view themselves as activists; they used fairly conventional terms to explain their roles. They did not quite endorse what William H. Simon (1978, 36–38) has described as the "principle of neutrality"—the view that lawyers should remain detached from their clients' ends and hold themselves unaccountable for the clients' purposes. Most of them indicated that they generally sympathized with the causes they served. A lawyer in a large firm said of his regulatory practice, "I'm very comfortable ideologically being on this side of the aisle, on this side of the divide in private practice. . . . I won't say I've never handled a case that I didn't agree with ideologically, but, by and large, since I'm skeptical of government regulation, I'm very comfortable fighting off [agency] action, which frequently I think goes beyond what it should." Another large firm lawyer said, "I am a passionate advocate for my clients' interests in almost all of the areas that I'm doing. I seldom find myself being neutral about something, or sort of disagreeing with something we have to say. I tend to believe in it." A lawyer who had been a strong advocate for civil justice reform well before he began to practice law noted with delight that his clients "pay me to do what I wanted to do anyway." Another tort reform advocate said that he believed that his work furthered good public policy by helping policy makers draw the right balance between competing objectives—compensating victims, while also ensuring that consumers can find affordable insurance and access to health care:

> I personally don't see it as, I want to be unfair to people that have been injured or to deny them their rights. But I'm also looking at, What about the rights of the people who aren't injured but do need access to doctors? Or you could apply it to manufacturing and say, I don't want to be unfair to people who have been injured, say, because of a drug, pharmaceutical product or something. But what about the people that may need the next vaccine that's developed on the market?. . . . That's really what has drawn me to this debate long before I ever had a client involved in it.

A lawyer active on the management side of labor issues said that even in his "raging liberal days" he had always "looked askance at the unions." They were on the wrong side of the issues he really cared about—civil rights and the Vietnam War. Moreover, unions were incompatible with his long-standing perspective that "the business owner owns the business and they really ought to be able to run the business that they want as long as they don't step over some really egregious lines. . . . " He noted that even in college, he was "not real big on having to be protected by a union or loading up the law with all kinds of employment protections." Instead, he had "always" believed "if somebody doesn't like working somewhere they just go somewhere else." Another lawyer who handled punitive damages appeals in a large firm said,

> I really do believe that what I'm doing is in the public interest. I feel as if the pendulum has swung far too far in favor of the plaintiffs' bar and that they are doing things that are injurious to the well-being of our country. That certain activities are no longer available, or easily available because of the fear of liability. That insurance premiums or the price of products have gone up unduly because of excessive liability. . . . So, when one thinks of public interest law, one doesn't typically think of well-heeled lawyers in fancy suits working at large law firms. But I do. I think that a lot of what we do is beneficial to the long-term economic health and happiness of this country.

These lawyers' expressions of comfort with their roles are consistent with Robert Nelson's (1988, 12) finding about large-firm lawyers—that "on questions of law and policy related to their own practice [large-firm lawyers] strongly identify with positions favorable to clients"—and with the finding of Heinz et al. (2005, 190–91) that large-firm lawyers tend to hold conservative views on economic issues.

Nevertheless, these business lawyers generally indicated that they viewed the organizations they served as clients rather than as beneficiaries of their personal political commitment. They appeared to accept the conventional view that they serve justice by selling their services in the market and playing their assigned roles in adversarial processes. The counsel to a business advocacy organization said that he cares about the issue on which he is active "because that's what clients pay me to care about." A large-firm lawyer who handled high-profile regulatory matters said that there were "lots of these issues where I would be glad to be on the other side": "I find the issues interesting and I like being a lawyer," but "there are not too many things that I've done that I'm necessarily all wrapped up

in personally; that's just not the way I look at things." Of one large litigation victory, he said, "Should I be proud of this? I don't know if I should
or not, but this case really killed . . . efforts to regulate a lot of substances
under that statute. It was a big case, an important case." Another business
advocate expressed confidence that "vigorous advocates on both sides" in
his area of expertise produced good public policy: "That's how, ultimately,
we probably as a society end up in the middle, with the best result, or the
most fair result."

These lawyers did not view their embrace of conventional practice
norms as a type of professional ideology; they rejected the idea that they
might be "cause lawyers" for business interests. A lawyer who described
himself as a "dyed-in-the-wool moderate" said that he was "not ideological at all": "I really think there is a distinction between groups like us that
fall within the conservative camp because of the interests of the clients we
serve and those who are pushing an ideological agenda." Another business
lawyer indicated that she viewed her task as advancing her clients' con-
crete objectives rather than promoting a coherent set of ideas or commitments. She counted herself a "very practical person"—not an ideologue:
"I'm looking at what the solution is. How do you fix the thing?. . . . Unlike
the Federalist Society and the Taxpayers Union and some of these other
groups, or if you would want to, on the other side, Joan Claybrook's group
and Ralph Nader's. . . . I [am] very much focused on doing my job—on
the pragmatic approach of what we're doing, how we get from A to B and
what we get done."

These lawyers for business interests styled themselves as political moderates, who could work across political lines and sectors and would not
allow conflict in their professional roles to become personal. Several said
that they sometimes voted for Democrats. Some emphasized that they enjoyed friendly relationships with their opponents. One lawyer said, "Oddly
enough, sometimes it's easier to be friends with the other side because you
just kind of know your role. You gotta put on your battle gear and . . . take
shots at each other and go have a beer afterwards." Another reported that
he had "a very good rapport" with his legislative opponents—"total professionals" who "do a great job representing their clients," and he noted
with dismay that an opponent had once refused to shake his hand. Another lawyer asserted that his group's success was partly attributable to
their good relationships with opponents and to not being perceived as
"ideologues or crazies." Another said of his past legislative work, "I always
liked it when we were able to cut across [party] lines." A lawyer for a large
trade association who had previously worked in government said, "I didn't

feel any compunction about moving from government to the private sector, because one is good and the other is bad. I don't believe that. There are bright public-spirited people in both arenas, and there are people not to be trusted in both arenas."

Business lawyers' distinctive professional identity corresponds with their exceptional position in the income hierarchy. I did not collect salary data, but these lawyers' offices and dress strongly suggested that they earned substantially more than their counterparts in advocacy organizations, think tanks, clinics, and small firms. They are paid well for their service to causes. Even when they pursue causes pro bono,[3] they do so from economically secure positions.

Lawyers for Social Conservative and Libertarian Interests

Lawyers who worked for social conservative and libertarian advocacy organizations generally appeared to be passionately committed to the causes they served. As described in chapter 3, many lawyers who worked for religious conservative groups invoked religious "calling" to explain their political activism. A lawyer who worked for a Christian advocacy group on abortion issues, for example, said that he believed that he had been "called" to serve "our fellow men and women" and that, while "secular people" often think of that as a "social change orientation, it was a much larger position for us." Another lawyer remembered that "one of the Bible verses that really weighed heavily on me . . . was the one about, to whom much is given much is expected. And I had realized that I've been really blessed . . . education at an Ivy League School, and a stable family and loving family, and going to a good law school and getting good grades and having a clerkship and all the rest. . . . And I was wondering how should I use that? How does God want me to use that?" Three Christian evangelical lawyers who had left private practice to work full time for religious advocacy groups described their decisions in religious terms. One said, "The idols in my life were money and prestige and people being proud of me and having a fancy job and making money. And I had always heard in church the claims that God makes about himself and that he is worthy of worship and devotion of one's life to him and started thinking, 'Maybe you're supposed to take that seriously.'" Another lawyer recalled that a "religious epiphany" set him on a "collision course" with his service to a wealthy client who appeared to have engaged in wrongdoing.

Lawyers for libertarian groups also offered earnest and ambitious accounts of their purposes, but they described their commitments in secular political terms. A lawyer who focused on "economic liberty" issues said that he wanted "to make some real changes in the world" by vindicating constitutional rights against governmental power through lawsuits and by persuading the public to view property rights as they do human rights or other individual rights. Another said that his work experience before attending law school showed him that government bureaucrats "need to be fought": "A lot of environmental rules and regulations were being driven by the mindset that whatever touches the land is bad and somehow environmentally wrong. I didn't agree with that . . . I thought it might be nice to be a lawyer who uses the law to help support good environmentally sound projects." A lawyer who pursued First Amendment cases said that "preserving the right to speak freely—that's what it's still about for me." Another lawyer described his "passionate commitment" to the libertarian vision—"to allow, to empower individuals to live their lives to the fullest in terms of applying their talents, their abilities without government coercion." A lawyer who had been tortured as a prisoner of war in Vietnam saw the right to self-defense (and thus the right to own guns) as "a natural right of a human being by virtue of his birth." An opponent of affirmative action stated emphatically, "It's wrong to discriminate against African-Americans. It's wrong to discriminate against other groups, too, on the basis of race." A prominent libertarian recalled taking a local government course in law school and experiencing "a total epiphany" when he learned "how to sue local governments" to advance his libertarian ideals. A property rights lawyer characterized his work as fighting "ham-handed regulations that back people into a corner where they have no alternative but to file lawsuits because you've wiped them out." Another property rights lawyer reported that he handled eminent domain cases on a contingency basis, often knowing that there was no possibility of recovering any fees, because the government's exercise of eminent domain power was a "moral sewer."

Some lawyers for religious and libertarian groups described themselves as champions of especially vulnerable groups or individuals. Abortion opponents, for example, viewed themselves as protectors of unborn children, and religious liberties advocates claimed that they were asserting the rights of religious people to express their views in an oppressively secular and morally corrupt public domain. One said of his decision to devote himself to opposing abortion, "We felt we had to use our small tools to confront the age and confront the culture and protect the innocent as best we could." A lawyer who spent years "keeping people who were home-schooling out of jail" later brought equal access cases challenging government officials who determined that "everybody can have their meetings in our public school or this government auditorium except religious groups." A pornography opponent asserted that local governments were "outgunned" by the industry and that his organization sought to "level the playing field." Several lawyers involved in criminal justice issues said they believed that they were serving the interests of innocent crime victims. An advocate for a group opposed to compulsory union membership trembled as he described how his client crossed a picket line and was beaten unconscious by union members; his role, he said, was to "stick up for" workers against people who "use their power to mess around with people's lives." Affirmative action opponents asserted that they were challenging employment and educational admissions processes that systematically disadvantage poor and working-class white males. Several libertarians identified their constituencies as disadvantaged minorities thwarted in their entrepreneurial ambitions by burdensome laws and consumers harmed by misguided regulation. A property rights lawyer described himself as an ally of small property owners who are vulnerable to local government's abuse of eminent domain powers.

Like liberal cause lawyers, who have been criticized for caring more about advancing causes than serving clients (e.g., Cahn and Cahn 1970; Bell 1976), some lawyers for religious and libertarian advocacy organizations indicated that they were more interested in developing favorable law than meeting particular client needs. A libertarian described how his organization had convened scholars to develop litigation blueprints, and another said that her organization was working to "build our body of case law." A religious liberties advocate was glad to move into a well-funded organization where attorneys could "cherry-pick a little bit": "We were able to sort of develop a much larger, overall game plan. . . . We always have half of our eye on the Supreme Court." Another lawyer said that he was "looking for places to take up Second Amendment cases."

Lawyers engaged in law reform readily acknowledged that they were selective about the clients they accepted. One noted that "the cases are carefully screened to make sure that they do move our legal objectives forward. A lot of people have very meritorious cases. . . . We can't take every single case that comes our way." Another reported that when asked to represent someone who is "really not interested in pursuing the law," she and her colleagues "suggest they go somewhere else, because we really want to move the law forward." Another said of the many requests he received for representation on constitutional matters, "if it's not a case going in the direction I want to go, I turn it down."

Activism for these lawyers sometimes involves recruiting clients through whom to pursue the cause. A libertarian said, "One of the great things . . . about being a nonprofit group is you can blatantly solicit people to do this." Another described "finding the plaintiffs" as part of his organization's "three-step process" for launching new litigation. Several lawyers reported contacting people about whom they had read in the newspaper to ask whether they wanted to litigate. A lawyer who worked for a mediator organization said, "Right now I'm fishing for a commerce power case." Others indicated that they relied on networks of individuals and organizations to feed them plaintiffs. The founder of one libertarian group said, "Every one of [our] cases is produced by a network that you just have to have in place and that you have to work on. . . . It's not like trolling for clients, but you have to have a reputation." A lawyer who launched a religious liberty litigation group recalled, "We started letting churches and people know that we were available to represent them . . . at no charge to them."[4]

Many lawyers who served libertarian and social conservative interests emphasized that they valued having work they believed in. One said of his decision to join a libertarian advocacy organization rather than a large law firm, "I knew I would do something I believed in, which is more fun than working on cases because someone is paying you to." A lawyer who quit his job with a private firm to join a think tank noted how "liberating" it was to pursue one's own causes, "to gear up for battle and to do that about something you strongly believe in is fantastic, really intense." Another said that it was important to him "that what [he] did professionally would at least be consistent with [his] libertarian beliefs." A social conservative in a small firm said that he always had been "highly motivated regarding [his] political and moral views" and that work advancing those commitments was "where [he found] satisfaction in law." An abortion opponent reported that he had disliked his elite law school, where most of his classmates were selling out to make money, and he was thrilled to discover an anti-abortion advocacy group in which he could invest his time and energy: "[f]inally I . . . saw something to do in law that I would enjoy, that I would believe in."

In their identification with their work, these lawyers shared more with public interest lawyers of the Left than with most of the business advocates. A religious liberties advocate said that his commitment to pursuing work he believed in gave him a grudging admiration for the lawyers he typically opposed in the courts; he admitted to a "weird respect" for ACLU lawyers because "I know they are dedicated to their cause." A libertarian spontaneously remarked that he shared with "colleagues on the other side" the luxury of pursuing work he believed in. An attorney who had joined a firm in which many of his clients were nonprofit Christian organizations reported that "many of his prayers had been answered" because his professional work and his interest in serving Christian groups "were meshing together rather nicely." A lawyer who worked in a small firm where he mixed paid with unpaid work said that he did not compartmentalize his life except as he was required to do so by professional ethics: "I see the pieces of my life forming a coherent whole. . . . I see a connection between my religious beliefs, my political involvement, the kinds of cases I work on, my appetites for other types of civic involvement. There is a coherent fabric to my life."[5]

Several lawyers for libertarian and religious interests described incidents that had offended their political sensibilities and prompted them to leave previous jobs. An attorney who now works for a libertarian organization left his law firm when a client asked him to pursue government protection for his industry—a position that conflicted with the lawyer's libertarian commitments. Another libertarian was fired from his job with an advocacy organization when he refused to dismiss a lawsuit that threatened the financial interests of a board member's friend. A lawyer who now works for a Christian organization resigned from his firm after his partners asked him to stop representing an anti-abortion group pro bono and to cease praying at the office, and another left private practice to establish a religious liberties group around the time he began "seeing some things [he] really didn't like" from one of his primary clients. Several lawyers in advocacy organizations said that they had lost patrons for their organizations because they took positions that conflicted with donors' interests. One boasted that he has been "personally responsible for losing a good deal of money for" his organization because his position on a large commercial case had "antagonized to no end" a major donor and because his criticism of another public policy outcome had made a sometime supporter of his organization "apoplectic."

Eight of the lawyers who appeared to identify most strongly with the causes they served were in solo or small-firm practices where they mixed paid and unpaid work for social conservative or libertarian causes. One of these lawyers indicated that he spends 50 percent of his professional time on uncompensated work, all of which dovetails with his commitment to "faith-based" approaches to social problems. He runs a conservative public interest law foundation, serves on boards of numerous state and national organizations, and is heavily involved in the Republican Party and the conservative movement. Another lawyer said that he spends significant amounts of time on uncompensated activities such as "testifying to the House Judiciary Committee . . . or testifying on some civil rights measure, or on the flag-burning amendment—something I'm doing [because I believe in the cause], not because somebody is paying me to do it." He explained that "the main reason" he left a large firm to pursue a more politically oriented practice was that he "didn't really care from anything other than a professional standpoint how the disputes [he] was working on were resolved." Another lawyer in a small practice had run for the U.S. Senate, played central roles in the passage of state referenda, litigated dozens of high-profile cases, and served on boards of numerous libertarian organizations. He had negotiated upfront with his firm for the "opportunity to do things on my own that I believed in" and to "discuss my extreme classical liberal libertarian views" in the press. A lawyer who helped establish several religious groups and served at a high level in the Reagan Administration worked in a small firm that serves churches and not-for-profit Christian groups and attracts like-minded Christian evangelicals. Yet another lawyer established a small firm that allows him to pursue his pro-life activism by mixing pro bono with paying work: "I could never imagine myself in a big firm, slaving away for some business interest. . . . I wanted to put together the kind of practice that allowed being happy and satisfied, which I have." The founder of a libertarian advocacy organization established a private firm to pursue cases that did not meet the organization's eligibility criteria but involved "taking the principles [that the organization has established] and making them stick in other situations." Another lawyer moved from a large law firm to a small firm where almost all of his clients are nonprofit religious groups.

In small private firms, lawyers describe a close and sometimes complex relationship between pro bono work and paying matters. Some say that their work for causes—some of which they pursue pro bono—has helped build their practices. A libertarian reported that, when he began his career, he sought a firm that would provide "space to do my thing . . . that [would] be tolerant." But he discovered that his libertarian work was a business asset: "While I originally thought that my views . . . were a liability, it turned out—one of the happy discoveries for me—[that they were] a plus because I ended up developing business as a result of the people who knew me from my libertarian activities." Another small-firm lawyer opened a storefront practice without a single client, but soon thereafter he received work and ultimately the general counsel's position for a large advocacy organization with which he had been associated through his involvement in politics. When I asked whether he received pay for this work, he responded, "There was a lot of pro bono associated with my practice but you cannot take on the chunk of business that they had for me without being paid. Now I certainly—as I do with many of my conservative clients— [ ]charge them less than I do the tobacco company, but that's the way it is." The same lawyer noted that his work on behalf of one cause had drawn him into an area of practice in which he has become one of the nation's leading experts; that practice area is now a major part of his business. Another said, "We take cases sometimes where we either believe in the cause that is being advanced enough that we make it our own, or perhaps make it partially our own, where we're paid some portion of the fees that we would normally be paid according to our usual and customary billing rates." A lawyer in a property rights firm described a type of pro bono amicus work designed to benefit no particular client but the general class of "one-shotters"[6] they represent:

> [Other firms with different types of practices] have clients on retainer, and relationships with them, and call all the time. We don't have that. We have a very small handful of people who have repeat business with us. . . . So in contrast to other firms, which every now and then I look at enviously where I know that when some issue comes down, they have the ability to pick up the phone and say, "Sam, there is this case coming up and it's really going to bite you in the ass. We need to try and do something about it. Will you hire us to do an amicus brief to try to push the court in your direction so you don't get hurt when they come down with an opinion?" We don't have that. So sometimes we see something coming down like that, that we know we are going to have to fight in the future. We'll do it anyway.

The same lawyer said that such work could be "a useful business-getter," but that deciding when to take pro bono cases required careful planning. It was "a constant subject of discussion, and should be, because it's a business." "If we can't keep enough coming in to keep the doors open, then we can't do any of that stuff. So it's a balance that has to be struck."

It appears, then, that small firms may give conservative and libertarian lawyers greater freedom to select work consistent with their political commitments than large law firms do. The suggestion that small firms may be particularly attractive practice settings for lawyers who wish to pursue causes part time is consistent with research by Scheingold and Bloom (1998, 236) on left activist practice, by Heinz et al. (2005) on social and political values in the Chicago bar, and by Mather, McEwen, and Maiman

(2001) on communities of divorce lawyers. Service to causes from small practices involves neither the for-profit versus pro bono dichotomy that underlies the predominant conception of pro bono service and public interest practice today (Carle 2001) nor the total cause orientation of salaried practice in public interest law firms and advocacy organizations. It is a hybrid of sorts that seems to be particularly congenial for lawyers who want to "do well by doing good" (Garth 2004; Wilkins 2004b).

Many lawyers in advocacy organizations and small, specialized practices indicated that they found great satisfaction in their work for causes. One said that his pursuit of libertarian causes had been "a great crusade for me personally that's very exciting and very fulfilling." Another lawyer said of his work for a religious liberties organization, "It's one great ride after another. I just love this job . . . You couldn't have scripted a more exciting job for a civil rights lawyer than this. It's been a blast."[7] The founder of a libertarian group said that the organization's first five years of operation were "the most fun I ever had in practicing law." A lawyer for a mediator organization who reported working roughly seventy hours per week claimed that "when your work is a labor of love it doesn't bother you." A libertarian said of himself and his colleagues, "It wouldn't be out of the ordinary for one of us to bring home a Supreme Court case or something in an area that we're interested in and just kind of read it in the evening for pleasure reading almost." A lawyer who founded his own public interest law firm "with a shoestring budget and all volunteer lawyers" said that he was having "an enormous amount of fun." A lawyer who worked part time for a libertarian think tank said of his work, "It can't pay my mortgage . . . [but] it's the most stimulating environment. . . . I've not worked anywhere that matches this. Everybody's happy even though we're always losing." A lawyer in a think tank said that he would not trade his current position even for a seat on the Supreme Court—"except maybe for a day": "On the whole, this is a very fulfilling life."

Unlike the business lawyers, who worked in financially lucrative positions, many of the lawyers for religious and libertarian organizations described financial hardships associated with their service to causes. Lawyers for the early religious conservative groups seemed to have endured especially difficult beginnings. One, who had left a lucrative practice in a large firm to found a Christian law group, described moving with his family from a large house to a studio apartment. He recalled that he had excellent cases and overwhelming evidence on his side but suddenly found it difficult to pay his hotel bills. (As he began losing cases for the first time in his career, he also concluded that, in the past, his business card and clients' economic strength had mattered more than his own skills.) A founder of an evangelical religious liberties group said that he launched the organization in a ten-by-fourteen foot room in his home, answering his own phone and depending on his wife to type pleadings; he drew no salary and survived on book royalties and fees for speaking engagements. Two other religious liberty advocates said that they had been paid nothing and lived in other lawyers' basements when they began taking cases, and they claimed to have been the lowest paid members of their law school's graduating class even after they started drawing salaries. One remembered the working conditions: "We had a shoestring, terribly equipped, underfunded, holding up paychecks [organization]—everything associated with your classic public interest organization." Several lawyers for religious groups still worked in extremely modest surroundings at the time of the interviews.

Lawyers associated with libertarian organizations also described financial strains during their organizations' early years. One said that for the first few years "we never at the beginning of any month had the payroll in the bank," and another remembered "breathtaking financial problems, which required the pilfering of both toilet and fax paper and [included the] constant threat of having our equipment repossessed." A lawyer who joined a think tank to develop a plan for a new public interest law group discovered that the organization that had hired him was bankrupt. A libertarian recalled that he had taken a substantial pay cut when he left a midlevel federal government position to join a think tank, and the founder of another libertarian group said that both he and his cofounder took salary hits when they left their previous public interest jobs to establish the new organization.

Lawyers for religious and libertarian advocacy organizations reject the conventional model's claim that lawyers are morally unaccountable for their service to clients. For these lawyers, decisions about what clients and causes to serve are personal. A lawyer who directs a Christian law group asserted that conventional professional ideals are "all a game to escape responsibility." A lawyer active on abortion issues who learned that I had a young daughter leaned toward me and asked, "Wouldn't you want to know if your daughter was about to have an abortion?" Several lawyers questioned the integrity of those who took positions contrary to their own. A lawyer who fights pornography said that he could respect lawyers who disagreed with him about whether and how to regulate pornography but not those who denied that pornography causes harm; he said that anyone who took that position "either has to be a fool or a damn liar."

Another lawyer acknowledged that the ACLU has good lawyers who "may even be sincere in their beliefs," but he charged that their position on child pornography was totally "outrageous." An opponent of affirmative action said, "[I]f there were any justice in the world, all these people would be disbarred that were involved in propagating these myths and lies [about differential admissions standards in universities]."

Lawyers for Mediator Groups

Lawyers for mediator organizations appeared to hold a distinctive professional orientation that was neither the ardent devotion to particular causes displayed by social conservative and libertarian lawyers nor the client orientation typical of business lawyers. Their interests exceeded the boundaries of the issue agendas of particular constituencies. As noted in the previous chapter, this was an elite group with remarkable credentials and political connections. Six had served in senior positions in the Reagan Administration, and another was appointed to a high post in the Bush II Administration. An eighth had been nominated for the federal bench (but denied a hearing).

These lawyers were intellectually engaged, politically wired, and focused on the fate of the conservative movement. Several commented on their roles in building coalitions. One stressed his interest in promoting dialogue across religious boundaries, and another emphasized his strategy of building coalitions "across the spectrum." They also described grand personal ambitions. One hoped to help persuade his profession to view law primarily as a restriction on government, and another aspired to build "a community of lawyers committed to the founding principles." One devoted much of the interview to identifying four "strategic" goals for the conservative movement, including recruiting Asian-Americans to "go the way of the Cubans, not the way of the Jews" and reorienting conservative philanthropy to ensure that businessmen and other wealthy people pass control of their fortunes ("whatever it is—$20 trillion . . . in the next twenty to twenty-five years") to foundations committed to advancing and perpetuating their values. Several of these lawyers emphasized the role of ideas and persuasion (as complements to money and organization) in American politics. One said that his conservative mentors "were very much interested in the battle of ideas" and had encouraged him to "contribute to that war." Another remarked that he "really loved ideas" and believed that they were an important source of power in the public policy process.[8] Several lawyers for mediator groups stressed the value of civility as an element of persuasion. One called civility a "traditional virtue" to which he was strongly committed, and another had stopped working with an organization that had become "too strident." The lawyers for mediator organizations were not only prominent conservatives but also elite members of the broader legal establishment, concerned about maintaining their stature in that larger community and defending its values.

SHADES OF GRAY

The preceding sections of this chapter have shown that lawyers for social conservative and libertarian groups generally identified much more strongly with the causes they served than did their business counterparts in large firms and trade associations. But the differences between the professional orientations of the business lawyers and advocates for social conservative and libertarian interests were not always stark. Some lawyers for social conservative and libertarian groups described mixed motivations for accepting their current jobs and more conventional professional orientations.

Just as many lawyers for liberal causes receive nonpecuniary benefits from public interest work (Komesar and Weisbrod 1978, 87–89), so too do lawyers employed by conservative and libertarian advocacy groups. Several indicated that they liked their jobs because they offered more interesting work and greater responsibility than conventional practice. One lawyer for a libertarian group, for example, said, "I took the job because I thought it would be intellectually interesting. . . . I would have a lot more responsibility for cases than I would ever have, even as a partner, in a private firm, and that they would be cases that would get a lot of public notice." Another lawyer for a libertarian organization reported, "I went into public interest practice because I believed in the cause and wanted to advance it, and I stayed because I found that I had the responsibility for handling major cases that I could never have had, or would have been very difficult to have, had I been in private practice. I've argued four cases in the United States Supreme Court. Very few attorneys in private practice get to do that." Several lawyers observed that their jobs in advocacy organizations called for hours that were more compatible with family commitments than law firm practice would have been. One lawyer left private practice to teach and work for think tanks because he wanted "flexibility to basically be with my [child]." He noted that his previous position, as a litigator in a prominent law firm "just eats you alive." Another left a high-level political position in the Justice Department when President Clinton took office, and he accepted a job with an advocacy organization where he could meet his family responsibilities and avoid travel. A lawyer in a religious liberties organization said that his group "tr[ies] to make sure that family is not sacrificed on the altar of the job," and another religious liberties advocate had his young child at the office when I arrived for the interview. Two religious conservatives indicated that flexible arrangements with nonprofit groups allowed them to home-school their children. A lawyer who took a position with a libertarian advocacy organization after graduating from law school explained that she "liked what [the organization] was doing" but also wanted to be near her extended family, who lived in the area.

Some lawyers' job changes within the nonprofit sector reflected concerns about their professional development rather than any assessment of how they could best serve a cause. One lawyer made such a move because he had "peaked on the learning curve" in his job and needed to "raise [his] own profile . . . specialize more." Another recalled (tongue in cheek) that he had missed the rough and tumble of litigation when he served as a political appointee in the Reagan Administration: "After a year I had to leave because I just wanted to sue somebody, anybody." Another lawyer changed positions when he became apprehensive about impending staff cuts, but he acknowledged regret that one of his cases was reassigned to a colleague who eventually argued it before the Supreme Court: "I gave away the envelope that had the winning ticket."

Several lawyers for conservative and libertarian advocacy organizations indicated that they were committed to their clients' goals but not personally invested in them. Unlike most lawyers for religious conservative groups, the general counsel for one large religious organization said, "I remind myself and I tell my clients that I am their lawyer. It doesn't matter, it shouldn't matter to them, whether I agree or disagree with them. . . . They pay me to advise them. I give them advice and they decide." He said that he had no experience with religious matters before taking the job and was not particularly drawn to the organization's agenda: "What drew me to the job was to find something as different as I could from what I was doing"—litigating for a large federal agency. Another lawyer for the same organization said that he was an agnostic. A lawyer who worked for an organization that opposes affirmative action said that he believed in the organization's goals, but he added, "I don't think any of this stuff is the be all and end all of the universe."

PRACTICE SETTING AND PROFESSIONAL IDENTITY

Unsurprisingly, there was a strong relationship between the types of causes lawyers pursued, the practice settings in which they worked, and their professional identities. Large law firms attract lawyers who are comfortable serving corporate clients and other moneyed interests. Those firms' clients demand technical expertise and committed advocacy from their lawyers, and they may also expect their lawyers to sympathize with the institutional arrangements that maintain "their clients' favorable position in society" (Nelson 1988, 243). However, corporate clients and the firms that serve them also derive value from ideals of lawyer independence and neutral partisanship, which allow lawyers to claim distance from their clients' ends (Simon 1978). The center-right politics and mainstream professional ideology of these organizations suit their clients' needs and preferences well, just as they are uncomfortable environments for lawyers who do not share those political views and professional norms (cf. Wilkins 2004a, 1586–89). Advocacy organizations and think tanks—which pursue primarily symbolic interests—sell messages about how public policy must change to accomplish some public good. They need and attract salaried lawyers who strongly identify with the organizations' agendas—not advocates who might take the opposite side of the issue tomorrow. Some of these organizations—especially the mediator groups—cast their nets broadly to appeal to a large variety of conservatives, but most of the advocacy organizations and think tanks look for lawyers who share a particular philosophy. One libertarian lawyer said of his organization,

> [It] is ideologically driven. There's no question about it. It has an identified mission, and there is a natural selection process at work from both sides. People don't apply here unless they are libertarian, and people don't get accepted if they do apply unless they are libertarians. [The organization] is looking for people who advance the libertarian agenda, and people that come here are looking for an organization like [this one] to help them pursue what they perceive to be their ideological drives.

Solo practices and small firms are generally better able than large firms to accommodate lawyers who seek to develop practices reflecting their political commitments. Lawyers in such practices have large numbers of clients and tend to be less dependent on any particular client than lawyers in large firms (Heinz et al. 2005). Moreover, their clients are more likely to be "one-shotters" who have little long-term influence over the lawyers' practices

(Heinz et al. 2005). The publicity and political connections that small-firm lawyers cultivate through their work for causes may help them build their reputations and generate business (Wilkins 2004b; Garth 2004). More flexible institutional arrangements and the smaller likelihood of disqualifying conflicts of interest also may help explain why small firms attract lawyers who wish to pursue causes consistent with their values.

THE MAKING (AND UNMAKING) OF PROFESSIONAL IDENTITY

Chapter 3 emphasized continuity between the social worlds from which lawyers come and the values and political commitments they hold. This chapter has shown a strong correspondence between the constituencies that lawyers serve and their conceptions of professional role. But individuals' identities and their commitments to groups sometimes emerge and transform over time (Ellemers, Spears, and Doosje 1999; Turner 1999). Social identity sometimes changes through participation in collective action (McAdam 1989; Drury and Reicher 2000), and involvement in social activism often deepens participants' commitment to causes (McAdam 1989). Lawyers' professional norms develop in the workplace and reflect the "arenas" in which those values evolve (Nelson and Trubek 1992; cf. Bellow 1977). This section considers evidence that some of these lawyers' professional identities and political commitments changed during the course of their careers.

The prototypical cause lawyer selects law as a profession or chooses a particular area of practice in order to advance a predefined social or political agenda (Bisharat 1998b, 477); their activism and causes are simply given. Some lawyers interviewed for this research fit the profile of the classic cause lawyer who decides early to devote his professional life to particular political ends. A libertarian said, "I decided to attend law school to one day apply my legal training to changing the world"—to "vindicate the libertarian principles that I was increasingly holding dear," and another libertarian asserted that changing social policy "was all I was really interested in doing career-wise." An affirmative action opponent said, "I . . . always have thought it would be right if I could have a career [through which] I could advance the conservative cause." An abortion opponent said of his pro-life advocacy, "That's what I went to school for." Another lawyer reported that he went to law school to "get[] the courts back in a business that they had been out of since 1937" of enforcing constitutional restrictions on congressional power.

Most lawyers, however, described less direct and deliberate routes to their work for causes. Many said that they attended law school without a clear sense of why they were there or what they would do with their training. Several prominent lawyers denied that they had expected to become leading conservative advocates. One recalled, "By the time I left college I pretty much knew what I thought and I had access to the thinkers who crystallized what I believe, but I didn't go into law school intending to really be very politically active." A libertarian litigator said, "I've always had very strong beliefs towards the conservative or libertarian side, but I didn't necessarily go to law school to litigate those issues." One social conservative said of his views when he graduated from law school, "My idea of being a good citizen was sort of a negative thing—avoiding doing bad things. It wasn't about doing positive things and doing positive things that would affect change in a community or society as a whole." Many lawyers for religious groups reported that they had hoped that becoming a lawyer would enable them to help people, but few had imagined the types of practices they later pursued, perhaps because most evangelical Christian legal advocacy organizations are relatively new (den Dulk 2001).

Many lawyers said that they had not become involved in the causes they now serve until late in their careers. The general counsel for an antipornography group had previously worked for a large business for twenty-seven years. Another lawyer worked for a poverty law clinic before deciding that he wanted "to go into some type of Christian work." Several Christian lawyers were in private firms when they experienced religious epiphanies that triggered their flight to activist practices. One of them was a successful partner in a large firm who had argued several cases in the U.S. Supreme Court and was protecting "all the scalawags in [a major commercial center]" before he resigned. A business lawyer became involved in conservative causes late in his career as he felt less concerned about his stature in the law firm and freer to express his political commitments; he gradually lost interest in the "big deal" regulatory cases that had built his professional reputation and "thought it would be fun" to handle more controversial cases.

Several lawyers said that they were not even conservatives when they graduated from law school. As described in greater detail in chapter 5, many lawyers who were in college and law school during the 1960s and early 1970s served causes of the Left before shifting (or drifting) toward conservative and libertarian causes.

But a few lawyers had moved in the opposite direction. One said he had been raised in a conservative Mormon household but now was repelled by causes of the religious right. He worked in a firm representing mostly business interests:

> [My background] formed a very conservative person. And I was rather proud of that . . . as a new lawyer. And as time went on my views changed and attitudes changed. And now, I would just hate to think of myself as being grouped with some of the more conservative lawyers in the country that espouse some of these right-wing—or especially religious right-wing—causes, because they trouble me a great deal. I just don't see myself as that type of person or in that group.

A lawyer for a mediator organization who had held a high-level political appointment in the Reagan administration indicated that his conservative commitments had become more moderate in recent years.

Many lawyers indicated that their allegiance to the causes they now serve evolved over time through their work for those causes. The president of an anti-abortion group said that he first became interested in the issue in college when he read about *Roe v. Wade* and concluded that it was flawed jurisprudentially but that his interest later "evolved from a more legalistic view to more of a cultural commitment." Another lawyer said that his Supreme Court clerkship had awakened his interest in constitutional law and that his commitment to changing public policy intensified "as I've gotten deeper into these issues that I found I care very much about." A lawyer who works for a Christian evangelical group began prosecuting pornography cases to gain trial experience; "I wasn't particularly religious. I got into these cases, not because I had a passion for the work, but because I just wanted the jury trials." At first, he tried to distance himself from some of the evangelical Christians associated with the fight against pornography: "I was really good at my job, but I didn't really connect with the spiritual side of things." Years later, well after he had become a well-known pornography prosecutor, he experienced a religious epiphany and became an evangelical Christian himself. Another lawyer said, "I would never have thought in a hundred million years that [pornography] would have been my issue." In 1973, when he was a law student volunteering in a prosecutor's office, his boss asked him to parse the U.S. Supreme Court's new obscenity decision in *Miller v. California,* which established a three-part test for determining whether state statutes designed to regulate obscene materials were constitutional. He was assigned responsibility for answering dozens of defense motions challenging the constitutionality of obscenity prosecutions under the new standard. After graduating from law school, he became the office expert on obscenity. At first he viewed such work in conventional professional terms; it was simply part of the prosecutor's obligation to enforce the law. Over time, however, he became convinced that pornography had harmful social consequences, and he is now among the most prominent advocates for regulating Internet pornography. A lawyer who served as in-house counsel to a large religious group said that the organization's agenda had almost nothing to do with his decision to take the job but that "the more I learned about it, the more that I read, the more I become a part of it and am responsible for achieving it, the more I identify with it."

Several lawyers claimed that chance had shaped their careers more than strategic planning. A lawyer who was active on religious liberty issues said, "People who are ten years old and fifteen years old . . . come up to me and say, 'I'm inspired by you' and 'What steps did you take to get here?' And I feel like I just sort of fell into this. . . . I'm embarrassed to say there was no orderly way or conscious, deliberate way that I moved into this." An abortion opponent said that he had no intention of pursuing causes when he went to law school: "I had some pretty strong political opinions at the time; I had a strong sense of right and wrong. But at the time, I did not connect going to law school with those feelings and beliefs. Later on, they sort of merged. But at the time—at the age of twenty-one—my interests in life were pretty simple, really. I just enjoyed eating and I enjoyed drinking beer, traveling . . . I didn't have a huge social or political agenda." Another lawyer said that he had taken a job with an advocacy group in part because his search for an academic job was not going well: "It was . . . very fortuitous that I came into this position. . . . I would like to tell you that I had a brilliant plan, which I executed with clarity and vision, but, unfortunately, I did not." Some of these lawyers, then, became lawyers for causes without self-consciously embarking on such a course; their current roles may say as much about where they found opportunities as they do about where their political commitments led.

Finally, although I have emphasized how lawyers identify with and respond to causes, the interviews demonstrate that lawyers also influence the causes they serve. As Shamir and Chinksy (1998, 231) have noted, lawyers "are not simply carriers of a cause but are at the same time its producers: those who shape it, name it, and voice it." The interviews are full of stories about how lawyers have helped to define causes—for example, how they have helped give "tort reform" its name, linked free enterprise theories to the interests of disadvantaged minorities, and recast the culture wars as matters of federalism. They established new organizations to pursue these agendas and often served as their principal advisors and spokespeople. These lawyers, then, often were primary architects of their causes, and their identification with those causes likely increased as they shaped them to their own visions.

CONCLUSION

This chapter highlights another fault line within the conservative coalition—the division between lawyers for whom work for conservative causes is a by-product of client service and lawyers whose service to causes reflects their own fervent religious and political commitments. Lawyers for business interests generally described their roles in conventional professional terms. They asserted that they supported their clients' positions but did not feel strongly personally invested in them, and they may have valued their standing in the legal establishment more than their ties to the movement's populist elements. Advocates for social conservative and libertarian groups, like the left activist lawyers on whose models they draw, challenge conventional models of professionalism by "commit[ing] themselves and their legal skills to furthering a vision of the good society" (Sarat and Scheingold 1998, 3). However, the visions to which social conservative and libertarian advocates dedicate themselves are radically different. Both sets of lawyers insist that they are responsible for the ends to which they devote their professional skills, and they share a passion for work they believe in. But their engaged service frequently points them in opposite directions and leads them into conflict with one another.

5

How Much Common Ground?

Much divides lawyers for the different constituencies of the conservative coalition. They come from different social backgrounds and hold different views about relationships between political commitments and professional role. What, if anything, draws them together? This chapter examines common experiences and goals that unite at least some lawyers interviewed for this research. It reveals no unifying philosophy, but it does identify several factors that might provide bases for understanding and perhaps cooperation: generational effects, shared disapproval of liberals, overlapping policy agendas, a common interest in remaking the judiciary, the Republican Party, shared professional status, and perceived disadvantage in the legal establishment. The first five of these have little connection to lawyers' occupational roles; they might also apply to the larger pools of elites within each of the constituencies of the conservative alliance. The last two elements, however, relate directly to lawyers' professional identities and the prestige and opportunities available to them within the conservative movement and legal profession.

GENERATIONAL EFFECTS

The ages of the interviewed lawyers ranged from the thirties to the eighties. Six lawyers who were in their seventies and eighties were leaders in the first wave of conservative public interest law groups. A much larger group was part of a generation that came of age in the 1960s. The boundaries of this sixties generation have been defined in various fairly arbitrary ways by political sociologists,[1] but if one includes those aged twenty-one to thirty-six in 1975 (see Davis 1980), thirty-six of the interviewed lawyers qualify. These lawyers were part of a cohort often associated with civil rights protests, opposition to the Vietnam War, and the feminist movement, but the same era produced a generation of leaders on the political right, many of whom helped to mobilize opposition to the New Left and prepare to take control of sources of institutional power in the 1980s (Klatch 1999). The remaining thirty lawyers were twenty-six years old or younger at the time Ronald Reagan won the presidency in 1980. They were part of an age cohort that accounted for the largest shift in votes from Democrats to Republicans in the 1984 election (Himmelstein 1990, 177).

Karl Mannheim's essay, "The Problem of Generations," argues that periods of rapid social change produce "generational units" connecting people of the same age who have experienced the same events as young adults (1952). Although members of these generational units may "work up" these common experiences in different ways, depending on their social backgrounds, they share "a specific range of potential experience" that "predispos[es] them for certain characteristic modes of thought and experience, and a characteristic type of historically relevant action" (1952). Rebecca Klatch's research on two wings of political activists who were young adults in the 1960s—members of Students for a Democratic Society and Young Americans for Freedom—found "striking parallels" in the stories of these opposing activists (Klatch 1999, 3). Although they held "diametrically opposed views of the world," they shared a sense of historical location and a common passion for politics (Klatch 1999, 5).

My research was not designed to test the salience of generational effects or the interaction of generational effects and life-course politics (e.g., Braungart and Braungart 1986). But lawyers in each of two age cohorts— the sixties generation and the Reagan/Bush I generation—share a common historical location, which may help create mutual understanding among lawyers from different social backgrounds.

The Sixties Generation

Some of the interviewed lawyers of the sixties generation participated in causes of the Right during their early adult years. They worked with conservative student groups—such as Young Americans for Freedom, Intercollegiate Studies Institute, and the National Right to Life Committee— conservative student newspapers established as alternative media outlets, and Republican political campaigns. One lawyer noted that he was active in a student organization for which Milton Friedman was the faculty sponsor, and through that group he had met other budding conservatives with whom he remained in contact. A libertarian founded "Radicals for Capitalism" at his college. Another lawyer was a member of a controversial all-male honorary society.

Some of the interviewed lawyers of the sixties generation recounted their dismay about the social unrest of the times. One recalled the difficulty of his transition to an elite college from a "hard-core Mormon household":

> When I arrived on the shores of California as a freshman at Berkeley and met Mario Savio and his lieutenants from the Free Speech Movement, they invited me to spend the evening with them before my dorm was ready. I was shocked to see this dope-smoking, wild group of students and hangers on. So that was my first awakening coming from this very conservative background. . . . My fellow students were burning the flag. I was horrified by that. And then I listened to the news breaking about the success or failure of American forces in Vietnam, rooting for them, while my fellow students were opposed to them.

A lawyer for a mediator group also remembered his unease about the protest politics of the 1960s:

> I guess the most formative thing for me I can say is my grandfather, who would tell me every day, just about, never to forget that America is the blessed land. . . . And when I came to [an elite law school] and saw guys spelling America with a K . . . It was so profoundly wrong. Because I knew the promise of America because I had seen it, whereas they were so distant from the generations in their families that had . . . gone through the sacrifice precisely so that they could live as they did. But I saw it. I was privileged to see what could happen to me in two generations—a generation and a half behind my grandfather, who was working for $5.00 a week, sixty hours a week . . . in some New York City sweatshop. And it would seem to me an act of contempt for my grandfather's love and efforts for me to start to spell America with a K, because what I had was not some privilege that would rain on me because I happened to be white where other kids were black, or it was some act of luck or good fortune. It was the direct result of a grandfather whom I loved, whom I saw work and struggle, to be able to provide this for his grandchildren. And I never took it for granted, and his example has never allowed me to take it for granted. . . .

A Christian conservative remembered the early 1970s as a "radical time" when the law school faculty focused on "ideological recruitment" and when the only professor who mentored students was available only to those who "bought into his left-wing politics." He felt equally disaffected from his classmates; as president of his law school's environmental law society, he had supported nuclear energy development, and for that offense he was officially impeached from his position. Another social conservative recalled that he "was not particularly taken with" the "left of center ACLU-oriented professors" who, "because they rode motorcycles, had long hair, and nontraditional clothing, were popular with some students."

Several lawyers of this generation who were neither part of the Left nor involved in the opposition recalled how the times had shaped their political views. A libertarian who attended college in the late 1960s said that he had disagreed with those who were taking over university buildings ("it was a bad war" but "a lot of [the protest] was anti-American") and with social conservatives who "were basically involved in defending the war and opposing drugs and trying to resurrect traditional values and so forth." An abortion opponent recalled how debates with his college classmates had influenced his own views about abortion:

> [It] was the Vietnam era and I was opposed to the war. We got into a lot of debates on consistency issues. At the same time, the abortion movement had begun at that point, and I was aware of that because some of the people I knew were involved in it. . . . . I thought that there wasn't a consistent theoretical basis for opposition to the war . . . , and I tried to develop one on my own. . . . . I had gone to traditional Catholic schools . . . I wasn't religious at the time, but I sort of related to the idea of a consistent natural law approach to life. And that was the way I approached the whole Vietnam thing. And so I became interested and I thought, I have to be consistent about this. So I became consistent about it . . . There was an awful lot of concern that was expressed by people during the antiwar era about causing death and destruction indiscriminately. And I felt like that would be the basis for opposition to any war, if you were a total pacifist, or on this war in particular, then you had to have some very good reason to go around killing people or offering yourself to be killed. . . . [T]here was also a lot of talk about how they were treating those folks differently than we treat ourselves because they were gooks or whatever. And so there was opposition to any kind of discriminatory idea that you would treat Vietnamese people differently than you would treat your next door neighbor. And I agree with all that. But at the same time, I wanted to be able to define what a human being was precisely and

broadly in order that you could say, "You do not kill." And I couldn't draw the line at birth, which some people were doing.

Some lawyers of the sixties generation who had participated in causes of the Left during college and law school described how their commitments had drifted rightward thereafter. A lawyer for a mediator organization who had been active in desegregation efforts in the South and in Democratic politics immediately thereafter said that he gradually lost faith in liberal answers to the issues of social justice to which he remained committed. He attributed his change in attitude, in part, to his experience as a young lawyer in New York City:

The ordinary course would have been for me to have gone, like all my classmates, to a Wall Street firm where in some noblesse-oblige, patronizing way I would have reached my hands across the backs of that racist, resistant middle class into the ghettos, like we were trained and conditioned to do. And as luck would have it, there I was representing [various public employee unions]. . . . And I saw virtue in those middle-class values and aspirations. And saw them as the place where the poor could be moving. And saw the city—which had been such an engine for me and could have been such engine for social progress on the part of the new waves of people who were next up at bat to achieve the American dream—I saw the city descend into bankruptcy. And I saw, most of all, endless examples in the John Lindsay administration of total moral corruption, as New York City sank. . . . And, I don't know, maybe I would have just been another million-dollar-a-year partner at a law firm, driving my Volvo, and listening to National Public Radio, just like everybody else . . . had I not had that wonderful opportunity as a lawyer to have been representing the very people I would have thought to have been standing in the way of social progress. But I saw the Lindsay administration sell out the city with contracts to labor unions in exchange for political support. And I saw poverty programs enriching the worst crowds. . . . I then knew that my reservations about the trendy politics of the sixties and the seventies . . . were not merely practical. . . . There was a moral component to conservative politics. Because there was nothing moral in a city that had been this engine of progress for so long descending into bankruptcy. Where CCNY, which had trained . . . prior generations to all sorts of possibilities, was now descending into these open admissions programs where intellectual content was not competitive. . . . Where our foreign policy lacked any confidence in what America had to offer the world. Where we were blaming ourselves, when I sensed us to be the last best hope of mankind, and still do.

This lawyer declined to seek an appointment in the Carter Administration after concluding that the Democrats he knew did not "share [his] most basic assumption about the goodness of America and its capacity to achieve social justice" and "held contempt for the middle class from which [he] came": "When Jimmy Carter was elected, I started to make phone calls to friends of mine in the Carter Administration, hoping to get some fancy job . . . I stopped myself short, because I didn't vote for Carter and I had stopped believing in that stuff. . . . "

He thereafter switched political parties:

> In the . . . most morally courageous act of my life, I went to get the card—a registration card, checked the box called, gulp, Republican. Signed the form and went to the postal box and stuck it in, and became, as I said at the time, the only Republican I knew, and having done it I didn't feel Jewish for six months. . . . [Later], of course, I starting associating with people who had gone through pretty much the same emotional identity experience I went through.

He recalled his anxiety about this shift in political allegiance: "How could I leave the world of my classmates, where everybody's shared assumption was that Nixon was a fascist pig?"

Another lawyer for a mediator group said that she was "anything but conservative" when she attended law school and that she was "insufferably self-righteous about how liberal" she was early in her career. But she described a series of experiences that led her to redefine her political commitments. She was sympathetic to the political goals of campus activism in the 1960s but uncomfortable with the "strategy of destruction" that characterized some of that work. She began reading books that challenged her assumptions that "government is the answer to poverty and government is the answer to injustice and . . . everybody else is wicked and government is good; I had sort of accepted that completely on faith almost the way I had unquestioningly accepted God when I was a child." Later in her career, she found herself at odds with feminists who thought that gender should play a larger role in how she defined herself. Eventually, she said, "Things just converged and I began to think of myself more as a conservative." A libertarian who had "come out of the Left in college" and had "been involved in demonstrations and the like after Kent State and Cambodia" described those experiences as "eye-opening": "[They] caused me to question my assumptions and, I suppose, my naive worldview and to reject the dichotomy of just left and right, or Republican and Democrat, liberal and conservative, as the only alternatives. And I began to give it a lot of thought and struggle along the way to develop a philosophy that I felt would be appropriate in these times. And that led me to be a libertarian."

A pornography opponent whose childhood heroes had included William Kunstler and ACLU lawyers, and who had always thought of himself as a liberal and invariably voted for Democrats, specialized in obscenity cases as a young prosecutor. He began focusing on the interests of crime victims, the adverse effects of pornography on poor neighborhoods, and "judicial appointments and how they would affect my life as a prosecutor." A Jewish lawyer who had been active in causes of the Left was dismayed when the ACLU adopted a pro-choice position, which he found incompatible with basic tenets of his religion, and he thereafter helped establish and lead an anti-abortion group.

Several business lawyers reported that they too had worked for causes of the Left during their college and law school years but had become more conservative since then. A business lawyer described himself as a "George McGovern liberal Democrat" when he took his first job after law school with a government agency that handled various social and poverty-related programs:

> I . . . really had this kind of naive view that government can solve problems. And I held to that view until I really had an understanding of what government does. And in that job . . . I was really awakening to how money gets wasted and doesn't really accomplish anything and it is just a whole lot of bureaucracy and a lot of people get employed by it but they really sort of push paper around, push money around. And at the end of the day it doesn't really seem to be what's solving problems like poverty and crime. Oddly enough, I don't think I've lost any of my concerns, I like to say compassion. That's a little self-serving, but I think I still do care about things like that. But I really don't see government as being the solution. I mean, I think it has more to do with people's relationships with each other and the family. And, I'm not a big religious freak so, but, yeah, I think the church can, too, to the extent people participate in that.

These changes coincided with increasing financial responsibility for his growing family: "I didn't want to work for anybody there [who] would make me gag, but I really was mostly interested in the work, and, with a family, I was getting very career-oriented and really not ideological at all." A business lawyer who was active in the civil rights movement and had spent a night in jail in connection with his work in the Chicago Freedom

Movement recalled that he went to law school "to use law to make changes in the world." His interest in labor law had reflected his "very 1960s view of the world that labor unions were not only the way to improve the working conditions of ordinary people but were the bulwark against communism." After law school, he went to Washington to work for the federal government, and he eventually served at a high level in the Carter and Reagan administrations. He said that he had become frustrated with the Carter Administration's "ideological-driven positions" and impressed that "some very progressive stuff which [the Carter Administration was] afraid to touch we actually got done during in the Reagan Administration because there was an understanding that there was a problem that had to be resolved and that required negotiations." Thereafter, he switched his registration from Democrat to Independent.

These varied accounts of the transformation of lawyers' professional ideals are consistent with a literature on the conservative influence of professional socialization (Granfield 1992; Stover and Erlanger 1989), although that research emphasizes shifts from liberal public interest commitments to a more conventional practice orientation, rather than changes from political left to right. These accounts also reflect a rightward shift in public opinion, a growing disaffection with legal activism during the early years of these lawyers' careers (Galanter 2002), and a broader move of Jewish intellectuals (e.g., Norman Podhoretz, Irving Kristol, Nathan Glazer, etc.) from the Left to the Right during this period.

The Reagan/Bush I Generation

If turmoil over civil rights and the Vietnam War defined the sixties generation, the generation that came of age during the Reagan/Bush I era was defined by its reaction to 1960s activism and "political correctness." Many of the interviewed lawyers who attended college and law school during the Reagan and Bush I years expressed distrust for the social activism of the 1960s and the legal liberalism that followed in its wake. One Christian conservative said, "When I went to college, where I went to college, most of the people who wanted to further social change did so from a liberal perspective, and most of the conservatives were more interested in freedom from the agenda of liberals who wanted to further social change that they didn't necessarily agree with":

> My disagreement with [liberal legal activists] on their political views had turned me off in a way to the whole idea of public service. I thought it was

just people cloaking themselves in this mantle of trying to do good, when really they had what I considered to be an ill-advised political agenda. . . . I was even turned off to the idea of people saying, I want to go into public service. I thought that was largely a smoke screen.

An opponent of affirmative action said, "One of the reasons why I got into conservative public interest law to begin with [was] to expose the hollowness and the shams behind [liberal public interest law]." Another conservative recalled that he was motivated to attend law school to oppose the kinds of legal activism celebrated by liberals in the 1970s:

[W]hat drove me to study law was that law was an important vehicle for preserving our system of government. . . . I had an inkling in college, based on some of my course work, that law could be an instrument for driving our institutions in different directions. . . . Our governing institutions could be driven in directions they weren't meant to be driven in, and that law was a very powerful instrument for doing that. But law could also be a very powerful instrument for preserving the rule of law, and maintaining the separation of powers and federalism and a proper role for courts.

Many of these younger lawyers said that they had always been conservative and had been active in conservative causes since they were young. A lawyer of the sixties generation spoke with evident delight about "this young generation" who "had seen activism turn to anarchy" and, unlike his own generation, "didn't have to go through emotion and identity contortions to be conservatives." One of these younger lawyers said, "I was conservative from early on and I had definite opinions, opinions that, I must say, haven't changed a lot over the years. . . . I'm not somebody who has traveled from left to right or right to left or anything like that. I've definitely always been conservative." Another reported that he was "always a conservative": "I started out as a fourth grader being a conservative—I used to read the op-ed pages and I always agreed with the conservative columnists." He explained that even in high school he read "giant economic tomes of classical free market liberals" and foresaw devoting himself to furthering such "broad-scale change." Another recalled, "By the time I went to [college] . . . I was pretty aware that I was politically conservative": "I was always skeptical, at least from the time I remember, . . . skeptical of 'big' government, in part because I grew up New York City in the 1970s. . . . Our taxes were unbearably high. There were no services; I mean, they didn't pick up the garbage, they didn't shovel the streets when there was snow. It was hard to have a lot faith in 'big' government." Many of the interviewed lawyers of this generation had worked for well-known conservative politicians, conservative newspapers, and other conservative institutions during their high school and college years.

Many younger lawyers suggested that their conservative impulses had been reinforced through conflict within the predominantly liberal universities they had attended. One said that going from his conservative community in the Southwest to an Ivy League university "was a big cultural shock." He worked on the student newspaper, where most of the other contributors were "very extremely left" and his views "were basically anathema":

> There were two schools of thought at [this student paper]. One was the liberal school, which was, "Well, even though [respondent] is crazy, we believe in freedom of speech, so he has a right to publish." And the other school was the Marxist school, which was, "Next time he comes in here, let's take him in the back and beat the crap out of him so he won't come back." And there were just enough liberals to hold off the Marxists so that I never really got beat up, and they did publish my stuff, with great disdain.

A libertarian recalled that he was "the token conservative columnist" for his college daily paper and served as a leader of an organization that was a "strongly conservative" alternative to the Republican Party and a counterweight to an organization that was pushing "a whole series of things you would typically think of as politically correct." Another lawyer remembered his dismay about a college course he had taken "called Capitalism and Socialism, in which the class spent twelve out of fourteen weeks studying socialism and basically one week reading Schumpeter, Friedman, and Hayek." A social conservative indignantly recounted receiving a mediocre grade on a paper about abortion regulation, which he later published in a reputable law journal. Some lawyers who complained about their law school environments also indicated that their experiences during those years had fueled their determination to become active in the conservative movement. An abortion opponent credited his decision to enlist in pro-life work to a professor who declined to counsel him about public interest opportunities once he discovered respondent's position on abortion. Other lawyers described how conflict with professors and classmates led them to establish conservative advocacy organizations, journals, and debating societies.

This generation of conservative lawyers appeared to view themselves as beleaguered minorities in the legal academy even as their side was winning elections and making large cultural gains. They benefited from the growing infrastructure of the conservative movement, which provided opportunities for them to work for conservative public interest law groups, participate in conservative political organizations and journals, interact with older conservatives, and land jobs in Republican administrations.

DISTASTE FOR LIBERALS

In the interviews, conservatives were generally united in their disapproval of liberals, although business advocates and lawyers for mediator groups offered less than their share of criticism. Social conservatives claimed that liberals' support for birth control, abortion, gay rights, and pornography debases sexual intimacy, threatens the traditional family, and jeopardizes the interests of children and the unborn. Religious liberties advocates characterized liberals as foes of religion, and school voucher proponents characterized them as enemies of educational opportunity. Several lawyers for mediator organizations argued that liberals' Great Society programs worsen conditions for minorities and the poor by undercutting their authority to make decisions for themselves. Property rights advocates asserted that liberals' failure to appreciate the relationship between strong private property rights and political freedom contributes to the erosion of economic opportunity, and affirmative action opponents argued that liberals betray the principle of equal opportunity. Business advocates complained about liberals' tendency to overregulate.

Some of these lawyers suggested that liberals were not just wrong but hypocritical, illogical, or stupid. One social conservative who had defended homeschooling parents from government interference said,

> I think conservatives can have totalitarian and authoritarian impulses that you have to guard against, and that's why we have the Bill of Rights. But it is amazing to me how many liberals are in total denial that they have authoritarian tendencies. . . . Some of the liberal opponents we get are so inconsistent and just do not at all see any inconsistency because they feel basically that they've got a good motive for promoting their authoritarian thing that absolves them of all guilt for any constitutional violation.

A libertarian complained about liberals' selective application of university speech codes to "anybody who would challenge the liberal leftish orthodoxy. . . . It was perfectly all right for gay and lesbian students to call Christians bigots, or members of certain racial or ethnic groups to make all sorts of insensitive or inappropriate remarks about other nonpreferred minority groups." Another libertarian referred disapprovingly to "enviros" whose antipathy for the profit motive led them to oppose market-oriented strategies for protecting the environment. A property rights lawyer described a case he handled in which "hot-headed environmentalists" had delayed the development of coastal property for housing that he believed would have benefited the owner, the county, and people who would live there. A pornography opponent complained that feminists were "confused" and unreliable allies because "many of their leaders came up through Eastern liberal colleges, where they were told that any kinds of restrictions on speech are censorship." A lawyer for a religious conservative group described as "Id-ee-o-tic" the position of his opponents in litigation over a religious organization's practice of hiring only employees who shared its religious beliefs. A lawyer for a mediator organization complained that young "progressive" lawyers were intellectually flabby. Unlike young conservatives, who had been forced to go "toe-to-toe" with the "intellectual brown shirts of the law school faculties," he said, liberals have received "rotten training" and "are unprepared to think for themselves because they are on God's side and the answers are easy."

Other lawyers criticized liberals for failings that had more to do with attitude and tone than substance. One said that "sometimes the more liberal intellectual types are so conceited or so taken with their own intelligence that they really don't have a whole lot of respect for minorities. They talk down to them. They act like they're trying to take care of them and they patronize them . . . ": "I think that a lot of the high falutin sort of intellectual liberals aren't as compassionate or as active in doing practical things for their supposed minority constituency. . . . [They want to] tell everybody else what to do. . . . I don't need a bunch of white liberal guys telling me they're going to take care of me." Another social conservative described liberals as people who "want to micromanage your life" and who "feel that they have a monopoly on intelligence and morality." A lawyer who had been nominated for the federal bench but denied a Senate hearing said, "the more I know about the other side . . . the less I like them . . . the less persuaded I am by them, and the less I feel that they are—that their views are, or their strategies, their tactics, the way they engage, how they do things, are ways I [could support]." A business advocate asserted that the Bush Administration had restored civility to the White House after the Clinton years, when matters of common courtesy, particularly as they applied to the treatment of staff, had been slighted.

OVERLAPPING ISSUE AGENDAS

Communism and socialism were the enemies around which all strands of the conservative coalition could coalesce through the 1980s, and some of the interviewed lawyers commented on how antipathy for those movements had shaped their political commitments. One lawyer interviewed for this research had been a prominent advocate for purging communist sympathizers from government and challenging communist activities abroad from the 1950s through the 1980s. A libertarian said that his experience as an immigrant from an Eastern bloc country had forged his political outlook. Another libertarian ascribed great importance to being the child of Russian émigrés. A gun rights advocate who had served in Vietnam and had been imprisoned and tortured there recalled that when he returned to the United States he "wanted to kill communism by whatever means it was possible to do it; I wanted to just absolutely forestall any further spread of this type of thinking—of arbitrary government, and to restrain all government within reasonable bounds. . . . " A lawyer for a mediator organization said that he was "always fighting the communists" during his college years[2] and that he continued to mistrust all "utopian solutions." A libertarian recalled that when he was an undergraduate "the Soviet Union was the major—in my view, was *the* major threat—to everything I held dear."

But the power of communism and socialism to unite the conservative coalition has diminished since the collapse of the Soviet Union and the economic liberalization of China. At the time of the interviews, a variety of other domestic and foreign policy issues had become the primary concerns. The end of the Cold War and the loss of a unifying enemy has worried movement insiders (e.g., Gottfried 1993), including some of the lawyers I interviewed.

But there remains some shared ground in the issue agendas of the constituencies. As each pursues its own agenda, it finds common cause on particular issues with constituencies that are similar. Business interests and libertarians are the most natural and reliable allies. They generally agree about reducing taxes and limiting government regulation, although business advocates depart from that position as it suits their clients' interests. Libertarians and religious conservatives agree on school choice and religious expression in the public sphere. Recently they have found common cause in resisting "eminent domain abuse." In the wake of *Kelo v. City of New London,* which approved the condemnation of private property for use in a comprehensive community redevelopment plan, religious conservatives began to fear that local governments would use eminent domain power to seize church property, which does not generate tax revenue, for use in development projects that do (Kirkpatrick 2005b; Lampman 2005). They have mobilized to support state ballot initiatives to curtail eminent domain power and to require full compensation for regulation that diminishes property values (Gilroy 2006; Schlafly 2006).

Despite these elements of agreement over policy priorities, articulating a coherent and stable set of common commitments among these constituencies has proven difficult. Grover Norquist, President of Americans for Tax Reform and coordinator of Wednesday morning meetings of Washington activists (including but not limited to lawyers), has asserted that conservatives and libertarians are united in their desire to be left alone: "The guy who wants to be left alone to practice his faith, the guy who wants to make money, the guy who wants to spend money without paying taxes, the guy who wants to fondle his gun—they all have a lot in common. They all want the government to go away. That is what holds together the conservative movement" (Cassidy 2005). In his introduction to a collection of essays about advocates for conservative and libertarian advocacy groups, Edwin Meese similarly claims that participants in the "freedom-based public interest law movement" share a commitment to "ordered liberty—the prudential blending of individual freedom and political order" (Edwards 2004, i). A lawyer interviewed for this book asserted that there was considerable agreement among social conservatives, business advocates, and libertarians about issues of personal liberty and limited government. For the Christian Right, he argued, the desire to be left alone reflected the idea that "you've got to make your decisions" and that "God will judge whether your choices were right." A libertarian also expressed optimism about the compatibility of the policy preferences of various types of conservatives:

> [O]n the issues that bring [conservatives] to politics, on the issues on which the preferences are most intense, even social conservatives, or old Right conservatives, tend to be libertarian.... I'm sure that lots of NRA members, gun owners, are also union members and hold very strange views on free trade— they're probably against it. But that doesn't matter, because the one issue that brings them into politics and that shapes their conduct and their voting behavior and their advocacy—on that issue they're libertarian. And I think that is true about a ton of constituencies out there. So, I think, despite some sparring and somewhat childish behavior on both sides of that particular divide, I think there's a lot of agreement and, I think, a fairly, a remarkably stable and coherent, lasting coalition.

There is clearly truth to the claim that conservatives care about having government leave them alone. Libertarians generally oppose government planning. Business interests resist regulation that does not contribute to their bottom line, and they tend not to characterize the basic institutional and regulatory frameworks that sustain market capitalism as "regulation." Some burning public policy issues for social conservatives can be described in similar "leave us alone" terms. They want freedom to home-school their children, to express their religious convictions in the public sphere, and to hire employees whose religious views and sexual practices conform to their own commitments. Indeed, many of Christian litigators' victories during the past few decades have resulted from their choice to reframe church-state issues as matters of free speech.

But not all of these constituencies consistently endorse the "leave us alone" position. Religious conservatives want government to fix our corrupt society and prevent further erosion of traditional social mores. Some of them seek to criminalize gay sex and prohibit gay marriage, outlaw abortion, ban pornography and obscenity, infuse education with religion, and prevent terminally ill patients from ending their lives. These initiatives are not in harmony with libertarian ideals. They reveal, instead, the sharp limits of religious conservatives' commitments to individual freedom as libertarians define it. One lawyer I interviewed said that religious conservatives draw the line on individual freedom for behavior that amounts to "taking a sledge hammer to the foundation." In that sense, he said, they are fundamentally different from libertarians, who are such "slaves to their philosophy" that they are prepared to take "really wrongheaded" positions on issues such as sexual behavior and drug use. Social conservatives embrace freedom for religious expression, but they also want to use law to advance their values. As Kevin den Dulk has described the tension, evangelicals "seek more than cultural space to practice religion in private; they wish to transform the culture as a whole by using public means to influence individual behavior and direct others toward their understanding of God's will" (den Dulk 2006, 212). Their conception of individual freedom is a bounded one whose limits are found in God's law (den Dulk 2006, 212). Similarly, business interests sometimes do not want government to stay away; despite their general mistrust of government, they seek regulation and government support when it promotes their purposes (Key 1964, 77; Vogel 1978).

Differences in policy agendas of the constituencies represented by the interviewed lawyers are reflected in the organizations' patterns of participation in legislative hearings. Using the LexisNexis Congressional database, which contains comprehensive legislative records about the U.S. Congress, I compiled records of testimony submitted to federal committees by the sixty-nine organizations represented by the interviewed lawyers from January 2003 through August 2007. The represented organizations submitted 823 pieces of testimony during that period. In thirty-two sets of committee hearings, organizations from more than one category participated, and most of these overlaps involved mediator organizations and groups in the other categories. Business and libertarian organizations participated jointly in eight sets of hearings. Libertarian and social conservative groups did not overlap at all, and only one issue, religious expression in the workplace, attracted participation by both business and social conservative groups.[3] Thus, the primary constituencies of the conservative coalition tend to pursue different legislative agendas.

In addition to substantial disagreements about broad policy goals, differences in attitudes about politics and compromise also inhibit cooperation. Business lawyers' pragmatic understanding of their roles and their clients' objectives makes them willing to build alliances with a broader range of people to advance economic goals that matter to their clients. One business lawyer said that sometimes "there can be what you might call unholy alliances, but it's based upon the need that is being addressed. Do you need to have your nontraditional ally to make something happen? . . . So the issue determines it, not the philosophy." She said that she had once attended a meeting called by Federalist Society members to discuss cooperation on amicus briefs but that her participation was "based upon the pragmatic issue" and "not upon a philosophical approach." Another lawyer for a trade association said he believed that "negotiations among adults recognize that you win a little, you lose a little, and you leave a little on the table. And to the extent that you can find adults, that's what you do." He said that it is critical to understand that

> The . . . industry doesn't pay us to be ideologues. They pay us to solve problems. . . . All politics is mathematics and all successful politics is addition. . . . We just don't have the votes anywhere to be able to get things done without bringing other people into a coalition of some type or another. That's often within the business community, but we often have to—we *need* to—go beyond that to people who are coming at an issue from a different perspective.

Even some libertarians indicated that they were prepared to work with allies who did not share their principles. One said, "Ad hoc alliances, that's very critical, and I have no compunction, no qualm about working with nonlibertarians in order to move the ball forward." Another libertarian said "there is a lot of strength in nontraditional alliances, including groups that libertarians don't generally count as allies." Advocates for social conservative groups are generally less inclined than lawyers for the other constituencies to view politics as an arena for give and take and striking deals. Many religious conservatives view their organizations' goals as God's mandates rather than merely compelling policy objectives, and they are not inclined to compromise. One lawyer for a large religious organization told me that his client was "not prone to . . . use political expediency as the benchmark." As Rozell and Wilcox found in their examination of the Christian Right's transition from an ineffectual social movement to an influential political force, "For those who tie their positions on political issues to inerrant Scriptures, compromise may literally be seen as making a deal with the devil" (1996, 285). One long-time observer of the conservative legal movement noted such a reluctance to compromise by conservatives who took a "priestly view of the law"—for example, a strong position about the proper interpretation of the Constitution: "The most interesting tension is not [between] the libertarians and the moralists, although that's an interesting one. The much more interesting tension on the part of the lawyers is between the priests and the counselors, the principled guys and the political guys."

Differences in the policy agendas of the different constituencies sometimes result in open conflict. Such strains have appeared in controversies over affirmative action, immigration, gay marriage, broadcasting obscenity, abortion, and the treatment of "enemy combatants" in the War on Terror. Immigration reform proposals also have split the conservative coalition, as business interests have supported the Bush Administration's plan to combine increased border security with guest worker programs to create a path to citizenship for illegal immigrants already in the United States and social conservatives have vigorously opposed plans that would give illegal immigrants "amnesty" (Silva 2006). The administration's proposed constitutional amendment to prohibit same-sex marriage appeals to the party's social conservative base, who have charged that the Bush Administration has lagged in its commitment to goals they regard as fundamental (Kirkpatrick 2006a), but it has alienated liberal and moderate Republicans, whose support for Bush has sagged significantly since his reelection (Hulse 2006). The administration's policies with respect to domestic surveillance and the treatment of enemy combatants have divided some libertarians from social conservatives and law-and-order advocates.

A measure to increase fines for obscenity in broadcasting has similarly divided business advocates from Christian conservatives (Kirkpatrick 2006a).

REMAKING THE COURTS

In assessing how conservatives managed to avoid conflict with one another during first five years of the Bush presidency, conservative activist Richard A. Viguerie said, "[W]e did that because it was all about the courts, all about the courts, all about the courts" (Weisman 2005). Although my interviews did not specifically ask lawyers for their views about constitutional interpretation or the judiciary, many of the interviewed lawyers indicated that they favored the appointment of conservative judges. Some had worked on judicial appointments for Republican administrations. Many asserted that liberal reformers had illegitimately used the courts to thwart the outcomes of democratic processes and had been assisted in that effort by judges willing to construe ambiguous constitutional provisions to support activists' claims. A libertarian recalled his distress as he began studying constitutional law as a first-year law student: "I started reading these cases and, frankly, they didn't make a whole lot of sense to me—the more, if you will, liberal decisions. They seemed to me to be not following the law. And I thought it was important to follow the law." A pornography opponent said that he stopped voting for Democrats "towards the end of Carter's administration when I started getting exposed to more of the opinions and decisions of the judges who were getting appointed": "I didn't like the sort of attitude of a lot of the more liberal, activist judges . . . who, I thought, wouldn't follow the existing law. . . . I started voting for Reagan because I thought he would appoint more by-the-book judges, and he did." A tort reform advocate expressed dismay about how elected judges are engaging in "judicial nullification of state tort law": "if the public understood what's going on, they wouldn't stand for it. . . . [It's] just an absolute example . . . of ignoring the rule of law and creating new rules to achieve a result." A social conservative suggested that the rule of law, whose ultimate authority came from God, had given way to tyranny by the courts.

Disapproval of "judicial activism" gives conservatives a common grievance around which to rally, and it helps to mask significant policy differences among them. Religious conservatives, for example, disagree with many libertarians and business advocates about whether abortion should be allowed, but focusing on their shared disapproval of the reasoning of

Roe highlights common ground. One Christian advocate observed that "one of the intellectual mechanisms" for keeping peace within the conservative coalition is to focus on judicial activism because conservatives are "uniformly offended by" it. He claimed that "100 percent" of conservatives, including even "the libertarian guys at Cato" would agree that *Roe v. Wade* was wrongly decided.

Even if lawyers of the conservative coalition agree that left-leaning judicial activism is bad, however, they are less united about how to define judicial activism and what approach to constitutional interpretation judges should apply. All of them would endorse broad language in the Federalist Society's mission statement asserting that judges must "say what the law is and not what it should be" (Federalist Society 2006). They agree (as do most Americans) that judges may not impose their will in defiance of the Constitution. But they disagree about what that *means*—how judges should find the law, whether and to what extent they are bound by precedent, and when judges are justified in striking down state and federal laws.

During his years as attorney general in the Reagan Administration, Edwin Meese launched a campaign to persuade the public that the Constitution had been interpreted by courts and Congress in ways inconsistent with the founders' understanding of the document. In a speech at an ABA meeting, Meese criticized judges who "roam at large in a veritable constitutional forest," producing decisions that were "more policy choices than articulations of constitutional principle" (Silas 1985).[4] He urged the appointment of judges who would "judge policies in light of principles, rather than remold principles in light of policies," and called for a "jurisprudence of original intention," according to which Supreme Court justices should seek to implement "deference to what the Constitution, its text and intention, may demand" (Silas 1985). Meese pledged that the Reagan Administration would "endeavor to resurrect the original meaning of constitutional provisions" and the founders' views "as the only reliable guide" (Kamen 1985). He argued that judges should seek to implement the original meaning of the authors and ratifiers of the Constitution and the Bill of Rights—a view that generally accords less power to the federal government and fewer protections for individual rights.[5]

Originalism has proven to be a powerfully attractive jurisprudential philosophy for conservatives. It would reduce federal governmental power, protect business interests from regulation, restrict the rights of criminal defendants, expand property rights, invalidate affirmative action programs, diminish privacy rights, and eliminate the abortion right found in *Roe v. Wade.* The Federalist Society built its 2005 Annual Convention around the theme of originalism, presumably because its leaders thought that this topic would help to generate consensus among members.

But faithful application of originalism would quite radically change the law because it would require overturning hundreds of established precedents.[6] Conservatives who endorse this strong version of original-ism tend to disapprove when judges defer to precedents that contradict the "framers' understanding of the constitution," and they applaud (and do not regard as improper judicial activism) decisions invalidating legis-lation that is inconsistent with the original meaning of the constitution (Sunstein 2005; Keck 2004).

Despite rhetoric to the contrary, then, many conservatives, including many interviewed lawyers, do not believe in judicial restraint in the sense of upholding established precedents and deferring to legislative judgments. The judicial activism they deplore is illegitimate because it is not based on the founders' original meaning. It is distinguishable from the dramatic changes they ask the judiciary to undertake to correct illegitimate prior judicial activism and to restrain and reverse the work of other governmen-tal actors. Several social conservatives and libertarians expressed varia-tions on this view that courts should more aggressively seek to institute the founders' understanding of the Constitution. One said,

> The judiciary should be neither active, the way the Warren/Burger Justices were active in discovering rights in the Constitution that were not there to be discovered . . . Nor should the judiciary be restrained as the conservative jurisprudes who were reacting to judicial activism were urging. Rather, the proper role of the judiciary is that of responsibility to the Constitution, which means they should be active in the sense of limiting government where it is to be limited and finding rights where they are there to be found.[7]

He argued that the judicial activism he favored was "itself a product of prior legislative activism following the New Deal . . . which had led to the decline of private sovereignty for which the proper remedy was principled judicial activism." Another lawyer said that his goal was to "get courts back in the game of policing the boundaries of congressional authority and the Constitution." A property rights lawyer complained that "by and large the courts have failed miserably in enforcing the Constitution in this field" and that, in the rare instances when courts have properly en-forced constitutional property rights "it is deemed by the establishment to be something radical and new and horrific and whatever." A libertarian said that the *Slaughterhouse Cases* (1873) and their progeny "must be overturned," and another acknowledged that implementing his view of the founders' understanding of the Takings Clause of the Fifth Amendment would invalidate much regulation of the twentieth century. Several guns rights advocates sought to overrule a nearly seventy-year-old line of precedents holding that the Second Amendment does not give individuals the right to keep guns unless the individuals serve in an organized militia. All of the abortion opponents advocated overturning *Roe v. Wade.*

Among lawyers who support overturning Supreme Court precedents, there are sharp disagreements about which precedents are wrong. Many of the social conservatives argue that honoring the framers' intent means rejecting rights claims that do not find explicit support in the Constitution. Thus, the right of privacy, which has no textual basis in the Constitution, is illegitimate, and the long line of decisions finding and applying that right cry out for correction. Libertarians, in contrast, emphasize the Declaration of Independence's invocation of natural rights. They argue that the framers intended to protect not only rights specifically enumerated in the Constitution but also other rights rooted in the liberal philosophy that prevailed at the time, especially property. Social conservatives and libertarians also tend to disagree about the framers' understanding of the First Amendment's religion clauses, with social conservatives seeking to overturn Supreme Court case law imposing constitutional limits on the government's endorsement of particular religious messages and libertarians insisting that such limits implement the founders' commitment to religious pluralism.

Some of the conservatives I interviewed, however, including many of the business lawyers, did not endorse large-scale rollbacks of judicial precedent. Some of the lawyers for business interests sought to persuade the courts that large punitive-damages awards violate due process, but they did not advocate revoking the New Deal or dismantling the regulatory state, as some libertarians did. They certainly did not favor stacking the courts with jurists committed to overturning *Roe v. Wade* or injecting more religion into public education. For them, judicial restraint meant generally deferring to precedents on the books, perhaps because their clients valued stability and predictability (cf. Rabin 1986) and because they earned their livings selling their regulatory expertise (cf. Epstein 1988, 313–14; White 1992). The business advocates, then, were much more cautious and "lawyerly" than their social conservative and libertarian counterparts; they were more inclined to prefer slow, incremental change to radical reform.

Thus, while lawyers of the conservative coalition might agree on the goal of sacking liberal judges and appointing more conservative ones, they are not of one mind about the values those judges should hold, how far they should go in reversing the work of courts and legislatures in the twentieth century, and which nominees exhibit the "right" credentials and values.

THE REPUBLICAN PARTY

The design for this research selected organizations and lawyers on the basis of their service to one of the constituencies of an alliance that has coalesced behind the GOP. Unsurprisingly, therefore, most of the interviewed lawyers indicated that they were Republicans. But many of these lawyers, particularly libertarians and social conservatives, displayed little real loyalty to the party, and their disaffection usually focused on the party's commitments to competing constituencies within the alliance.

Although some religious conservatives were active at the highest levels of Republican politics, many indicated that their commitment to the party was weak. One pro-life activist said that he was "probably more Catholic . . . than conservative or liberal" and that he was deeply disappointed with the Bush Administration's approach to poverty. Another Catholic abortion opponent reported that although he had voted more often for Republicans than Democrats in the past twenty years, he did not "identify as Republican at all . . . especially on economic issues." An evangelical Christian said that, while most people think of him as a Republican, he considers himself a Protestant Christian first: "As you get into my life, it's hard to characterize my politics, but if you follow my faith-based commitments it makes much more sense." A Catholic anti-pornography activist said that he had switched from Independent to Republican as the Democrats became "the party of the sexual revolution," but he noted that the Republican Party was involved in some "pretty unsavory things." Another social conservative said, "I don't think of myself as a Republican, Democrat, or Independent. I think of myself as conservative—a Christian first, and then, in ideological or political terms, conservative." Another Christian advocate said that he was not registered to vote: "I don't like politics . . . I stay . . . away from it." According to Federal Election Commission records, only seven of the twenty-five lawyers for religious and pro-life groups had made individual contributions to Republican candidates from 1993 through October 2007.[8]

Few of the lawyers for libertarian advocacy organizations described themselves as strong Republicans. Five identified themselves as Independents, and another said, "My party is the Libertarian Party." Another described himself as "estranged from the political system." Even some libertarians who said they usually voted for Republicans indicated that their commitments to the GOP were weak. One noted that "the Republicans tend to have some views that I don't necessarily agree with," particularly on drug laws. Another lawyer who reported that he was a registered Republican nevertheless insisted that he "adhere[s] more to principle than to party." Others said that they frequently voted for Republicans but felt no loyalty to the party—for example, "I usually I do end up voting Republican just for lack of a Libertarian candidate"; "I've never really looked at party lines"; "party affiliation for me is a meaningless thing; I'd probably be a libertarian if I thought that there was any chance that they could actually do anything"; "I vote for the Republican; I am a registered Republican; but I have no illusions that it represents my interests." The founder of one libertarian advocacy group indicated that he regards himself as "an apostate Republican," and he noted that most of his colleagues are "militantly nonpolitical." Another lawyer characterized party loyalty as an impediment to responsible voting: "I think your commitment always has to be to principle and to ideas, and [you] make your political determinations based on what values you think are the most important in a particular election." Another libertarian said that he had not voted in many years, partly because "there is nobody running that really represents what I believe." He added, "there is no question . . . that I would favor Republican positions more than Democratic positions on a large variety of issues, but . . . I'm certainly not in favor of George Bush's education bill, faith-based initiatives, and a variety of federalized crimes. These are things that just roil me." A property rights lawyer said that he was a registered Republican but also "a liberal Democrat" as that label was used thirty years ago:

My views would fit very comfortably into the views of the Democratic Party about the time John Kennedy entered the White House. And that is, people like Scoop Jackson, Dean Acheson, on taxes even John Kennedy. On affirmative action and such, even Hubert Humphrey. I have no problem with those views. In fact, I suggest that if you have nothing better to do, you listen to the Kennedy speech on economics . . . Except for the funny Kennedy/Boston accent, you'd swear it's Ronald Reagan. He is talking about a party platform which stood for a militarily strong America, ready and willing to project its force around the world to protect its interests and its allies' interests. A certain degree of government intervention but kept well within checks. So

that the government could . . . abolish legal impediments to individual freedom by ethnic groups and maybe to circumscribe nongovernmental overt
discrimination, but otherwise then leave people alone to find their way. As
I already said, Kennedy was for lower taxes. Of course, Scoop Jackson was
for military strength. Dean Acheson for a policy of containment. . . . So you
discover what I have described for you is the position of today's conservative.
So I haven't changed. What has changed is that at the time of the McGovern
campaign, the Democratic Party was taken over by a bunch of wacko radicals who have not relinquished control to this day. I have no hesitancy in
saying that. Those people are not Democrats. They're essentially left-wing
radicals who have absolutely no commitment to, or concern for what is generally perceived of as the classic American values of equality and fairness,
and so on. . . . So somewhere along the line I decided that I wouldn't want
to be identified with them, and I reregistered as a Republican. But my views
haven't changed one bit.

Nine of the twenty-three lawyers for libertarian organizations had made
individual contributions to Republican candidates or GOP party organizations since 1993, according to Federal Election Commission records, but
two of those lawyers had also contributed to Democrats. One lawyer had
contributed exclusively to Libertarian candidates.

Most of the business lawyers indicated that they generally vote for Republicans, but none expressed enthusiasm for the party. One said, "There
are people here whose lives are tied up in being Republican. That's not
the way I am. I just happen to have certain beliefs based on having seen
the way the government works—not antigovernment, but government has
extraordinary power and I think in too many instances puts its own fief-
doms, with their self-interest, [ahead of] the rest of us." Another said that
he sees himself as politically "right down the middle, that would be just
right of center" although he "generally support[s] Republican initiatives."
Several lawyers for business interests expressed ambivalence or distaste
for the Republican Party. One said that she did not like either party because "extremists . . . call the agendas":

> It's the very liberal left of the Democrats or the trial bar, which I *do* think
> owns much of the Democratic Party, and the Christian Right for the Repub-
> licans. To me they are not representative of the political philosophy of the
> majority of the people in the United States. . . . I am by philosophy a fiscal
> conservative with a social conscience. I do not believe government should
> be paying for everything, but should provide assistance for everybody to
> help themselves.

A proponent of tort reform said that he was "totally fed up with the two-party system": "I don't feel either party represents my beliefs, so I have to just hold my nose and choose." A business lawyer who described himself as an Independent noted that his wife was active in Emily's List, an organization that seeks to elect pro-choice Democratic women: "Sometimes we wind up writing competing checks." He said of the people he hires for his organization, "We have Republicans, Democrats, liberals, conservatives. I only care about whether you're smart, you're hard working, and you're fun to be around. And I find that political persuasion is not a determinant of any of those things." Although most of the lawyers for business interests had made individual contributions to GOP candidates, four of the eleven had contributed to Democrats as well as Republicans. According to records of the Center for Responsive Politics, one of these lawyers had even contributed to Senator Ted Kennedy's campaign in the 1990s.

Many of the lawyers for mediator organizations were active in Republican Party politics at the national level, and presumably they valued the party as a vehicle for drawing conservatives and libertarians together. All of them had contributed to Republican candidates.[9] But even some of the lawyers for mediator organizations expressed considerable detachment about the fate of the Republican Party. One said, "Well, I think of myself as not a Democrat. I guess that means I'm a Republican, because I'm not a Democrat, [and] I'm not all that independent. That's really my political conviction—anyone but them." Another said, "I take issue with [Republicans] when I think they do bonehead things, but my criticism of them usually comes from the Right." A lawyer who was particularly well connected in conservative circles answered, "I vote Republican. Do I think of myself as a Republican? I think of myself more as a conservative than I do a Republican, [but] if given the choice, I vote Republican."

SHARED OCCUPATIONAL INTERESTS AND PROFESSIONAL IDEOLOGY

As suggested in chapter 1, lawyers' professional bonds might provide some basis for understanding and cooperation. Legal education is remarkably uniform throughout the country (Abel 1989, 212; Stevens 1983). All law schools teach students to "think like lawyers," a process that may tend to promote analytical, rational habits of mind (Erlanger and Klegon 1978; Provine 1986). Some have suggested that legal training leads lawyers to like rules and procedures (Scheingold 1974, 159; Stevens 1983, 55–56), to value stability and predictability (Scheingold 1974), and to resist proposals for radical change (Scheingold 1974; McCann 1986, 204). All law graduates endure a common ordeal—a bar examination—administered by the states in which they plan to practice.

Therefore, while the interviewed lawyers were stratified on many dimensions, their shared education and experience as lawyers might create mutual understanding. Woven throughout the lawyers' accounts of their roles in the conservative movement are bits of evidence of their common training, professional socialization, and views about the boundaries of proper advocacy. As will be described in chapter 7, they used a broad range of strategies, but all of the policy arenas in which they operated had long traditions of lawyers' participation. Not all of their arenas were solely the province of lawyers; many participated in lobbying, media work, and public education, where they interacted with nonlawyers. But none of the interviewed lawyers advocated "extralegal" or illegal strategies. That was true even of lawyers associated with pro-life and property rights activism—two causes that have spawned radical and sometimes violent elements (Blanchard 1994, 51–60; Culhane 1994).

Some of the interviewed lawyers indicated that they valued the special status and opportunities they enjoyed as lawyers. One said that he went to law school to position himself to participate in public policy debates: "I wanted to talk to reporters. I wanted to appear on talk shows. I wanted to write op-eds . . . To be part of the debate. And it's hard to do that unless one is a lawyer in America today. That seems to be the path." Another recalled that when he worked on Capitol Hill as a junior legislative assistant to a conservative senator, he saw that "the people who were really . . . in the interesting positions . . . were all lawyers. It was a lawyers' world." Another said, "I decided [to go to law school] when I was four years old. . . . I was watching John F. Kennedy on television, and I said, 'Gee, what he does is cool,' and I asked my mother, 'What do I have to do to do that?,' and she said, 'You have to go to law school.'"[10] A school-choice proponent reported that he "wasn't willing to lick envelopes" but found it highly satisfying to write briefs. A lawyer who had been a social conservative activist before attending law school remembered that she had "never done any debating before really and . . . they started putting me up against [opponents who] were lawyers and they acted like they knew more than I did, so I figured I would go to law school to get my union card."

Several lawyers for pro-life groups emphasized their disagreement with the more radical elements of the cause they served and their roles in couching the religious right's positions in legalistic and politically saleable terms. One noted that his work typically emphasized "how religious tradition can inform the Court's decision making" and satisfied neither hard-core activists nor inward-looking religious people; it was "frustrating to the more politically active" but "probably equally frustrating to those who believe that prayer is enough—that we ought to be praying for conversion." Several pro-life advocates said that they and the groups they served were committed to the rule of law and disapproved of extreme groups that resorted to violence. Another abortion opponent spoke disparagingly of some of the "more radical or uncompromising pro-life groups":

> People who . . . will not in principle support a constitutional amendment that would overrule *Roe* and turn abortion issues to the states because that's not good enough. It has to be an amendment banning *all* abortions. . . . And because these things are regarded by the groups as matters of theology or matters of life and death . . . they are almost worse today to their 80 percent allies than they are to their 100 percent enemies.

Another lawyer said, "I don't think that the activist side of the pro-life movement—by that I mean the protesters and demonstrators—I don't think they're achieving a lot. They may actually have achieved the opposite of what they think they've achieved, because I think the public image of a pro-life movement is bound up with people who blockade clinics and prevent ingress and egress. . . . " He complained that radical activists played into the hands of the liberal media, who were not inclined to cover abortion litigation fairly:

> On the pro-choice side, they interview some lawyer—maybe the lawyer who argued the case. . . . On the pro-life side, do they interview Jim Bopp [General Counsel of the National Right to Life Committee] or somebody like that, or Clark Forsythe [President of Americans United for Life], or somebody who could talk intelligently about this? No. They interview Randy Terry, who's just a complete flamer as far as I'm concerned. I think he's useless. But what are his credentials to be talking about it? None. He's not a lawyer. He doesn't think like a lawyer. This is a legal issue!

These lawyers' common professional experiences and socialization, then, may help to draw them together. But the wide range of issues in which they engage and differences in their political perspectives push them apart and impede their cooperation. Terence Halliday has suggested that American lawyers find it difficult to mobilize around common professional goals because they are divided by the varied normative projects in which they participate (1987, 48). Moreover, while there are substantial similarities in the legal education and professional socialization of all American lawyers, there also are important differences. Lawyers attending elite law schools and working in major metropolitan areas generate substantially different contacts and adopt different perspectives than their counterparts from local law schools working in social conservative advocacy organizations in rural areas. These differences in experiences, networks, commitments, and values may inhibit cooperation among lawyers for the various constituencies of the conservative coalition.

PERCEIVED DISADVANTAGE IN THE LEGAL ESTABLISHMENT

Many of the interviewed lawyers remarked on their dissatisfaction with what they viewed as the pillars of the liberal legal establishment: law schools and especially law faculties, legal services programs, the liberal public interest community, and the ABA. Their relationships with, and perceptions of, those institutions appear to have strongly influenced their professional identities.

Although law students of all political stripes experience alienation in law school (Granfield 1992, 41–42; Stone 1971; Stover 1989), many of the lawyers interviewed for this research described a special type of discomfort associated with holding conservative views while attending law schools whose students and faculties leaned left. As already suggested, many of the interviewed lawyers said that their professional identities had been forged through conflicts with liberal and radical professors and classmates. One reported that "most of the professors [at his law school] were pretty left-wing . . . some of them pretty militantly so." Another lawyer said that the faculty at his law school was "typical" in its hostility to conservative viewpoints, and he claimed that there was "[n]obody . . . there that I felt particularly politically or intellectually in tune with." Several lawyers also reported that they had felt estranged from their law school peers. A Christian conservative who described his law school as "an intolerant left-wing environment" expressed fury that the pro-life group he founded was the only student organization to be chartered but not funded by the student bar association. A woman who was an outspoken conservative in law school said that "[o]ther women were really ugly to me." A lawyer who recalled that he was "the only vocal conservative" in his law school class said that he "was very unpopular, extremely unpopular." Another recalled, "After writing pieces excoriating *Roe v. Wade* and some of the other sacred cows of liberal jurisprudence, I was sort of a marked man."

Several lawyers had attended law schools known for their high concentrations of conservative faculty. A lawyer who went to George Mason said that he appreciated that his professors had not examined every legal issue from "square one"; they did not, for example, analyze the concept of private property—and instead focused on what he characterized as "more interesting" issues "where there are legitimate disputes at the margin." Lawyers who had attended Yale and the University of Chicago also noted that they had found important conservative mentors at those schools.

Several of the older lawyers remarked on the absence of any group like the Federalist Society to help them find companionship with fellow conservatives during law school, and many of the younger lawyers said that the Federalist Society had generated ties among conservative students. One of the older lawyers recalled, "I was in law school in the pre–Federalist Society era. The organizations were all on the other side. . . . There weren't that many conservatives." Another, who described himself as "one of, if not the lone conservative voice" in his law school observed, "We didn't have anything like the Federalist Society to kind of crystallize around." Another said, "I think it's gotten better now, but my law school education was at a time when [we were not] . . . provided with alternative viewpoints. There was no Federalist Society on campus. . . . " Many of the interviewed lawyers who attended law school after 1982 were active in the Federalist Society, and eight of them led or participated in establishing chapters at their law schools. One lawyer attributed the "uneasy peace" among different types of conservatives within Federalist Society student chapters to "the fact that we're quite outnumbered in the legal academy."

Several lawyers who had sought but failed to land law faculty positions believed that their conservative political views had hurt their prospects. One said that "being a conservative white male didn't help," and another recalled of his unsuccessful search for a tenure-track position that "invariably ideology . . . would raise its ugly head." Several conservative law professors expressed the view that they were part of an underappreciated and small minority. One described himself as "the only conservative Christian on any law faculty within a four-hundred-mile radius," and a libertarian asserted that he was one of only four or five Republicans on his law school faculty. A conservative who had clerked on the Supreme Court said that he had expected to receive an offer from a major law school but found instead that his options were quite limited. Another reported that conservatives on law faculties often felt isolated because "there's this tendency to say conservative—you're a bad person. . . . "

Several of the interviewed lawyers expressed disapproval of the federal legal services program, which has received qualified support from the ABA since its creation in 1974 (Auerbach 1976, 270; Marks et al. 1972, 42). Lewis Powell, author of the "Powell Memorandum" (described in chapter 2), was president of the ABA at the time the program was founded, and he agreed to cooperate with the initiative only if it used the "expertise and facilities of the organized bar" as much as possible and required lawyers to comply with the "ethical standards of the profession" (Auerbach 1976, 270–72). But critics from the Right have persistently charged that legal services lawyers have departed from their mandate to serve the poor and have pursued controversial law reform work at the expense of individual client service (e.g., Brookhiser 1983; Moore 2000; Rowley 1992). They led a campaign over several decades to restrict the activities of legal services grantees. Among the regulations designed to ensure that legal services lawyers stick to individual representation and uncontroversial matters are prohibitions on political organizing, class action lawsuits, lobbying, litigation on behalf of prisoners, challenges to welfare reform, abortion litigation, and the representation of some categories of immigrants.[11] Congressional restrictions imposed in 1996 also prohibit Legal Services Corporation (LSC) grantees from using other sources of funding to pursue any of the banned activities.[12]

Complaints about the federal legal services program arose frequently in the interviews. One lawyer for a mediator group recalled his frustration in the 1970s with opponents of welfare reform, led by "left-wing forces including a lot of the ultraliberal think tanks and also liberal so-called legal services lawyers." Another lawyer for a mediator organization asserted that the Legal Services Corporation had "lost its way," becoming "out of touch with what the needs of poor people really were—basically individual needs." He argued that legal services lawyers should give poor people the same types of services that lawyers in the private sector perform for individual middle-class clients: "We should come into people's lives episodically, do the best we can, and let them move on." The same lawyer blamed legal services attorneys for a series of decisions finding that due process requires a hearing before government benefits and entitlements are suspended. He called the first of these, *Goldberg v. Kelly*, "the most devastating, anti-poor, anti-Black decision of our lifetime":

It's a *Plessy v. Ferguson* decision in terms of its [impact] . . . It substitutes *us* [lawyers] for communities and community institutions. And it's a hypocritical decision—not intended to be so by Justice Brennan—but, in the end, a hypocritical decision, because we who have money don't rely on public institutions, and we operate on the basis of contract. So we get our neighbor evicted who plays the piano too loud. And they can't—somebody who's shooting dope or peeing in the hallways—because legal services lawyers are out there making it impossible to do so. . . . They can't suspend or expel some kid who is monumentally disruptive in public school. . . . "More of us means more justice," is this bizarre view that lawyers have. We began a rights revolution that undermined middle-class values and the ability of middle-class institutions to make their own damn mistakes and to recover from them and to learn from them and be strengthened by the process.

A libertarian said, "I'm very supportive of a properly motivated legal aid group that is out to assist poor people. I'm very uncomfortable when they choose to establish their own political forum as to what is good for poor people, and use those funds and monies, rather than provide neighborhood legal assistance, to follow their individual political agendas."

Other lawyers complained that prevailing conceptions of public interest law and pro bono tend to promote liberal rather than conservative causes. A professor claimed that law school clinics and law firm pro bono committees continue to define "public interest" to mean "indigent only or left-leaning political cause oriented." Instead, he argued, the concept should apply "across the whole [political] spectrum," to ensure that "it isn't only a particular political ideology that thinks they get to do public interest work": "And I think that is very important because there a lot of, believe it or not, public interest minded conservatives that would love to do public interest work, just not for causes that undermine what their principles are." A property rights lawyer described a recent disagreement with his alma mater over a flyer he had received for a public interest lecture series:

> Every name that I could recognize on the list—and I recognized most of them—were left-wing political type people. I looked at that and I said, "You're giving the kids a skewed view of what the public interest is when you tell them that there is a lecture series dealing with public interest law, and all you're bringing in is the left-wing firebrands." [The] response was, "Well, we have other lecture series where we bring in people from the business side." I said, "That doesn't work for me. That's fine. Bring in the business people and have a business roundtable or whatever you want to do, but you still are not offsetting the idea that public interest means liberal politics." I'm concerned that there is too much of that that goes on in academia.

A libertarian said that he believed that his career reflected a commitment to public service defined in a way no longer endorsed by law schools: "[P]ublic service [once] had much less of the sectarian meaning than it has acquired now. . . . Then it meant public service in the grand sense. . . . So you didn't have to merely help people who were poor. You didn't have to help trees or chipmunks and things like that. You could actually do things that represented an interest in bettering the role of government vis-à-vis the individual, in terms of expanding personal liberties. . . . " In response to my question about whether he had attended law school to pursue social or political change, another lawyer said,

> No. This was in the 1950s. In the 1950s, a lawyer was a fella—usually a fella, there were very few women—who was supposed to know the law, and was supposed to bring that law to bear on his client's affairs. . . . It was decidedly not the idea among lawyers then that it was our job to save the whales or to save the world. That was inappropriate for lawyers. That was essentially a policy/legislative sort of thing. It was a whole different world.

Several lawyers talked about unsuccessful battles to persuade their law firms to allow pro bono work for conservative causes. One lawyer left his firm in the wake of such a disagreement when the firm rejected his request to handle a controversial Supreme Court argument.

Several of the interviewed lawyers insisted that lawyers for conservative causes were greatly outnumbered by, and much less organized than, lawyers for causes of the Left. A founder of one of the earliest conservative public interest law groups complained, "[T]here is a tremendous manpower discrepancy between the liberal and radical public interest law firms and the conservative [public interest law groups]. I don't know what the current balance is, but the last time I checked it was considerable. Years ago, there were like fifty attorneys versus a thousand. It would be more attorneys on both sides now and it wouldn't be quite as much of a spread, but it's a gigantic spread." When I asked about communication among lawyers of the conservative coalition, a property rights lawyer said, "the other side seems to be much better organized than we are. You've got all this vast right-wing conspiracy crap coming out," but "this is the most disorganized conspiracy I have ever seen if there is such a thing." Another property rights lawyer argued that "the people who are arrayed against [us] are highly organized": "There is a massive, highly organized, very competent movement [composed of] a curious kind of amalgam of three . . . seemingly very dissimilar groups, [including] good faith environmentalists, traditional suburban aristocrats, [and] the NIMBYs,[13] who may be of modest financial circumstances but they're not stupid and they realize that the status quo has set them up for life." Property owners, he said, "don't understand that they are in a major war," and trying to organize them to challenge regulation was "like herding a bunch of squirrels. . . . From what I see, if any kind of . . . conspiratorial approach [exists], it would be on the other side. . . . " A libertarian said of his organization in its early years, "you quickly find out that [conservative public interest law groups] are really autonomous and inward looking. And there's not a lot of [collaboration]." Another libertarian offered this comparison of cooperation among legal advocacy groups of the Left and Right:

> Groups on the Left cooperate very closely. Groups on the Right do not, because the conservatives are all individualists and conservatives also always feel like they've been losing. So every time someone decides they're gonna get active they just come in with the attitude, "I'm gonna do it all, I'm gonna come in, I'm gonna fix it. Everybody that's done it before has just done it wrong." And they always start from scratch. . . . If you get a guy on the Left . . . the first thing he'd ask is, "What's the party line? What's been done on this before?" And they cooperate. A conservative comes in and starts his own foundation, writes his own book on all the subjects he's interested in, without reading anybody else's books, they just don't cooperate. And that may be philosophical because they're individualists. They don't think in sort of this social way.

The ABA was another popular target of criticism. One libertarian stated, "I am not a member of the American Bar Association. I wish I was [sic] so I could resign again." Another libertarian described his decision not to join the ABA as an act of "silent protest." Several lawyers specifically objected to the ABA's practice of lobbying and testifying on abortion and the death penalty. One business lawyer said, "I don't really understand, as a lawyers' advocacy group—I'm sure if they polled the ABA members, they're split right down the middle—how the organization can develop a consensus to testify." Another lawyer said, "I'm deliberately not a member of the ABA because of their political stands and doing things that I think ought not to be done by that kind of trade organization."[14] A libertarian reported that he had "gotten into bumps and battles with the ABA over the years" and that now "basically my bar association is the Federalist Society."

Several lawyers had been involved in judicial confirmation battles— several on behalf of other conservative nominees and one fighting on his own behalf to secure a spot on the federal bench. These lawyers accused the liberal legal establishment, including the ABA, of blocking the confirmation of highly qualified conservatives by injecting political ideology where it did not belong.

The perception of lawyers for all strands of the conservative alliance that they are at odds with law schools, the public interest community, and the organized bar gave these lawyers a joint grievance around which to rally. But these lawyers were not all similarly situated with respect to the legal establishment; many of the elite lawyers were on the fringes if not actually part of it. Elites of the conservative movement sometimes identified with other elites within the bar at the expense of their lawyer comrades within the alliance.

CONCLUSION

There are several sources of ties among lawyers for the different constituencies. Many of these lawyers belong to the same "generational units," and they are united in their disapproval of liberals. There is some overlap in their issue agendas, and they share a commitment to changing the judiciary. All of them work for constituencies that have longstanding ties to the GOP. Their common occupational experiences and interests and their perception of disadvantage within the legal establishment also help to bind them together.

But it is unclear whether any of these elements of common ground is sufficient, independently or in combination, to unite these lawyers. Factors that might once have led them to find common cause despite substantial differences among them may no longer provide sufficient glue. As the movement has matured and acquired influence, disagreements have emerged over priorities and tactics. Today, generational bonds among these lawyers appear to be weak counterweights to the social, cultural, and professional differences that divide them. Their shared distaste for liberals is nearly matched by their distaste for one another. The Communist threat around which conservatives previously rallied has disappeared, and other overlapping aspects of their issue agendas are now swamped by differences. Conservative lawyers' joint interest in remaking the judiciary has occasionally foundered over questions about just what it means to be a conservative jurist and what types of conservative commitments a nominee must publicly embrace. The Republican Party may sometimes succeed in disciplining politicians within its ranks, but it does not appear to command much loyalty from most of the lawyers interviewed for this research. A common underdog identity may once have tied together lawyers for the different conservative constituencies, but it has become more difficult to sustain as conservatives have founded dozens of public interest law groups, gained control over executive branch appointments, and created an impressive lawyer network. Despite their shared occupational experiences and interests, then, these lawyers are fractured by differences in ideology and values.

However much Republican Party loyalists and "mediators" might seek to bind social conservatives, libertarians, and business interests together into a stable and enduring coalition, the alliance is unstable. Differences among lawyers of the conservative coalition present real problems for those who would hope that lawyers might help unite the constituencies. We consider next the conservative movement's institutional response to this challenge—the creation of mediator organizations that focus especially on maintaining a network of influential conservative lawyers.

6

Mediator Organizations: The Heritage Foundation and the Federalist Society

This chapter focuses on mediator organizations and their role in integrating the conservative coalition. It pays special attention to two such institutions—the Heritage Foundation and the Federalist Society—and how they seek to unify and mobilize lawyers for conservative causes. These organizations appear to have succeeded in drawing elite lawyers into the conservative movement, and they have made considerable progress toward fostering cooperation across constituencies.

Mediator organizations attempt to appeal to all strands of the conservative alliance. The American Enterprise Institute, for example, combines research on a range of economic policy and foreign and defense issues with programs on culture, religion, law enforcement, and welfare reform. Its scholars include an eclectic group of prominent figures, such as Irving Kristol, Richard Perle, Michael Greve, Lynne Cheney, Charles Murray, author of *Losing Ground* and *The Bell Curve,* and Michael Novak, who has written dozens of books on religion and public life, including *The Naked Public Square, Catholic Thought and Liberal Institutions,* and, most recently, *Washington's God.* The American Conservative Union, a grassroots lobbying organization, "supports capitalism, traditional moral values, commitment to a strong national defense, and jurisprudence based on the original intent of the framers of the Constitution" (American Conservative Union 2005). The Ethics and Public Policy Center, another mediator organization, seeks to "clarify and reinforce the bond between the Judeo-Christian moral tradition and the public debate over domestic and foreign policy issues." It hosts projects focusing on various religious traditions: "Catholic Studies," "Evangelicals in Civic Life," and

"Jewish Studies." It also houses a separate program on "the relation of modern economic theory to its Judeo-Christian and Greco-Roman origins, its practical application to personal, family, and political economy, and the interaction of economics, philosophical worldviews, and religious faith." The organization's emphasis on limited government appeals to the business constituency, and its attention to moral values attracts social conservatives.

The Committee for Justice applies this integrationist formula to the judicial appointments process. C. Boyden Gray—an establishment icon who served as White House counsel to President George H. W. Bush—formed the organization in 2003 to unite the conservative coalition around the goal of confirming President George W. Bush's judicial nominees. Gray did so at the request of Karl Rove, Bush's top political strategist (Rosenbaum and Clemetson 2005). He enlisted support from business organizations, which had previously resisted engaging in confirmation battles that revolved primarily around social issues rather than the economic matters that concerned their members (Hamburger and Wallsten 2005). He also recruited leading lawyers for social conservatives, including Jay Sekulow, chief counsel of the American Center for Law and Justice. Other prominent lawyers associated with the Committee for Justice during its first few years included Leonard Leo, executive vice president of the Federalist Society, and Edwin A. Meese III of the Heritage Foundation (Edsall and Milbank 2005).[1]

Table 3.4 in chapter 3 presented data suggesting the value and influence of mediator organizations; it showed that conservative foundations have invested heavily in these groups. Recall that in 2003–2005 foundations gave mediator organizations more than twice the amount of money given to any other category. Chapter 3 also showed that these organizations attract the most elite lawyers and that the lawyers who serve these organizations are particularly invested in identifying common ground among the constituencies. Thus, conservative leaders, philanthropists, and prominent lawyers appear to believe that mediator organizations are institutions of real consequence.

Although all of the mediator organizations contribute toward the goal of uniting the conservative constituencies, this chapter highlights two organizations that are distinctive in their emphasis on promoting communication and cooperation among *lawyers*. Like the other mediator groups described in chapter 3, the Heritage Foundation and the Federalist Society define their missions in terms designed to attract all elements of the conservative coalition. Heritage's Web site says that the organization seeks "to formulate and promote conservative public policies based on the principles of free enterprise, limited government, individual freedom, traditional American values, and a strong national defense. . . . " (Heritage Foundation 2006a). The Federalist Society calls for "reordering priorities within the legal system to place a premium on individual liberty, traditional values, and the rule of law" and "restoring the recognition of the importance of these norms among lawyers, judges, and law professors" (Federalist Society 2007c). Like other mediator groups, Heritage and the Federalist Society attempt to promote cooperation and discourage conflict. But these organizations distinguish themselves by focusing on the special role that lawyers might play in binding together the elements of the conservative alliance. They seek to promote communication among lawyers, to mobilize lawyers' participation in conservative and libertarian causes, and to elevate legal over extralegal strategies.

THE HERITAGE FOUNDATION

The Heritage Foundation was established by Paul M. Weyrich in 1973 with money from Joseph Coors and Richard Mellon Scaife. At the time of Heritage's founding, there were only two major conservative think tanks— the Hoover Institution and the American Enterprise Institute (AEI). Its founders designed Heritage to be less cerebral than Hoover or AEI and more focused on giving policy makers timely information in easily comprehensible form. According to one lawyer interviewed for this research, Heritage "came in to fill a void, which was the day-to-day development of policy ideas and the quick turnaround time and dissemination of this information to Congress . . . and then, later, with a conservative president, to the executive branch as well." The organization's primary activities would be producing targeted publications—including books, newsletters, articles, and policy papers—and sponsoring meetings and symposia. Heritage gained significant public recognition in 1980 with its $100,000, 3000-page "Mandate for Leadership," containing several thousand specific policy proposals pitched to the incoming Reagan Administration. Edwin Feulner, Heritage Foundation president since 1977, described the "mandate" as a "blueprint for the construction of a conservative government" (Omang 1980). Heritage continues to produce a steady stream of publications.

Although initially associated primarily with libertarian and neoconservative policies, Heritage later embraced cultural conservatism. It did so at the urging of founder Paul Weyrich, who runs his own family values think tank, the Free Congress Foundation, and Richard Larry (Archibald 1991), who served as the Sarah M. Scaife Foundation's president through 2001 (Lewin 2001). That move culminated in 1991 in the hiring of William Bennett, secretary of education in the Reagan Administration and drug czar in the Bush I Administration, to lead a new project on the study of cultural policy (Stefancic and Delgado 1996, 55). Heritage now sponsors projects on crime, family, marriage, and religion, as well as dozens of projects on economic and regulatory issues. Its DeVos Center on Religion and Civil Society, created in 2004 with a $1.8 million gift from Richard and Helen DeVos, seeks to "focus scholarly attention on the interplay between religion and public policy in America" (Heritage Foundation 2007).

In addition to serving up digestible analyses for policy makers, Heritage plays an important role in promoting cooperation and suppressing conflict within the conservative movement, primarily by convening meetings and fora of diverse activists. George Nash, a historian of the conservative movement, has called the Heritage Foundation "an ecumenical presence"—"the institutional equivalent of Ronald Reagan" (Nash 1996, 335). A lawyer interviewed for this research said that "[o]ne of Heritage's purposes when it was founded . . . was to be kind of a clearinghouse for what we might call, for want of a better name, 'conservative' organizations." Its annual Resource Bank meeting attracts more than five hundred "think tank leaders, academics, legal experts, and activists" from around the world (Heritage Foundation 2006d, 22). The "main function" of these meetings, according to Heritage's Web site, is "building the conservative movement" (Heritage Foundation 2006b).

Heritage regularly convenes meetings of lawyers associated with various causes of the conservative coalition. It conducts semiannual "Legal Strategy Fora" with lawyers from about thirty organizations around the country. It also holds a monthly meeting of legal organizations in the D.C. area to "keep[] them informed about each others' activities," to educate them about "what's going on on the Hill," and to promote cooperation on amicus briefs and seminars. These meetings could conceivably exacerbate rather than reduce conflict. Harold Lasswell observed that discussing contentious issues is as likely to sharpen disagreement as to resolve differences (Lasswell 1960, 196–97), and participants in Heritage meetings report that the gatherings sometimes do generate testy exchanges. Participants also assert, however, that these sessions tend to promote order within conservative ranks. One lawyer reported, "Back in the seventies, conservatives were at war with each other. The Heritage Foundation came along, and their goal was peace, and they accomplished it. . . . [A]t one time your greatest enemies were within your philosophical spectrum, not without, and that's no longer the case. . . . Ed Feulner put pressure on groups, using the resources available to him: people, powerful people, board members, what have you. Just said, 'This is going to stop.'" Another lawyer said that the purpose of Heritage meetings was to "talk about cooperation among the groups" and "how litigation and legal-oriented groups can work with policy groups." He explained that participants often disagree about policy, but they "develop those areas of agreement that we can work together on without being in controversy. . . . In areas where there isn't that agreement, then . . . [Heritage] encourage[s] the groups to go separately and work on those issues more or less by themselves or with groups with which they agree. So I think that has helped to defuse a lot of what might otherwise be controversy within the [movement]."

The key figure in Heritage's attempt to coordinate the work of lawyers of the conservative coalition is Edwin Meese III, who joined Heritage in 1988, at the end of his tenure as U.S. attorney general in the Reagan Administration. He now serves as the Ronald Reagan Distinguished Fellow in Public Policy and Chairman of the Center for Legal and Judicial Studies. With the center's director, Todd Gaziano, Meese oversees meetings of lawyers of the various constituencies and is widely credited with encouraging bonds among lawyers with divergent political commitments. A social conservative said that these meetings facilitate "philosophical interfacing," allowing him to test his arguments with other smart lawyers "who are not necessarily in our circle." A lawyer who worked for another mediator organization said that Heritage meetings serve "an exceedingly valuable function" in coordinating the conservative movement and enabling diverse constituencies to operate as "a loose community." Yet another lawyer credited Meese with transforming Heritage's function from merely averting war among conservatives to facilitating cooperation. He explained that Meese's "legal background and stature" allowed him to "[take] it to the next step, which is once you had peace that maybe you could do something with your mutual groups."

Heritage's goal of mediating among competing constituencies is facilitated by Meese's reputation as an affable and disinterested broker. His background gives him credibility with each of the constituencies he seeks to engage. As an active Lutheran (Barone 1984), who has delivered speeches about the importance of "people who believe in God" (Melton 1987) and who appointed a Commission on Pornography when he served as President Reagan's attorney general, he is able to connect with the religious right (Meese 1992, 312–13). His law enforcement background appeals to law-and-order conservatives, and his endorsement of school vouchers and his opposition to affirmative action have earned him favor with libertarians. His elite credentials (a B.A. from Yale and J.D. from the University of California, Berkeley), connections forged during his years as counselor to the president and U.S. attorney general, and business experience (as vice president for administration of Rohr Industries) give him credibility with business advocates.

In addition to convening meetings of conservative activists, Heritage also supplies selective benefits to cooperating organizations. The Heritage Foundation's Job Bank seeks to place conservatives and libertarians in academic posts, civil service positions, congressional offices, faith-based organizations, lobbying groups, media organizations, think tanks, political groups, and trade associations. Heritage issues a weekly Supreme Court alert—a prompt summary of decisions delivered by e-mail to organizations around the country, and it sponsors moot court sessions judged by "the best appellate lawyers from the law firms downtown and from some of the public interest groups" to prepare conservative lawyers of all stripes for arguments before the Supreme Court. In 2005, Heritage helped ten advocates prepare for U.S. Supreme Court appearances (Heritage Foundation 2005, 9).

One lawyer recalled how the idea for the moot court program hatched during a Heritage meeting and drew upon Meese's connections with accomplished appellate litigators. Until recently, this lawyer explained, "there was no support system. . . . If cert got granted in a case, basically everybody was left to fend for themselves. There was no structural way where we came around and embraced this conservative brother or sister who had gotten cert granted in a case. And people just sort of did it on their own. . . . " During one Heritage meeting, according to this lawyer, Meese noted that an important property rights case would soon be argued before the Supreme Court. Participants in the meeting observed that the lawyer who would argue the case had no prior Supreme Court experience, and one of them suggested that Heritage convene a moot court to prepare this green lawyer. Meese agreed. "[He] just gets on the phone and calls up these guys that had been his lieutenants at the attorney general's office in the Justice Department and says, you know, you clerked for Scalia, you've argued ten cases in the Supreme Court, or whatever. I want you to come and help this guy." The decision to sponsor these practice arguments, the lawyer said, reflected the view that "the good of the movement is helped by [the success of] this one guy."

In his position at Heritage, Meese also has continued a campaign against "judicial activism" that he began in 1985, soon after he was confirmed as attorney general. His Center warns against the "dangerous erosion of the proper role of the courts" (Heritage Foundation 2006c) and seeks to "educat[e] policymakers and the public about the proper role of judges and the true meaning of the constitution" (Heritage Foundation 2006c). In 2005, under Meese's leadership, Heritage published *The Heritage Guide to the Constitution,* "stressing the original intent of the Framers as the authoritative standard of constitutional interpretation" (Meese 2005b). This collection includes essays by 108 practicing lawyers, scholars, and judges. Like the meetings that Meese convenes, this volume draws participation from a variety of libertarians and traditionalists. Some of them are prominent public figures, such as Richard Epstein, Charles Cooper, Charles Fried, Douglas Ginsburg, Douglas Kmiec, John Yoo, and Roger Clegg. Less well-known but equally important in terms of building ties across constituencies, the book's contributors also include Thomas Berg, law professor at St. Thomas School of Law and codirector of the school's Institute on Catholic Thought, Law and Policy; Stephen Safranek of Ave Maria School of Law; and David Wagner of Regent University School of Law.

The Heritage Foundation's revenues in 2006 were $53,821,085—more than those of any other conservative think tank. (The American Enterprise Institute reported $27,796,809 in revenue in 2006, and the Hoover Institution reported a base budget of $36.7 million for 2006–2007.) Heritage's largest foundation supporters in 2003–2005 were the Samuel Roberts Noble Foundation ($5,000,000); Sarah Scaife Foundation ($2,400,000); Jay and Betty Van Andel Foundation ($1,800,000);[2] Lynde and Harry Bradley Foundation ($1,132,500); John Templeton Foundation ($843,000); Herrick Foundation ($750,000); and M. J. Murdock Charitable Trust ($600,000). Current board members include Richard Mellon Scaife, Steve Forbes, Edwin Feulner, Holland Coors, and Midge Decter.

THE FEDERALIST SOCIETY

The Federalist Society, like Heritage, attempts to draw together the constituencies of the conservative coalition by appealing to all. The founding documents for the Yale Federalist Society claimed that the organization would "provide[] a sense of community for its members who span a wide ideological spectrum which includes traditionalists, fusionist conservatives, libertarians, objectivists, classical liberals and Straussians" (Teles

2008, 142–43). The national organization continues to pitch itself broadly as "a group of conservatives and libertarians interested in the current state of the legal order . . . founded on the principles that the state exists to preserve freedom, that the separation of governmental powers is central to our Constitution, and that it is emphatically the province and duty of the judiciary to say what the law is, not what it should be" (Federalist Society 2007c).

Through the Federalist Society speakers' series, launched in 1983, thousands of law students and lawyers have been exposed to the views of a variety of prominent conservatives and libertarians, including Antonin Scalia, Edwin Meese, John Ashcroft, Kenneth Starr, Russell Kirk, Walter Williams, C. Boyden Gray, Jack Kemp, Jean Kirkpatrick, Orrin Hatch, Robert Bork, Alex Kozinski, Richard Epstein, Michael McConnell, George Priest, Roger Pilon, Linda Chavez, Michael Horowitz, Clint Bolick, William Kristol, and George Will (Federalist Society 2006c). From the start, the Federalist Society committed itself to sponsoring debates as well as lectures. The students who launched the Federalist Society drew inspiration from their experiences in Yale's Political Union, where the Party of the Right produced feisty exchanges among public intellectuals such as William F. Buckley, founder of the National Review, Richard Brookhiser, Senior Editor of the National Review, and Walter Olson, a journalist active on tort reform issues as a fellow at the Manhattan Institute. Just as Buckley hoped to shape public opinion from the top down by appealing to educated readers at the *National Review,* the founders of the Federalist Society hoped to alter the attitudes and commitments of elites in the legal profession and especially in law schools. And just as Buckley's *National Review* sought to achieve intellectual respectability for conservative ideas (Hart 2005), so did the Federalist Society seek to reach its objectives by prevailing in debates.

Soon after its founding, the Federalist Society hired Eugene Meyer as its executive director, and Meyer continues to serve as the organization's president. Meyer is not a lawyer, but he attended Yale as an undergraduate several classes ahead of the Society's founders: Steven Calabresi, Lee Liberman (now Lee Liberman Otis), and David McIntosh. Like the founders, Meyer participated in the Yale Political Union and the Party of the Right.

Eugene Meyer's father was Frank Meyer, who tried to forge common ground between libertarians and traditionalists in the early 1960s (Nash 1996, 321–22). A former Communist turned libertarian, Frank Meyer edited the Books, Arts and Manners section of the *National Review* from

1957 until his death in 1972 (Hart 2005, 225). In that role, Meyer recruited contributors to review the work of major intellectuals of diverse conservative perspectives. Frank Meyer also edited a volume of essays on American conservatism, *What Is Conservatism?*, which included contributions by Russell Kirk, Willmoore Kendall, F. A. Hayek, M. Stanton Evans, Garry Wills, and William Buckley (1964). In the first chapter, "Freedom, Tradition, Conservatism," Meyer attempted to articulate "the Common Cause" between two divided streams of conservative thought: "those who abstract from the corpus of Western belief its stress upon freedom and upon the innate importance of the individual person (what we may call the 'libertarian' position) and those who, drawing upon the same source, stress value and virtue and order (what we may call the 'traditionalist' position)" (Meyer 1964, 8). He asserted that individual freedom was "the central and primary end of political society" and that the State must be sharply limited. Traditionalists were rightly concerned with virtue but were wrong to endorse using state power to enforce virtuous behavior. Meyer criticized classical liberals for underestimating the importance of the "organic moral order" and for failing to "distinguish between the *authoritarianism,* with which men and institutions suppress the freedom of men, and the *authority* of God and truth" (Meyer 1964, 15–16). Meyer asserted that both branches of the divided conservative movement actually agreed fundamentally about the existence of "an objective moral order" by which "human conduct should be judged" and about the importance of limiting the power of the State. He also claimed that they shared an interest in promoting an understanding of the Constitution as originally conceived by the founders—as embodying conflicting claims about the relationship between virtue and freedom but with "an awareness of their joint heritage" (Meyer 1964, 19). Meyer argued that the libertarian and traditionalist strands "are arrayed against a common enemy" (Meyer 1964, 19)—"the Liberal collectivist body of dogma that has pervaded the consciousness and shaped the actions of the decisive and articulate sections of society over the past century or more" (Meyer 1964, 19).

Under Eugene Meyer's stewardship, the Federalist Society has pursued a consensus among conservative lawyers much like the "fusionism" that Meyer's father sought among conservative intellectuals decades earlier. The Society's focus on "individual liberty, traditional values, limited government, and the rule of law" mirrors Frank Meyer's claims about a basis for harmony among different strands of conservatism. Its call for the judiciary to "say what the law is, not what it should be" (Federalist Society 2007c) echoes Frank Meyer's claims about the unifying power of originalism. Just as Frank Meyer sought to build understanding by encouraging writers of diverse perspectives to write for the *National Review,* so does the Federalist Society under Eugene Meyer's leadership attempt to engage conservatives of diverse perspectives in conversation and debate. And just as Frank Meyer and the *National Review* sacrificed philosophical coherence to achieve political objectives, so does the Federalist Society.

The organization's executive vice president, Leonard Leo, is a bridge builder. Although younger and less well-known than Ed Meese, Leo too has multifaceted credentials and experience that may enhance his ability to work with lawyers from all constituencies of the conservative alliance. As a strong Catholic who served as the Republican Party's chairman for Catholic outreach in 2005 (DeParle 2005), he has credibility with religious conservatives. His past work on property rights and regulatory reform fosters ties with libertarians. And his establishment credentials, including undergraduate and law degrees from Cornell, two federal judicial clerkships, and large firm practice experience, encourage business elites to view him as one of their own. One libertarian interviewed for this research called Leo one of the "great figures in the movement—a great organizer."

How does the Federalist Society promote cooperation and a sense of shared identity among lawyers for these diverse constituencies? Although it does not attempt to forge policy compromises or to articulate specific positions on behalf of the organization, it nevertheless stresses common ground. It promotes conversation around several core principles. One person who was active in the Federalist Society asserted that there are "two different types of organizations":

> One I would affectionately call "bomb throwing" . . . an organization that is trying in a vigorous way to get its views on current issues heard and is aggressive about it and takes positions, and sometimes flamboyant positions, and I think this could play a very important role in political debate. The second type of organization is an organization that pushes the core ideas. The bomb throwing could come off of the core ideas, but that's not what the bomb throwing organizations do. I see [the Federalist Society] as an organization that discusses the core ideas. . . .

Another lawyer involved in the Federalist Society said,

> We do, I think, an effective job of bringing those various groups together, and having them better appreciate their shared commitment to a very fundamental set of principles that we think are the bedrock of our legal system.

So when you start digging under the surface and asking questions about specific policy questions, at some general level, if you ask these folks, what ought to drive the American legal system, I think all of these different constituencies, if you will, would say, "Well, we have a commitment to limited constitutional government. We believe in separation of powers. We believe in federalism at some level, although that may differ definitionally from person to person. We do believe courts have a limited role in our constitutional democracy. They're not supposed to make law, they're only supposed to interpret it. . . . The idea that economic and personal freedoms are both important to human dignity." You get agreement on those very general principles, and that is, I think, . . . what the Federalist Society is founded on.

The Federalist Society pursues its integrating mission indirectly, by sponsoring conferences, generating publications, convening practice groups, promoting lawyers' involvement in public affairs, and facilitating appointments of judges and government officials. Although the Federalist Society does not take positions on matters of public policy, it encourages its members to do so. One lawyer active in the Federalist Society said that the organization seeks to "inspire and motivate [its members] to become what we call citizen lawyers—to be active participants in the public policy process." He explained, "We believe that our members can decide for themselves where they stand on various issues, but we want to provide an infrastructure for them to learn so they will become motivated to do more as lawyers in our communities." The organization's *Journalist's Guide to Legal Experts* supplies the media with contact information and biographies for almost two hundred lawyers who are prepared to offer conservative and libertarian perspectives on 148 issues.

Although Federalist Society programs may tilt toward libertarians, the organization actively seeks to involve traditionalists as well. Its practice groups, for example, include a section on religious liberties, and its meetings cover topics of interest to religious conservatives—for example, school choice, "charitable choice" (government programs allowing religious organizations to receive federal funds to supply social services), the use of religious materials in public schools, and creationism. Recent speakers at Federalist Society events have included William Bennett, Alan Keyes, John Ashcroft, Phyllis Schlafly, and Justice Clarence Thomas. The 2006 annual Barbara K. Olson Memorial Lecture was delivered by Judge A. Raymond Randolph, United States Court of Appeals for the D.C. Circuit, on the folly of *Roe v. Wade* and *Lawrence v. Texas* (Randolph 2006). The theme of the 2007 National Student Symposium was "Law and Morality."

The Federalist Society claims to have succeeded in establishing "a conservative and libertarian intellectual network that extends to all levels of the legal community" (Federalist Society 2005). That assertion is consistent with what some lawyers told me in interviews. One social conservative who was active in the Federalist Society said that the group seems "to embrace both sides—traditional conservatives and the libertarians" and that "at least within the legal realm, that seems to be the vast connector. I think they have been very successful in what they have set out to do." Another lawyer said, "Of course there has always been a division in the Federalist Society between more traditional conservatives and libertarians," but "there always has been an uneasy peace in the interest of having a common group in order to find common purpose. . . . " Another noted that "traditionalists and libertarians could well disagree in certain areas" and that "business conservatives and religious conservatives . . . don't always see eye to eye." But he asserted that "the Federalist Society, at least for the legal movement, is a mediating institution for the center right." A senior lawyer stated that "the Federalist Society has made a major, major contribution to . . . communication" within the coalition, and another said, "The Federalist Society, in my view, is the key legal organization."

The Federalist Society now has 40,000 members, including lawyers, students, and professors. It has student chapters at more than two hundred law schools, lawyers' chapters in sixty cities, fifteen nationwide practice groups, and a law faculty division, whose director is Lee Liberman Otis, one of the Society's founders. The Society produces twenty-two publications. Its online Pro Bono Center matches lawyers to pro bono service opportunities consistent with the organization's broad mission. The Federalist Society also administers the Olin/Searle/Smith Fellows in Law program, which gives young conservative scholars funding for one year to write books and articles and thereby prepare to secure tenure-track faculty positions.

The Society's annual conventions in Washington, D.C., attract thousands of lawyers, law students, and scholars from all constituencies of the conservative alliance. Speakers at the 2005 convention included Karl Rove, the president's chief political strategist; Paul Clement, U.S. solicitor general; Theodore Olson, the former U.S. solicitor general who successfully argued *Bush v. Gore;* former Massachusetts governor Mitt Romney; Kenneth W. Starr, former U.S. solicitor general, independent prosecutor in the Whitewater investigation, and now Pepperdine Law School Dean; Edwin Meese III; Robert Bork, former Yale Law School professor, federal appellate judge, and failed U.S. Supreme Court nominee; C. Boyden Gray, White House counsel to the first President Bush; John Engler, president of the National Association of Manufacturers; and more than a dozen federal appellate judges. On the opening morning of the convention, President Bush met with the organization's leaders at the White House (Kirkpatrick 2005a). The 2006 annual meeting, organized around the theme of "limited government" and held one week after the midterm election, was less cheerful (Lewis 2006), but the roster of speakers was no less prominent. It included Vice President Cheney, Supreme Court justice Alito, U.S. senator and Republican presidential candidate John McCain; senator Arlen Specter; William Kristol; Solicitor General Paul Clement; Michael Chertoff, Secretary of Homeland Security; Charles Murray; Phyllis Schlafly; Ed Meese; and seventeen federal court of appeals judges. Speakers for the Federalist Society's 2007 annual meeting, marking the organization's twenty-fifth anniversary, included President George W. Bush; Supreme Court justices Thomas, Roberts, Alito, and Scalia; former New York City mayor Rudy Giuliani; Robert Bork; Edwin Meese; C. Boyden Gray; and Theodore Olson.

The organization's policy against taking positions may help explain its success in creating ties among the constituencies. By eschewing any effort to forge consensus beyond the very broad principles in its mission statement, it nevertheless promotes cooperation by keeping conservatives and libertarians engaged in conversation with one another. Interaction among different types of conservative lawyers through Federalist Society activities may promote understanding among lawyers with fundamentally different worldviews. One religious conservative said of Federalist Society meetings, "I like to go just to see what the other guys are talking about." He speculated that it "also broadens their horizons to have me around." These exchanges sometimes may cause lawyers to reformulate their positions in ways that make them more acceptable to their coalition partners. One lawyer claimed that the Federalist Society's indirect approach actually does facilitate cooperation: "Our commitment to . . . general principles, and our commitment to debate, freedom of thought, and not alienating . . . members by taking positions, has kept those groups together and has caused them probably to work more closely than they otherwise would."

Nevertheless, tensions among constituencies within the Federalist Society are evident in occasional hot debates at the organization's meetings and in published exchanges among members. The split between social conservatives and libertarians over gay rights is one area of disagreement. A Christian conservative said that his libertarian colleagues effectively told conservatives to "lighten up" about this issue, while Christian conservatives insisted that gay rights pose a "great threat." Policy disagreements among libertarians, law-and-order advocates, and neoconservatives have sustained a steady debate over the Patriot Act and the Bush Administration's domestic surveillance program (McGough 2003). The organization's Web site features "online debates" among members—for example, regarding the power of the executive branch to detain and try enemy combatants and whether terminally ill patients hold a fundamental constitutional right to access to experimental drugs (Federalist Society 2007a).[3] During a symposium panel entitled "Tort Law in the Federal System," a member noted a "conflict at the heart of the Federalist Society . . . between a belief in federalism as a method for governing ourselves, and the conservative or 'corporatist' goals that are advocated, for political reasons, by many members of the Federalist Society" (Bryant 2001).[4] He singled out for criticism the effort by business advocates to federalize tort law: "there is a fundamental conflict . . . between the interests of multi-national or national corporations and the basic principles of federalism. . . . Corporations want one set of laws because they provide uniformity, predictability, and reliability." (Bryant 2001, 734).[5] Other sharp conflicts among Federalist Society members have arisen over immigration reform, the scope of executive privilege, and the extent to which judges should disregard established precedents in order to fulfill originalist understandings of the Constitution.

Some of these strong disagreements have involved the Federalist Society's most prominent members. For example, Starr and Bork have sparred over whether wineries and distillers should be able to sell their products online, with Starr taking the free-trade position on behalf of wineries and Bork speaking for states-rights conservatives in favor of the bans (Kerwin 2003). Richard Epstein and Bork have engaged in public disputes about whether and when the Constitution allows individual liberties to be sacrificed to maintain public order (Howd 1999). C. Boyden Gray advocated Microsoft's position in antitrust litigation (Labaton 2001), while Bork was the most vocal of its adversaries in the lawsuit (Bork 2000). Leonard Leo served as the Bush Administration's point person for the Harriet Miers nomination, while Bork called her nomination a "disaster" (Savage 2005). At the 2006 annual meeting, Professor Richard Epstein debated with Berkeley law professor and former Justice Department official John Yoo and others over the scope of the president's power to conduct the War on Terror. Acknowledging that the issue was one that generates "deep division even within the ranks of the Federalist Society," Epstein said that the positions advanced by Yoo and other administration officials were "very dangerous" (Federalist Society 2007d).

The prospect of frequent sharp disagreements among lawyers within the conservative fold, and between lawyers of the Left and Right, clearly accounts for some of the Federalist Society's allure. One lawyer said, "I know that if I go to a Federalist Society conference, it's going to be a really interesting engaged debate." A business lawyer reported that he first became involved in the Federalist Society when he discovered that "the panels . . . had very interesting speakers on both sides of the issue—that whenever they had a panel with Ted Olson they'd have somebody who would be his intellectual counterpart on the opposite side on the same panel. And it was just neat to go see people who were icons or heroes on both liberal and conservative [sides], both on the same panel, and to see real pros at work arguing." A lawyer who eventually became active recalled his introduction to the Society; as an undergraduate he had attended a meeting at which Ed Meese offered his rejoinder to William Brennan's speech on originalism; "The meeting was a barn burner. I vividly remember [it]. . . . I loved it." Another lawyer who helped to organize Federalist Society debates in law school said, "I liked . . . the clash of ideas. That I found very, very pleasing." A conservative who decried the paucity of intellectual exchange between lawyers of the political left and right claimed that "Federalist Society icons are the ones who [are] debating *each other*. . . . That's where the serious juice is."

Admirers and critics alike assert that the Federalist Society's informal network has played an important role in vetting federal judicial nominees, staffing conservative public interest law groups and Republican administrations, and matching conservative students with prominent conservative judges (Broder 2005; DeParle 2005; Fletcher 2005). Executive Director Eugene Meyer observes that Federalist Society members frequently forge connections that lead to new job prospects and joint projects: "I think people by and large join the Federalist Society because they're interested in the ideas we're talking about. In the course of doing that, they also—as with any organization—meet people with whom they share ideas and they're going to end up working together not only in the Federalist Society but in projects in other areas of life" (McGough 2005).

Meyer reports that most lawyers hired by conservative public interest law groups have been involved in Federalist Society activities and that the Society "has encouraged many of its members to consider various forms of public service. . . . " (Meyer 2004, 198, 200). The Federalist Society gives conservative law students and newly minted lawyers opportunities to meet conservative luminaries (Bach 2001), and it provides a credential that some judges and other employers use as evidence of applicants' political leanings. Judge Alex Kozinski of the U.S. Court of Appeals for the Ninth Circuit has said that seeing the Federalist Society on a resume "tells me you're of a particular philosophy, and I tend to give an edge to people I agree with philosophically" (Bach 2001). Michael Luttig, until recently a judge on the Court of Appeals for the Fourth Circuit, was said to hire only Federalist Society members or students with comparable conservative credentials (Bach 2001). Several lawyers interviewed for this research reported that they had landed clerkships and other jobs through their Federalist Society connections. In the controversy surrounding the dismissal of United States attorneys in 2007, Bradley Schlozman, a senior Justice Department official, testified that he had recruited job applicants from the Heritage Foundation and the Federalist Society for career positions (Johnston and Lipton 2007). An e-mail message authored by D. Kyle Sampson, former chief of staff to Attorney General Alberto Gonzales, indicated that membership in the Federalist Society was a factor in the selection of candidates to replace the dismissed federal prosecutors (Johnston and Lipton 2007). The Federalist Society's membership solicitation cites the opportunity to "interact[] with prominent public officials, judges and scholars" as the first of eight reasons to join the organization (Federalist Society 2007b).

Although the Federalist Society disclaims any interest in replacing the ABA as the legal profession's primary bar association, it has long had an antagonistic and competitive relationship with the ABA. At the time of the Federalist Society's founding, the ABA had a reputation as a politically neutral or perhaps even an essentially conservative professional association (Abel 1989, 208; Rhode 1981). From the start, however, the Federalist Society sought to challenge that reputation and expose the ABA as an instrument of the liberal establishment. The founders' 1982 proposal for expanding the Federalist Society laid plans for organizing lawyers into chapters in dozens of cities where they would begin to shape the ABA's activities and push the ABA rightward (Miller 2006, 92). After Robert Bork's failed Supreme Court nomination in 1987, conservatives concluded that the ABA's divided rating had contributed to his defeat, and the Federalist Society launched an effort to end the ABA's semiofficial role in the judicial nominations process. In 1992, the Society began an investigation of the ABA, and in 1994 it published a critical book titled *The ABA in Law and Social Policy: What Role?*, which stated that "The role that the Association chooses to play in the coming years could have a profound impact on the public's perceptions of the legal profession, and, perhaps, on the growing tendency to treat law and legal process as politics by other means" (Federalist Society 1994). In the same year, the Federalist Society launched *ABA*

Watch, a semiannual newsletter dedicated to monitoring the ABA's activities. The inaugural issue questioned whether "the ABA presently cheapens the rule of law by improperly using its resources, respectability, and influence as a means to advance particular political goals" (Federalist Society 1996). In 1997, Senate Judiciary Committee chair Orrin Hatch (who serves as cochairman of the Federalist Society's Board of Visitors) ended the ABA's role in rating judicial nominees, and in 2001, White House counsel Alberto Gonzales announced that the Bush Administration would no longer consult with the ABA about judicial candidates. Although the Federalist Society does not play any formal role in the judicial selection process, its members participate informally and are widely believed to be influential (Lewis 2006).

The Society essentially serves as an alternative bar association for many conservative lawyers. Thirty-nine of the interviewed lawyers said that they were active in the Federalist Society. Like the ABA, the Federalist Society is organized into practice groups, which sponsor debates and conferences, disseminate information about legal developments in specialized practice fields, distribute articles written by Federalist Society members, and offer Continuing Legal Education credit to lawyers who attend their events (Federalist Society 2007b). Prominent lawyers, law professors, and leaders of conservative advocacy organizations chair the practice groups,[6] and each practice group, in turn, serves as an umbrella for numerous subcommittees chaired primarily by prominent conservative and libertarian lawyers and law professors. The organization sponsors special "projects" on judicial nominations, corporate responsibility, election law, international law, judicial nominations, state courts, and the war on terror. Its Web page includes dozens of audio broadcasts of commentary on Supreme Court cases.

The Olin Foundation was the most important sponsor of the Federalist Society during its first two decades; it contributed over $5.5 million to the organization during that period (Miller 2006, 94).[7] The Federalist Society's largest public foundation supporters in 2003–5 were the Sarah Scaife Foundation ($800,000), Lynde and Harry Bradley Foundation ($615,000), Lilly Endowment ($450,000), Brady Education Foundation ($300,000), Harry and Jeanette Weinberg Foundation ($200,000), Earhart Foundation ($170,000), F. M. Kirby Foundation ($130,000), and Marcus Foundation ($125,000). Its board of directors in 2008 includes Steven Calabresi, David McIntosh, Eugene Meyer, Gary Lawson, Brent Hatch, and T. Kenneth Cribb.[8] Its Board of Visitors includes Robert Bork, Orrin Hatch, Edwin Meese, William Bradford Reynolds, Theodore Olson, Donald Paul

Hodel, and Gale Norton (Federalist Society 2007c). The Federalist Society's annual revenue was $8,794,888 in the year ending 2006.

COMMON PREMISES AND ATTRIBUTES

The Heritage Foundation and the Federalist Society are similar in important respects. Both were founded during the lead-up to and early years of the Reagan era. The Federalist Society's founders—Calabresi, McIntosh, and Liberman—worked for Meese when he was attorney general in the Reagan Administration. Meese continues to serve on the Society's board of directors, and Gary Lawson of the Federalist Society's board served on the editorial advisory board for *The Heritage Guide to the Constitution*. The theme of the Federalist Society's 2005 annual meeting was "originalism"— one of Meese's pet projects. Several of their large foundation supporters are the same—the Lynde and Harry Bradley Foundation and the Sarah Scaife Foundation.

These organizations share the premise that, if one connects conservatives of different stripes who agree on core principles and share an interest in maintaining the coalition, they will find ways to cooperate. The two organizations focus primarily on highlighting areas of agreement, reinforcing common commitments, and identifying opportunities to work together. Their mission statements include language about individual freedom and traditional values, but neither organization seeks to resolve the tension between these goals. Both groups invest in creating and maintaining channels of communication through which individuals and organizations can exercise political influence.

Grover Norquist, president of Americans for Tax Reform, holds his own weekly meetings of conservative activists and is widely thought to play an important role in maintaining the conservative coalition. He extols the benefits of tabling differences and focusing on areas of agreement: "If you want the votes of people who are good on guns, good on taxes, and good on faith issues, that is a very small intersection of voters. But if you say, Give me the votes of anybody who agrees with you on any of these issues, that's a much bigger section of the population" (Cassidy 2005). A libertarian interviewed for this project offered a similar view about how to maintain the conservative coalition:

> I generally think that the alleged split between libertarians and conservatives is overblown. . . . I think there is much, much more common ground between libertarians and social conservatives than is commonly believed

because I don't believe that social conservatives on the whole have any stake at all in larger government. . . . And if you can manage to agree on 85 percent of the issues that are out there, that ought to be good enough and to sort of bracket the rest of it.

The Heritage Foundation and the Federalist Society apply this wisdom to organizing for conservative causes. They do not even attempt to articulate a consistent philosophy beyond the general points outlined in their mission statements. Instead, they bet on the cumulative power of the commitments on which they agree—even when alliances are temporary and deep disagreement lurks below—and on networks as vehicles for influencing public policy. One lawyer interviewed for this research ventured that the modus operandi of the conservative law movement was not to "bash heads" when advocates disagreed with their coalition partners but instead to urge dissenters to drop out of the debate and effectively say to the others, "You go fight for it."

Previous research on the communication network among a subset of

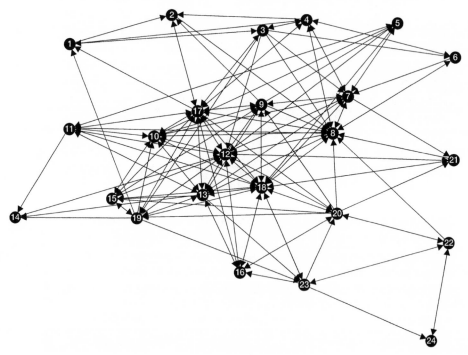

6.1: Contact links among notable conservative lawyers

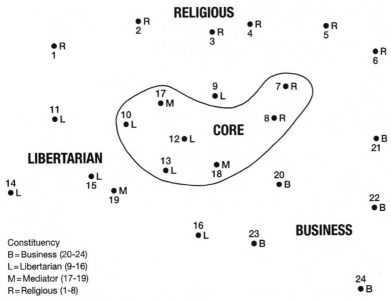

6.2: Constituencies of the twenty-four notables

the interviewed lawyers (Paik, Southworth, and Heinz 2007) lends support to the claim that the Federalist Society and Heritage Foundation play important roles in uniting lawyers for the different constituencies. In the interviews, I asked lawyers whether and how often they contacted each of fifty prominent conservative lawyers.[9] Twenty-six lawyers were both interviewed and included on the list of notables, and twenty-four of the twenty-six were in contact with at least one of the others during the twelve months prior to the interviews.

Figure 6.1 shows the connections among these lawyers (represented by circles) who were both interviewed and on the list of notables.[10] The overall pattern of the network shows a central core surrounded by a rim of less connected lawyers.

Figure 6.2 shows the constituencies served by the lawyers in figure 6.1, with the labels on each point reflecting the primary organizational categories served by each lawyer. The space is divided into regions defined by the constituencies represented. Lawyers in these distinct parts of the network communicated very little with one another. Ties between the religious and libertarian lawyers were especially sparse, as were ties between religious lawyers and business advocates. The "core" of the figure consists of seven lawyers who received ten or more contacts each. They include two lawyers for religious conservative groups, three for libertarian organizations, and two for mediator organizations. The religious lawyers were connected to the rest of the network primarily through the center.

We used three "positional" measures to assess the extent to which particular lawyers enjoyed power related to their network position: "in-degree centrality" (the number of contacts received as a proportion of all contacts that could be received within the bounds of the network), "out-degree centrality" (the number of contacts with others as a proportion of all possible contacts the actor could make within the network), and "number of brokered pairs" (which counts the number of cases in which an actor links actors who are not in contact with each other). On all these measures, the lawyers in the core had extremely high scores as compared with the others. These lawyers occupy a "structural hole" (Burt 1992; Padgett and Ansell 1993) that separates the business constituency from the religious conservatives, and they are well positioned to facilitate communication and cooperation within the coalition.

Figure 6.3 shows which of these lawyers actively participated in the Federalist Society. All members of the core were active Federalist Society members, while the eight lawyers who did not participate, all of whom were in the religious conservative and business constituencies, occupied less central positions in the network. Although I do not have complete

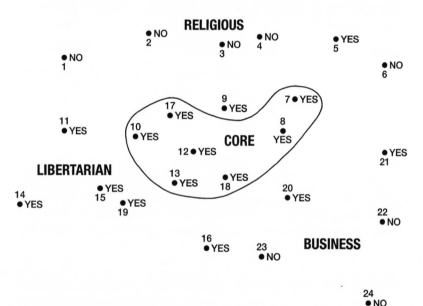

6.3 : Federalist Society participation of the twenty-four notables

data about participation in meetings convened by the Heritage Foundation, four lawyers in the core indicated that they regularly participated in those meetings. These data suggest that participation in Federalist Society and Heritage events may be associated with centrality in conservative lawyers' communication networks.

In interviews, some lawyers asserted that the effort by mediator organizations to knit social conservatives together with libertarians and business advocates into a cohesive network has not been entirely successful. Religious conservatives expressed reservations about forging connections to libertarians and business advocates. One said,

> Some of these religious organizations are a little more insular, a little less inclusive.... Places like the Rutherford Institute and Alliance Defense Fund would not seek to be inclusive necessarily. There is no room for a probusiness libertarian, pro-choice moderate conservative within an organization like the Rutherford Institute, and sometimes the religious conservatives tend to be distrustful of the country club conservatives.

A religious lawyer who regularly participates in Heritage meetings said that Heritage tends to draw fewer social conservatives than libertarians: "There are some like-minded people like me, but there's a lot more . . . kind of the libertarian lawyers . . . obviously people that really aren't totally on my same frequency ideologically." The lawyer networks in which social conservatives participated were relatively narrow. One observed that "there's a network of religious people and lawyers who work for them." A pro-life activist spoke of cooperation among major religious groups born "out of a common sense of what the Gospel demands of us." Several of the interviewed religious conservatives indicated that they relied heavily on such networks.

As noted above, more than half of the interviewed lawyers said that they were active in the Federalist Society, but lawyers associated with libertarian and mediator organizations were much more likely than social conservatives or business advocates to participate in Federalist Society events. Nineteen of the twenty-three libertarians and affirmative action opponents and all of the lawyers for mediator groups said that they participated, while only eight of the twenty-nine lawyers for religious, pro-life, and order-maintenance groups, and three of the eleven advocates for business organizations did so.[11]

Several lawyers suggested that the Federalist Society had not fully succeeded in integrating religious conservatives. One prominent religious conservative said,

The Federalist Society had a workshop about faith-based initiatives at their last big event in Washington. . . . They do have a religious liberty section . . . But my impression is that it's not the first thing that I think of where Christian religious liberty advocates or Christian lawyers, . . . cultural conservatives, . . . get together. It's gonna be something else, it's gonna be Alliance Defense Fund probably or informally.

A lawyer active in the Federalist Society observed that, although "all of the prominent evangelical lawyers are somehow involved with us, or we communicate with them, at least on a periodic basis," the organization had not yet reached as many evangelicals as it would like. He explained,

I think there are demographic reasons for that. They [evangelicals] are not practicing at Wachtel Lipton in New York City. They're practicing in Tupelo, Mississippi, okay, and our structure has really focused on major metropolitan areas. Evangelicals choose not to live in major metropolitan areas, and they choose not to make that their sort of their social home. So, they are out in communities like Mobile, Alabama, or Knoxville. It's hard to reach those people.

Another lawyer for a mediator group commented on the difficulty of coaxing Christian conservatives to engage in secular politics at all: "[W]ith these church groups, evangelicals, it's like herding cats, they are so easily spooked back into the enclave of the church."

The reach of the Heritage Foundation and the Federalist Society also may be limited in the evangelical community by lawyers' less influential roles in that strand of the coalition. As noted in the next chapter, the religious conservative groups represented by the interviewed lawyers used on average fewer lawyers than business and libertarian groups.[12] This finding is consistent with the observation of one Federalist Society member: "Does our evangelical community, as a proportion, track the size of that community within the conservative movement? Now, that probably is how I first thought about it, and I think in the end that's not the right way to think about it. . . . [T]here just might be a lot of evangelicals who don't practice law. I think that's where I am at this point."

Both the Heritage Foundation and the Federalist Society appear to be more closely aligned with the establishment than with populist rebels within the movement. The Heritage Foundation has long endured charges that it is too closely aligned with the Republican Party and has too much stake in continuing to exercise influence within the Beltway. The Federalist Society's Board of Visitors reads like a Who's Who of the conservative legal establishment, with members including Ed Meese, Theodore Olson, and William Bradford Reynolds. These organizations generally seem inclined to try to sooth and placate the more radical elements of the coalition rather than to side with them.[13]

Ambiguity about the real allegiances of leaders of Heritage and the Federalist Society probably helps them exercise influence within the conservative coalition. In their work on the rise of the Medici and the centralization of elite networks that helped to produce the Renaissance state in Florence, Padgett and Ansell explained how Cosimo de Medici's "multivocal identity" allowed him to "harness the power available" in the Medicis' network position (Padget and Ansell 1993). Medicean supporters were deeply divided by social class and neighborhood, and only the Medici family linked the segments (Padget and Ansell 1993, 1281). Padgett and Ansell attribute Cosimo's power to his "extremely multiple interests," the perception that he did not pursue self-interest, and his refusal to pursue specific goals. "Robust action"—the style of control they attribute to Cosimo—involves inscrutable or "sphinx-like" behavior, the ability to be perceived by multiple audiences as a potential ally, so that "control was diffused throughout the structure of others' self-fashionings" (Padgett and Ansell 1993, 1264).

Although there are many ways in which the American conservative coalition is quite unlike the Medicis' political network, there may an element of "robust action" in the Federalist Society and Heritage Foundation's approach to exercising influence. Both organizations have leaders who present themselves as sympathetic and trustworthy brokers, and they are able to present different faces to the different constituencies they hope to attract. Both occupy network positions through which they provide crucial links among deeply divided groups. Their power flows from their ability to bridge constituencies that fundamentally mistrust one another.

CONCLUSION

In the book's introduction, I suggested that lawyers might link the constituencies of the conservative alliance. The Heritage Foundation and Federalist Society are sites where ties among lawyers for the different strands of the coalition are forged. Both organizations target lawyers, and both convene meetings that encourage participants to consider shared political commitments. Heritage pushes lawyers who participate in its meetings to find ways to contribute to the mutual success of the organizations

they serve. The Federalist Society does not directly advocate cooperation on policy objectives but indirectly facilitates that goal by reinforcing
lawyers' shared identity and by generating contact among them. For some
lawyers, the Federalist Society operates as an alternative bar association
where lawyers congregate to talk about law, policy, and the future of the
legal profession. In the short term, these contacts may produce nothing
more significant than brief and casual conversation, but even idle chat
sometimes lays the groundwork for future cooperation. Such connections
may lead to joint political projects and coordination on policy goals. It
seems quite plausible, as one lawyer claimed, that the Heritage Foundation and the Federalist Society serve as the "cross-roads of the conservative movement."

7

What's Law Got to Do with It?

We turn now to the work these lawyers perform and the roles they play in the conservative movement. Are they simply activists who attended law school, or do they use skills that are distinctive to lawyers? To what extent do they and the organizations they serve pursue their goals through the courts, and how does litigation relate to broader political objectives? Are differences and divisions among lawyers of the conservative alliance reflected in their patterns of litigation? In what other arenas do they operate? Do professional norms constrain their choices of tactics and arguments?

Critics of public interest lawyers of the Left have charged that they tend to overestimate the importance and efficacy of law and to undermine progressive movements. Stuart Scheingold's classic examination of American law and politics, *The Politics of Rights: Lawyers, Public Policy, and Political Change* (1974), claimed that lawyer activists tend to believe in a "myth of rights"—a simplistic view of the interplay between law and social movements according to which litigation victories directly advance social change. He argued that lawyers' training and professional socialization, and the status and social capital associated with court-centered strategies, lead them to exaggerate their roles and to persuade other activists to invest too heavily in legal strategies. He compared this "traditional activism" (Scheingold 1974, 173) led by lawyers with a more sophisticated and promising understanding of the relationship between law and political progress—a "politics of rights"—according to which judicial decisions are merely political assets to be used strategically in other arenas (Scheingold 1974, 173).[1]

Other critics have offered similarly pessimistic accounts of lawyers' influence on social movements. Gerald Rosenberg has argued that "courts seldom produce significant social reform" (1991, 341). Instead, he claims, they "act as 'fly-paper' for social reformers who succumb to the 'lure of litigation'" at the expense of legislative alternatives (1991, 341). Other scholars maintain that litigation diverts resources away from political mobilizing (e.g., McCann 1986, 200; Bell 1986). Still others focus on relationships between lawyers and the constituencies they serve, arguing that lawyers tend to dominate clients (e.g., Alfieri 1991a; Cunningham 1992) and usurp leadership roles that should be left to clients and their organizations (e.g., Lopez 1992; Spann 1993, 166–68; Wasby 1995; White 1988). All of these criticisms proceed from essentially skeptical views about the power of courts and lawyers to deliver social change.

These critiques of reform litigation and lawyers who pursue it have spawned their own round of critiques. Some suggest that critics have paid insufficient attention to how litigation sometimes complements rather than displaces other strategies and how activists use litigation to influence other processes. Litigation campaigns can generate indirect or "radiating effects" on various social actors—not only the direct targets of litigation, but also legislators, potential allies, and the public (Handler 1978; Galanter 1983). Rights strategies can help to mobilize constituencies (Gordon 2005; McCann 1994, 281; Silverstein 1996) and unleash mutually reinforcing interactions between courts, legislatures, agencies, and other political actors (e.g., Feeley 1993; Schuck 1993, 1772; Siegel 2004; Sabel and Simon 2004). Litigation sometimes generates media coverage and transforms disputes in ways that reassign blame and responsibility (Mather 1998; McCann and Haltom 2004; Keck 2006); it can have "constitutive" as well as causal effects by influencing how problems are framed and events interpreted (Mather 1998; McCann 1994). Scholars also have shown that activist lawyers operate in lawmaking arenas outside the courts and that many of them are not fairly described as single-minded, politically naive rights crusaders (e.g., Coutin 2001; McCann and Silverstein 1998; Mack 2005; Olson 1984; Southworth 1999; Ziv 2001). The support structures that sustain law reform litigation also promote legal mobilization defined in these broader terms (Southworth 2000).

Research about the efficacy of court-centered strategies and the political sophistication of activist lawyers has focused primarily on lawyers of the political left (but see den Dulk 2006). But the questions posed in this literature are equally important for understanding lawyers' roles in conservative and libertarian causes.[2] This chapter shows that social conservatives are less invested in law-centered strategies than their libertarian and business counterparts; they generally used fewer lawyers and relied more on grassroots strategies. However, lawyers for all the constituencies used litigation flexibly for various types of instrumental purposes, and they expressed similar views about litigation's tactical value. Even the lawyers who were most optimistic about litigation's potential viewed it as just one of many available means of influencing policy, and they typically used it in combination with other strategies. In general, lawyers for conservative causes expressed confidence that their work contributed substantially to the causes they served.

LAWYERS AND LITIGATION

Litigation is quintessential lawyers' work. Unlike other types of activities in which lawyers sometimes engage on behalf of clients—legislative drafting and lobbying, research, media work, grassroots organizing, fundraising, and management, all of which are considered in this chapter—litigation is a policy domain that lawyers do not share with other occupations. Of course, client organizations may still "call the shots," making the primary decisions about when they will participate and what positions they will take, and they may rely on other types of political actors in making those judgments. But lawyers undoubtedly play especially prominent roles in litigation, and their influence on the conservative movement may be especially likely to be felt in that realm of work.

To assess in very general terms whether there might be differences in how constituencies of the conservative coalition use lawyers and litigation, I gathered two sets of data, which are reflected in table 7.1. First, I compiled a list of all lawyers who worked during the years 2003–2006 for each of the organizations represented by the interviewed lawyers. The list included lawyers who served the organizations in any capacity—as a litigator, advisor, board member, officer, or scholar. My sources included state and federal litigation records, Web sites for the organizations, board lists, and the LexisNexis database of legislative testimony.[3] I counted lawyers who filed briefs on behalf of the organization even if the organization did not employ them directly. This approach included lawyers in private firms who served either pro bono or for fees as well as lawyers who filed briefs on behalf of more than one group.

Table 7.1 shows that the business groups used the largest number of lawyers on average, followed closely by libertarian groups. Mediator organizations and religious conservative groups used many fewer lawyers, and order-maintenance groups, affirmative action opponents, and abortion foes used fewer still. These data are consistent with previous research,

TABLE 7.1: Lawyers Used by Organizations Represented by Respondents and Supreme Court Briefs Filed by Those Groups, 2003–2006[a]

	Mean number of lawyers	Mean number of Supreme Court briefs filed
Business	27	3.1
Libertarian	23	6.0
Religious	13	2.7
Mediator	12	1.4
Order maintenance	8	5.6
Affirmative Action	5	1.0
Abortion	4	0.8

[a]The lawyers data are current through September 1, 2006, while the briefs data extend through the end of 2006.

which showed that business and libertarian groups generally employed more lawyers than organizations that sought to advance social conservative causes (Heinz, Paik, and Southworth 2003, 17). Social conservatives' less extensive use of lawyers is also consistent with their more pessimistic accounts of the possibilities of producing change through law. They have pursued some of their goals by adapting liberal legal rhetoric to their purposes, offering an "alternative understanding of rights and equality" (den Dulk 2006) and advancing those views in the media and courts. They have framed their campaigns against abortion and restrictions on religious expression as rights claims—the right to life and the right to religious freedom (den Dulk 2006). But social conservatives generally do not believe that lawyers and courts can deliver the larger cultural transformation they seek.

The number of Supreme Court briefs filed during the same period tells a slightly different story. Libertarians filed the largest number of Supreme Court briefs on average, followed closely by order-maintenance organizations. The large mean number of briefs produced by order-maintenance groups was driven by one especially active organization, which focused on criminal justice matters and may have found the Rehnquist-Roberts Court particularly receptive to its agenda. Business organizations were the next most active participants in Supreme Court litigation, followed closely by religious conservatives. Mediator organizations submitted relatively few briefs, which is unsurprising since most of them were think tanks and lobbying groups. The *Grutter* and *Gratz* decisions probably account for the dearth of Supreme Court briefs filed by affirmative action opponents during this period, and the Supreme Court's consistent reaffirmations of

Roe v. Wade, until its recent partial reversal of course in *Gonzales v. Car-hart,* may help explain the absence of abortion opponents in the Supreme Court during that period.[4]

Litigation records of the organizations represented by the interviewed lawyers demonstrate that the constituencies of the alliance proceeded largely independently in the courts in the years following the interviews, but they also generally avoided open conflict. Table 7.2 shows that busi-

TABLE 7.2: Joint Participation in Supreme Court Litigation by Organizations Represented by Interviewed Lawyers, 2003–7[a]

| | | Participation (number of cases/splits) with other constituencies | | |
| | | | | |
Constituency	Cases	Cases	Splits	Constituency
Libertarians	73	20	6	Religious
		30	0	Business
		4	1	Order maintenance
		1	0	Affirmative action
		9	0	Mediators
Religious	32	20	6	Libertarians
		3	1	Business
		4	0	Order maintenance
		1	0	Affirmative action
		8	0	Mediators
Business	56	30	0	Libertarian
		3	1	Religious
		4	0	Mediators
		1	0	Order maintenance
		1	0	Affirmative action
Order maintenance	34	4	1	Libertarians
		4	0	Religious
		1	0	Business
		0	0	Mediators
		0	0	Affirmative action
Mediators	13	9	0	Libertarians
		4	0	Business
		8	0	Religious
		2	0	Affirmative action
		0	0	Order maintenance
Affirmative Action	2	1	0	Business
		1	0	Religious
		2	0	Mediators
		1	0	Libertarian
		0	0	Order maintenance

[a]Through August 1, 2007

ness groups represented by the interviewed lawyers filed briefs in fifty-six Supreme Court cases from 2003 through 2007 and that religious conservative groups participated in thirty-two cases during that period.[5] There were just three cases in which organizations from both of those constituencies appeared and just one case in which organizations from those competing constituencies opposed one another. Libertarian groups, which filed briefs in seventy-three cases during the same period, frequently appeared in the same cases as business and religious conservative groups, and they occasionally clashed with social conservative organizations.[6] The mediator organizations were not particularly active; they filed briefs in just thirteen cases during this time period. In all cases in which they appeared, organizations for other constituencies were also represented. Mediator organizations more frequently weighed in on behalf of business and libertarian concerns than on causes that mattered to social conservatives.

Sixty-five of the seventy-two interviewed lawyers—including lawyers in all of the constituencies of the conservative coalition—engage in litigation at least occasionally. Some of them, especially libertarians, express startling optimism about litigation's power to accomplish their clients' objectives, perhaps reflecting their considerable success in gaining the judicial appointments they seek. One libertarian recalled studying constitutional law as an undergraduate and "seeing a case like *Brown* where the world was changed overnight—it just was very, very heavy." He remembered concluding, "This is how you change the world—not through politics but through law." Another libertarian said that it was important "not just [to] talk about [libertarian] ideas, but also to try to bring them to fruition and try to make some real changes in the world, and I think that the law allows you to do that." A third libertarian reported that "law [is] . . . ideas in action . . . sort of in the way writing is, but you can force the result there. You can't get people to buy books, but you definitely can force them to respond to legal pleadings." A Christian who had litigated religious liberties claims in the European Court of Human Rights said, "[I]n Europe, it's like the Marshall Court of 1810. We're at the very early formative stages, and so there is a lot of excitement. We can write the road map in this area in Europe." A social conservative who had represented homeschooling parents in suits against social workers and school officials who tried to enter their homes without search warrants claimed that litigation had played a major role in allowing homeschooling to flourish. He recalled his intense satisfaction when his organization began winning cases and keeping government officials at bay.

These lawyers' expressions of confidence in litigation's power are consistent with the promotional materials of the organizations listed in table 2.1, many of which tout litigation as central to their purposes. Libertarian groups seem particularly hopeful about litigation's potential to secure favorable outcomes, including some that might be unavailable in other policy-making arenas. The Institute for Justice calls its lawyers a "Merry Band of Litigators" (Institute for Justice 2006b) and proclaims as a virtue that the organization's "successes don't depend on the compromise required by the political process, legislation and lobbying" (Institute for Justice 2006a). The Pacific Legal Foundation claims to be "the watchful sentry, the fervent warrior, and the beacon of hope" in "that arena where truly the individual can stand against overreaching government— the courtroom" (Pacific Legal Foundation 2006). The Washington Legal Foundation asserts that it has "shaped public policy through aggressive litigation of over 990 court cases [and] 710 administrative and regulatory proceedings" (Washington Legal Foundation 2006). The American Center for Law and Justice pursues its mission of protecting "God-given inalienable rights" in both the "courts and the legislative arena" (American Center for Law and Justice 2007). The Alliance Defense Fund claims that its "involvement in direct litigation" has "helped create a much stronger, more effective alliance to confront the challenges before us and to win for the kingdom" (Alliance Defense Fund 2007a). Other conservative and libertarian groups listed in table 2.1 that pursue law reform through strategic litigation include the Becket Fund for Religious Liberty, Center for Individual Rights, Landmark Legal Foundation, Liberty Counsel, and Claremont Institute for Constitutional Jurisprudence.

A recent collection of essays written by prominent conservative and libertarian litigators (Edwards 2004) expresses the authors' shared optimism about litigation's capacity to deliver real gains. Ronald Zumbrun, a founder of the Pacific Legal Foundation, argues that "there is more opportunity than ever before to use the courts to preserve and enhance individual and economic freedom" (Zumbrun 2004). Roger Clegg, vice president and general counsel of the Center for Equal Opportunity, claims that case law prohibiting racial preferences "protects the rights of millions [of] Americans" (Clegg 2004, 125). William Mellor, president and general counsel of the Institute for Justice, predicts that "put[ting] advocates for economic liberty in courtrooms across America" will help "roll back the excesses of economic regulation unleashed by the *Carolene Products* decision" (Mellor 2004, 92). Clint Bolick, cofounder of the Institute for Justice and now director of the Scharf-Norton Center for Constitutional Litigation at the the Goldwater Institute, writes, "As the Left recognized decades ago, and as we are now beginning to appreciate more fully, law is a powerful tool for social change" (Bolick 2004). He described his 2002 U.S. Supreme Court school voucher win as a landmark political victory:

> Of all the victories of the pro-freedom public interest law movement, none may have greater real-world impact—and none may ever be sweeter—than the ruling in *Zelman v. Simmons-Harris,* which lifted the federal constitutional cloud from school choice. In that case, the Supreme Court took a major step forward in vindicating the promise of *Brown v. Board of Education* and its sacred promise of educational opportunities. (Bolick 2004, 55)

Alan Sears, president of the Alliance Defense Fund, cites litigation to establish parents' right to homeschool their children as "one of the great successes" of religious liberties organizations (Sears 2004, 75). Thor L. Halvorssen, former executive director and chief executive officer of the Foundation for Individual Rights in Education, says that the U.S. Supreme Court's decision in *Rosenberger v. Rector* "meant that universities could no longer deny funds to students simply because they held religious or controversial points of view" (Halvorssen 2004, 134). All of these statements are consistent with a "strong-court" (Schuck 1993) view of the role of litigation in producing social reform—the belief that change initiated through the courts can be effective (e.g., Chayes 1976; Fiss 1979; Bork 1990).

Although many of the interviewed lawyers engaged in litigation and were sanguine about its potential, they did not adopt a simplistic view of the relationship between litigation and social change. None suggested that litigation alone could achieve the goals they sought. Social conservatives were particularly skeptical in this respect: they believed that law could protect religious expression and discourage immoral conduct but doubted that it could significantly advance their larger goal of transforming culture. Libertarians, who sought to use law primarily to constrain government, were more optimistic about accomplishing their ends through litigation. Lawyers for all constituencies appeared to appreciate the difficulty of planning, shaping, and executing litigation campaigns. When they litigated, they often proceeded with other strategies simultaneously, with the expectation that those tactics would reinforce each other. Lawyers also recognized the challenges of translating litigation victories into real change on the ground.

All but three of the lawyers who engaged in litigation pursued primarily impact work rather than individual service. Several commented on the difficulty of charting and implementing law reform strategies. One observed, "You can't always do as much as you want to develop the law . . . because there have to be clients whose cases would move the law in that direction." Another said,

> We've tried to work out . . . an overall litigation strategy. . . . It turns out that that's a very difficult thing to do because the litigations seem to have a life of their own. . . . Something will happen in the course of a case, and you'll find all of a sudden that that case has proceeded far more rapidly that you would have expected. So your litigation strategy of proceeding with case A first and taking that case to the Supreme Court has suddenly become . . . subservient to outside circumstances over which you didn't really have any control. Or a preliminary injunction was granted in case B and the other side is taking case B up to the court of appeals and the court of appeals has put in on an expedited basis. . . . So the overall litigation strategy stuff is something we try to do . . . but I've found over the course of time that it's very difficult to implement. The outside world, as in so many other areas of life, just doesn't want to cooperate.

A libertarian noted that "litigation, by its very nature, is a prolonged battle—not only individual cases but the whole crusade over time."

Lawyers described tactical choices about how best to shape legal doctrine. A religious liberties advocate said that he hoped to move away from largely defensive litigation in favor of advancing "affirmative constitutional position[s]":

> In the past, [the other side] have generally been able to play offense— challenge this law, challenge that law, that type of thing, and the traditionalists were more playing defense. . . . For years the ACLU would bring some case or some concept . . . and they would lose five, six, seven, ten cases. And then finally one judge would say, "You know, I think there's some merit to that." And then they would get a foothold and they would build upon that.

Another described why he had begun litigating cases at the trial level: "When you do an amicus brief at the Supreme Court, 90 percent of setting the terms of the debate is already prepared by people who don't know what they're doing. . . . You've got to, on occasion, get in on the trial level to take the case forward if you want to be raising certain issues. Otherwise it won't get to the Supreme Court at all." A libertarian offered a detailed description of how she tried to "build on" favorable precedents. A lawyer for a religious advocacy group noted that there were "cases . . . we want to keep away from the Supreme Court right now, because we know they'll lose."

Several lawyers commented on real world impediments to translating litigation victories into favorable and secure outcomes for the clients and constituencies. A religious liberties advocate complained about New York State's recalcitrance in the face of the Supreme Court's rulings on equal access to school facilities for religious groups: "There is uncommon and unbelievable resistance to this issue. . . . As Mississippi was to desegregation, New York is to equal access law. They are just in this defiant mode. I mean here they've gotten two major [decisions]—*Lamb's Chapel* and now *Good News Club* case—where they've been totally rebuked by the Supreme Court and they just cannot get the message." Thus, "bureaucratic contingency"—the difficulties that can thwart efforts to enforce court orders—(Handler 1978, 18–22; cf. Rosenberg 1991, 280–85)—sometimes frustrate religious liberties advocates just as they have civil rights and environmental lawyers. The founder of a libertarian group expressed skepticism about whether his organization's courtroom achievements would hold if conservatives lost control over federal judicial appointments:

> The composition of the Supreme Court could change tomorrow. . . . We were certainly helped by the fact that we did have eight years, arguably twelve . . . of [appointments of] judges to the bench, which did change the composition of the courts and made some of the arguments that we were making much more favorable. . . . [But] if you look to the long-term impact—that's why the verdict is still out—because no victory is ever secure.

Several of the interviewed advocates indicated that they looked for extrajudicial means of influencing litigation outcomes and agenda setting by the courts. Four had spent significant amounts of time on judicial confirmation battles. Many interviewed lawyers commented on the importance of shaping the views of judges, lawyers, and prospective witnesses and jurors, in accordance with political scientists' findings that courts have become sites of intense interest group competition (e.g., Epstein 1985, 148; Schlozman and Tierney 1986, 362–64). Collectively, these lawyers had written over ninety books (six lawyers accounted for sixty-nine of them) and many more journal articles. Most of this work was directed toward long-term change, but some of it targeted particular cases. One lawyer described commissioning a paper about a matter scheduled for Supreme Court argument: "[We] thought it important to get our spin out on that."

He adopted a title he "thought might catch the attention of the justices" and, six weeks before oral argument, sent the published paper to each justice and his clerks. An affirmative action opponent whose responsibilities involved mostly writing and speaking to the press indicated that judges were among the political actors to whom his organization targeted efforts "to change people's minds."

OTHER STRATEGIES

Many of the interviewed lawyers indicated that their work was not confined to litigation and other strictly legal tasks. Only a few lawyers engaged exclusively in litigation. They also counseled clients, pursued transactional work, drafted legislation and ballot initiatives, commented on proposed rules, advised public officials, organized coalitions, participated in fundraising and organizational governance, responded to media inquiries, wrote articles and columns for newspapers and magazines, and spoke at conferences. Most said that they pursued a broad array of strategies and that such tactics could reinforce one another.[7]

Legislation

Twenty-six of the seventy-two interviewed lawyers said that they regularly engaged in legislative drafting and lobbying. Twenty-nine of them testified before federal congressional committees from January 2000 through July 2007, submitting seventy-nine pieces of testimony during that period. Sixty-two of those submissions came from lawyers for the libertarian, business, affirmative action, and mediator groups, reflecting these groups' concentration in Washington, D.C., and their emphasis on "insider strategies." Libertarians were active on such issues as voting rights, judicial nominations, domestic surveillance, gun control, education reform, private property rights, prescription drug regulation, campaign finance regulation, the Endangered Species Act, and privatizing Social Security. Business advocates testified on defective products liability, medical liability, limitations on punitive damages, asbestos liability, and union organizing tactics. Mediator organizations weighed in on issues important to each of these constituencies, including the line-item veto, religious expression, federal funding for the delivery of social services by faith-based organizations ("charitable choice"), judicial nominations, campaign finance, the Defense of Marriage Act, and counterterrorism measures. Religious conservatives testified on political activities of tax-exempt organizations, religious expression, charitable choice, campaign finance, illegal immigration, and pornography on the Internet.

Some of the lawyers for social conservative groups discussed their roles in legislative campaigns to overturn adverse judicial rulings and push the constitutional boundaries established by the courts. One abortion opponent reported that his organization had participated in state legislative efforts to adopt statutes as restrictive as possible within limits set by the U.S. Supreme Court. Another said that he regularly advises legislators who want to criminalize fetal homicide and that he generally discourages them from "tak[ing] an approach that . . . is unnecessarily timid. . . . " A religious liberties advocate recounted helping school officials who want to go to the limits of the Establishment Clause in accommodating religious groups and injecting religious values into the curriculum. Another described his group's efforts to "correct" the Supreme Court's decision in *Employment Division v. Smith,* which upheld Oregon's refusal to award unemployment benefits to Native Americans who were fired for using peyote in a religious ceremony; it pushed for enactment of the Religious Freedom Restoration Act of 1993 and the Religious Land Use and Institutionalized Persons Act of 2000. Obscenity opponents worked with state and local governments to enact strong legislation, ordinances, and zoning provisions consistent with constitutional requirements. One social conservative reported that she had traveled the country and "testified at forty-one state legislative hearings" on a single issue.

Lawyers have no particular corner on the skills required to testify in committee hearings, and some of the categories of organizations that used relatively few lawyers were among the most active in submitting such testimony. Using the LexisNexis Congressional database, which contains comprehensive legislative records, I compiled testimony submitted to federal committees by the sixty-nine organizations represented by the interviewed lawyers from January 2003 through August 2007. The represented organizations submitted 634 pieces of testimony during that period. Table 7.3 shows that the mediator groups were by far the most active participants in federal committee hearings; they submitted on average almost thirty-two pieces of testimony per organization. Business and libertarian organizations, which were among the most active participants in Supreme Court litigation, also participated frequently in federal committee hearings. Religious organizations, abortion opponents, and order-maintenance groups submitted little testimony at the federal level. The location of most of these groups and their lawyers outside of Washington, D.C., probably reflects and partly explains their inattention to this "insider" strategy.

TABLE 7.3: Testimony Submitted by Organizations Represented by Interviewed Lawyers, 2003–2007

	Total	Mean
Mediator	254	31.8
Business	280	20.0
Libertarian	72	6.0
Affirmative action	5	2.5
Religious	20	1.0
Order maintenance	3	0.6
Abortion	0	0.0

As noted in chapter 5, the organizations represented by the interviewed lawyers rarely appeared in the same hearings, and, when they did appear jointly, they rarely tangled. Of the thirty sets of hearings from 2003 to August 2007 in which organizations from more than one category participated, four involved conflicting testimony among the represented organizations. In none of the six hearings in which more than one of the interviewed lawyers appeared did their testimony conflict.

Media

Advocacy organizations frequently pursue litigation and publicity simultaneously. As McCann has observed, "[m]edia-oriented stagecraft and legal advocacy . . . constitute the complementary tactics of modern professional policy advocates" (McCann 1986, 205). Indeed, it appeared to be common knowledge among lawyers for all of the constituencies that using the media strategically was a basic element of an advocate's job. A lawyer for a libertarian think tank said that his responsibilities include "publishing, speaking, debating, commissioning articles, running conferences, forums, doing radio and TV, [and] writing op-eds. . . . " Another libertarian stated, "We do a lot of work in the court of public opinion," and another asserted that "rhetoric matters; the terms of the debate have to be set not only in court but in the court of public opinion." An affirmative action opponent said, "We talk to the media, . . . write columns, . . . articles, . . . [and] books . . . publish studies, . . . appear on TV, . . . radio, at academic conferences, . . . [and] debates." A tort reform advocate explained that his efforts to inform the public about "things . . . that are not right in the judicial system" included "talk[ing] to reporters. . . . " A libertarian gives annual lectures to conservative public interest advocates on various strategic concerns, including how to "use the media." A lawyer for a mediator organization said that he responds daily to requests to participate in talk shows and talk to reporters. A lawyer who leads a grassroots social conservative group writes a weekly column and engages in daily radio commentary, and another social conservative hosts his own television show.

Several lawyers described their attempts to overcome what they characterized as the mainstream media's liberal bias. One said that he had begun working selectively with reporters several decades ago, partly in response to a plea by Michael Novak, a prominent Catholic intellectual, who had urged conservatives to engage with the "moral-cultural set"—the community of people who generate ideas:

> If you really want to influence the policy process, if you want to create a buzz about issues . . . , precisely as Michael said, it was so much easier than was commonly supposed. I only talked to five journalists and institutions. . . . The *New York Times* news side, the *Washington Post* news side, the *Washington Post* editorial side, the *Wall Street Journal* editorial side, and . . . the *New Republic*. . . . And I found that if you could talk to them one on one, you could get a good front-page story. It would be a matter of weeks before it would be a cover story in *Time* magazine. . . . And so, I would regularly, if I'd see some dispatch by a reporter from the *New York Times* or the *Washington Post* . . . I'd call these guys up, cold, and I'd say, "Listen I just read your story on civil rights" or on this or on that. And I'd say, "I don't give a damn about your politics. But, you know, you're a professional. And this is not good guys against bad guys. You know, some of us are struggling to find out what the right thing is. And it's no service to blacks or poor people or whatever classes of people you think you're protecting to report it as if it were a good guys against bad guys story."

Several lawyers said that they had created new media and publishing outlets to circulate and validate conservative and libertarian ideas. One described organizing a symposium at an elite medical school to lend respectability to his organization's position on assisted suicide. Another left a high-level political appointment in the Reagan Administration to serve as general counsel for an organization that sought to be an "intellectual clearinghouse" for conservative public interest law groups. He argued that "most of what gets written in law journals and so forth, tends to be from the left side of the spectrum," and he described his role as "principally helping to fill in that gap with writing by conservatives on legal issues. . . . " Another said that he had created a forum for "skeptical perspectives on gun control."

Many interviewed lawyers explained that their prospects for achieving political goals depended on winning battles over how to frame public policy debates. A libertarian claimed to have advanced his cause by popularizing the terms "judicial nullification" and "regulation through litigation." An abortion opponent said that he and his organizations were committed to "a long-term process of affecting culture and changing opinion." A libertarian said of his mission to rein in government, "The driving idea is this. It's captured in Richard Weaver's 1948 book . . . *Ideas Have Consequences*. . . . It was a change in the climate of ideas during the progressive era, which reached fruition during the New Deal, that brought us to the modern regulatory redistributive state. It is a change in the climate of ideas that will restore limited constitutional government." A libertarian wrote publications targeted to an audience of "about five hundred people who think about [his area of interest] seriously" but with the hope that "over time, this stuff will sort of percolate and eventually resonate" to change public policy. A pornography opponent said that he was working "to put the industry back in the gutter where it belongs rather than running down the mainstream of society." Doing so, he explained, would require changing public attitudes and priorities: "[M]y hope [is] that people will realize that" they have been "fooled" into thinking that they want readily available pornography and the "sexual jollies" it offers.

Many of the interviewed lawyers use the language of rights to describe their causes. Abortion opponents say that they are fighting for the right to life, and gun opponents cite the Second Amendment right to bear arms. Opponents of compulsory unionism describe themselves as champions of the right to work, and opponents of land use regulations invoke absolute conceptions of property rights. Religious conservatives proclaim the right of parents to educate their children and to express their religious views in the public sphere. Affirmative action opponents claim rights against race and sex discrimination, and proponents of tougher criminal laws refer to the rights of crime victims and a wary public. Business advocates assert that tort reform is necessary to secure their clients' due process rights.

Grassroots Organizing

Lawyers for religious, pro-life, and order-maintenance organizations are much more likely than lawyers for other types of organizations to be associated with grassroots advocacy strategies. The Web pages of many of these groups encourage visitors to sign petitions, write elected officials, call talk radio, and recruit friends. Some religious conservative groups urge visitors to involve pastors and other church leaders in their campaigns and to pray for the success of their efforts.

Very few of the interviewed lawyers were directly involved in grass-roots organizing strategies, but several discussed how organizing can complement litigation and legislative work. They also commented on the difficulty of reconciling broad-based grassroots efforts with well-planned legal strategies. A libertarian noted that "grassroots activism is a very potent combination when used with effective public interest law," but he emphasized the constraints of working with a constituency to whom one owes loyalty:

> Thurgood Marshall convened folks here in D.C. in the early fifties to really look at whether or not to go all out on separate but equal. And, as you know, that was a very divisive meeting in which he lost virtually all the representatives of the southern chapters of the NAACP because they thought that it was too radical. But you have to make the choice then and tell them what you're going to do and do it. You can't just sort of run the risk of finessing them or thinking, ah, they don't really need to know.

Another libertarian said that he liked the credibility that came from his organization's expertise and reputation for high-quality legal work but that he regretted that his group, unlike some grassroots and membership organizations, lacked "some constituency that could back us." Another libertarian said that his organization sometimes relied on grassroots groups to supply plaintiffs. A social conservative left a think tank to work for a membership organization because he believed that he could more directly influence judicial appointments from the latter type of group: "We've got one-half million members who can take action. . . . Think tanks don't have members; they just think. . . . It's a whole different dynamic where you have grass roots activists as the direct recipients of your work product." A religious liberties advocate noted that the free speech principles that underlie the Christian Right's litigation strategy for winning equal access to public educational institutions have sometimes been difficult for its members to accept. He described the tensions that arose when student-led gay-straight alliances—student groups created to promote welcoming environments for students regardless of their sexual orientation—began seeking protection under the Equal Access Act of 1984, legislation that social conservatives had worked hard to enact:

> In 1984 and '5, we start urging Congress to pass the Equal Access Act. They pass it in '85. We begin litigating in 1990 in the *Mergens* case. Jay Sekulow convinces the Court that it's constitutional. . . . So we're litigating little

secondary aspects of it, and all these student-led Bible clubs are starting up. . . . And then we start hearing about students organizing gay-straight alliances. And so, in the conservative Christian community . . . , the reaction is, "Well, we can't allow that. That's sinful behavior. That's wrong. . . . We shouldn't permit that, and so we're going to say no to them" . . . Lambda Legal Defense is litigating these cases under the Equal Access Act that we have put forward. And then school board members start calling us up . . . and say, "Tell us how to stop these groups from meeting." And so there was . . . a meeting [convened by the Alliance Defense Fund] . . . And we said, "What's our response for the gay-straight alliances?" Because everybody in the room felt that homosexual conduct is immoral, but they're using this law that we got passed. . . . So what do we do?

This lawyer described how he had helped to sell the view that evenhanded interpretation of the statute was unavoidable:

[W]e came to the conclusion that there was no principled way to say, the student-led Bible studies are in and the gay-straight alliances are out. That it would be hypocrisy. We would be contradicting everything that we had said. And that we can exist in an environment where the ideas that we think are correct are being espoused alongside the ideas we think are in error. That is preferable to a situation where the government can selectively shut down groups and say, you can't meet. So, and there was basically a collective agreement, although not at first at the beginning of the meeting. But we just said, "We just don't think that there's any principled way to say yes to Bible studies, no to gay-straight alliances."

As noted in chapter 5, lawyers for abortion opponents also worked to keep the movement's more radical elements under control and in compliance with the law.

Agenda Setting

Like lawyers for many advocacy groups of the Left, who generally exercise considerable autonomy in framing the organization's agenda, selecting clients, and setting strategy (Spangler 1986, 166–70; Olson 1984; Hosticka 1979; Southworth 1996), lawyers for legal advocacy groups of the political Right also claim to have substantial control.[8] Several lawyers for large organizations, including most of the trade groups and a religious group, said that the organizations' boards set strategy. But most lawyers for smaller groups indicated that they played major roles. One abortion opponent described himself as his organization's "primary strategizer, planner, and visionary." Another said that his role in setting goals for the organization was "very, very important" because "you cannot be talking about abortion and not talking about what the law will allow." A lawyer for a Christian group said the organization's board sets general policy and goals but then "leave[s] it to those of us on the line to help them implement that" because "obviously we are the ones who can see how the trends of the law are moving." Another said that he was constrained by the organization's mission—to pursue "religious liberty and sanctity of life"—but that "obviously there's a lot of room within those things and . . . the board looks to us to sort of set priorities and set strategy and they historically have given a lot of deference to the kinds of things that the staff like to do." Another libertarian recalled that "what was exciting about" his first public interest job was that he "had a blank check to really implement my vision of public interest law and civil rights in particular." A conservative who pursued litigation on behalf of a think tank said of his role:

> It's a benevolent dictatorship. . . . I've got just kind of a gut instinct on the kind of structural issues I want to work on . . . , and if I see something in the newspaper or something that comes my way that happens to fit that, or I think I can structure it in a way that lets me hit those issues, then I jump on it. . . . Then I call the president of the [think tank] and say, "Here's the case I have in mind. What do think?" He says, "Yes," and then we go with it.[9]

Another lawyer described the lawyer-director of the religious liberties organization he served as "a visionary par excellence": once he "determines where the [organization] goes, the rest of us try to hold on tight to the comet's tail and enjoy the ride." When asked who set strategy for several organizations she had founded, a family values advocate said, "I do it. I have boards, different boards, and they're all wonderful, but I guess I set the strategy." A libertarian said of her role in setting the organization's strategy, "I am an integral part of it," and another libertarian described his control over such matters as "virtually complete."[10]

CONCLUSION

The interviewed lawyers generally seem sophisticated about the relationship between law and politics and determined to play significant roles in advancing the causes they serve. They believe that litigation, and the coercive force that backs judicial decrees, significantly affected policy and culture in the twentieth century and is likely to continue to do so in the twenty-first. They use litigation, view it as an essential part of the long-term strategies of which they are a part, and appreciate its "interpretive" as well as "causal" potential. In the litigation arena, where lawyers exercise especially strong influence, there has been strikingly little infighting among the various constituencies of the conservative coalition.

But even if lawyers tend to emphasize litigation and to enjoy greater freedom in that realm to make their marks on the conservative movement, they do not focus single-mindedly on the courts. Most of the interviewed lawyers, across constituencies, use a variety of tactics designed to reach the various arenas in which law and policy are made. Religious liberties advocates and abortion opponents rely on litigation less than their libertarian counterparts and use grassroots strategies more. Advocates for all constituencies appear to understand that processes outside the courts influence litigation outcomes. They realize that their larger political purposes require sympathetic judges, jurors, legislators, and public audiences. All of these advocates believe that the battles in which they engage involve ideas and ideology as much as legal doctrine and that long-term success requires building institutions with committed advocates and expertise to pursue campaigns over time. Far from falling for a "myth of rights," these lawyers have absorbed sociolegal critiques of courts and lawyer activism, and they have used them to great advantage.

8

Conclusion

For the conservative movement and the lawyers who have shaped it, this book is primarily a success story. Conservatives have built institutions to check and contain the liberal public interest law movement, and, through that infrastructure, lawyers have acquired considerable influence within the conservative coalition. Lawyers for the several constituencies of the alliance have found common cause in opposing legal liberalism and challenging the liberal legal elite. They remain fundamentally divided by social background, values, geography, and professional identity, but lawyers' "mediator" organizations have partially succeeded in integrating the coalition and promoting strategies consistent with lawyers' investments in legal process. This chapter assesses the current status of the conservative law movement and considers larger implications of this account for debates about lawyers' roles in American public policy.

During the past three decades, conservative lawyers have made considerable progress toward righting the profession and professionalizing the Right. Lawyers' views overall have become more conservative since the 1970s, and the youngest lawyers are now among the most conservative (Heinz et al.2005, 187–88; cf. Hicks 2006). The campaign to repudiate liberal judicial activism has created a new prevailing orthodoxy that liberal judges threaten democracy. Conservatives have recruited a deep bench of highly competent, committed, and credentialed lawyers who hold prominent roles in law firms, advocacy organizations, think tanks, government, and law school faculties. They have established dozens of advocacy organizations and think tanks staffed by lawyers who generate books and articles, speak to the press, testify before Congress and agencies, and litigate in the courts. Republican administrations now have their pick of lawyers for judicial and executive branch appointments, and they have drawn on those pools to remake the federal judiciary and regulatory processes.[1] Those appointments, in turn, have significantly improved conservative public interest groups' prospects for success.

Conservative lawyers have managed to secure important roles in a movement that historically displayed hostility toward lawyers and legal activism. Although conservatives blamed public interest lawyers for many of the trends they mobilized to oppose, lawyers were essential to the strategy of fighting fire with fire. Just as lawyer activists and law professors were instrumental in the triumph of legal liberalism (Kalman 1996), so were they pivotal in its undoing. Their advocacy work ushered lawyers into leading positions in the conservative counterestablishment, and they are now among the most influential representatives of conservative ideas and values.

As lawyers have moved into the conservative movement, they have lent respectability to conservative positions and helped to translate them into law and public policy. Indeed, many of the lawyers interviewed for this book have seen concepts once regarded as fringy become part of the policy agenda if not established doctrine or law. Advocates of school vouchers, "free market environmentalism," "charitable choice," and the federalization of tort law have watched their positions move from marginal to mainstream. A lawyer who wrote a book advocating privatization of a major government program saw the Bush Administration endorse that proposal: "[It] was considered a crazy idea at the time but really has come to the fore now." A libertarian noted with glee how the Supreme Court unsettled Commerce Clause jurisprudence in *United States v. Lopez,* which held that Congress had exceeded its authority by passing the Gun-Free School Zones Act: "To the shock of official Washington, the Court came down saying that there were limits to what Congress could regulate under the Commerce power. That was something Washington hadn't heard in nearly sixty years." A lawyer for a religious conservative group observed that homeschooling was once regarded by school officials as "bizarre, kooky, harmful to children, something that should be put a stop to" but that "things have really changed for the better." Another lawyer noted that conservative litigation victories have established precedents that now appear in all law school textbooks: "Before 1987, there weren't any current [decisions]—meaning within the previous fifty years.... Now I think all of [the casebooks] have . . . some of the . . . major cases. . . . So it's impossible for a student not to be exposed to a more balanced presentation of philosophies. That's significant, and that affects government at all levels."

The causes these lawyers serve are in tension with one another; the issue agendas of social conservatives, libertarians, and business advocates sometimes conflict. One might expect lawyers' common professional training and interests to draw the coalition together. But the lawyers are themselves divided. They come from different social and geographic origins, attend different schools, and hold different views about the values that law should embody. They also disagree about the extent to which lawyers should be morally accountable for the ends and means they pursue on behalf of clients. Yet despite these differences and conflicts, conservative lawyers have created networks that reach all the constituencies of the conservative coalition, helping to bridge class, cultural, and ideological divisions within the alliance, and channeling energy and resources into lawyer-led initiatives. The organizations that facilitate these networks attract impressive foundation support and wield great influence within the conservative movement.

But the conservative alliance and its lawyers are not content with the progress they have made thus far. They continue to establish new legal advocacy organizations and think tanks and to pursue their positions in all arenas where law and policy are made. Despite their considerable success in remaking the judiciary—and evidence that they have acquired a working majority on the Supreme Court on a host of issues (Greenhouse 2007)—social conservatives still express urgency about the threat of an activist federal judiciary and promise a bruising battle ahead if they do not receive the judicial appointments they seek. Many of the Supreme Court precedents that traditionalists vow to overturn were decided by six-vote majorities, and social conservatives see at most four justices—Scalia, Thomas, Roberts, and Alito—as firmly in their camp.[2] Phyllis Schlafly's most recent book, *The Supremacists: The Tyranny of Judges and How to Stop It*, argues that "American institutions and culture are being undermined" by activist judges, who "are carrying out a revolution in our system of government" (2004). Mark Levin, President of the Landmark Legal Foundation, recently published a book asserting that the U.S. Supreme Court is a rogue institution that is "destroying America" (Levin 2005). In the afterword to Levin's book, Ed Meese called on Americans to respond to "the intensifying assault on our constitutional process and governmental structure by a relentlessly power-hungry judiciary" (Meese 2005a, 210).

Some religious conservatives have described *Roe v. Wade* as the *Dred Scott* of the twentieth century, and they are committed to overturning it.[3] Just prior to the Senate's confirmation of Justice Samuel Alito, Ed Whelan, president of the Ethics and Public Policy Center and a former Scalia clerk, said, "We have a Supreme Court that has been essentially lawless in so many respects for decades now, and a lot of work has to be done to restore it to its proper role" (Kirkpatrick 2005a). Grover Norquist has declared that "[t]he big fight—the Bork-style-battle—comes when Ginsburg, Souter, or Stevens steps aside. That is when the other side will make a stand, and our side will push for victory" (Cassidy 2005, 16).

On another front in their broad campaign to push the legal profession rightward, conservatives are focusing more attention on what they see as law schools' liberal biases. They are challenging practices of law school clinical programs, arguing that they tend to reflect the liberal political commitments of the clinical instructors who staff them.[4] A recent paper published by the Manhattan Institute charges that clinical programs "have been engaging in left-wing litigation and political advocacy for 30 years" (MacDonald 2006). It calls for "[o]pening up clinics to radical perspectives on the benefits of limited government and personal responsibility" and proposes alternative clinical projects serving small businesses, landlords, property owners, crime victims, police officers, and victims of reverse discrimination (MacDonald 2006). Several law schools now house legal clinics targeted toward conservative and libertarian students. Chapman University School of Law, for example, hosts a student Liberty Clinic sponsored by the Claremont Institute Center for Constitutional Jurisprudence. George Mason University sponsors a clinic affiliated with the Washington Legal Foundation, and the University of Chicago's Clinic on Entrepreneurship is a joint project with the Institute for Justice.

Conservatives also are pushing for the appointment of more conservative law professors, an effort that began in the 1970s (Kalman 1996, 77–82). Two recent studies suggesting that Republicans are underrepresented on law faculties (see McGinnis, Schwartz, and Tisdell 2005; Lindgren 2005) have fueled a drive to increase the appointments of conservatives to tenure-track positions (see Schuck 2005; Jacobson 2004).[5] As noted in chapter 2, religious conservatives also have created their own law schools to integrate religion with legal training.

Many of the interviewed lawyers suggested that conservatives' underrepresentation on law school faculties greatly disadvantages them in the competition over perspectives about law and policy. These conservatives apparently believe that increasing their ranks on law school faculties is important for selling conservative perspectives to law students early in the process of professional socialization. But not all of them agreed that the predominance of liberals in legal academia has significantly impeded conservatives' quest to win the upper hand in policy formation. Several suggested that the Federalist Society already provided a crucial counterweight by creating an arena for conservative students to test their ideas and supplying access to conservative mentors and professional opportunities. One lawyer argued that the "uniformity of law school faculties" had simply "marginalized them from law and public policy," giving experts in think tanks the pivotal positions in policy formation and inspiring a generation of law students to fight for conservative positions:

> It used to be that the universities were the source of ideas. You look at the Roosevelt brain trust, . . . the Kennedy Administration. But since the Kennedy period it's a fallow place. . . . And it's really sad that there isn't this debate. There's only one good part of it. The good part is that it gives spectacular training to conservatives in the Federalist Society—young men and women who at an early age learn to think for themselves going toe to toe with intelligent people. Thank God in one sense for the intellectual brown shirts at the law school faculties, because they have trained a generation of young lawyers who are going to be the Clark Cliffords, the Joe Califanos, the Lloyd Cutlers of the twenty-first century. And much of it is owed to the law school faculties. These people who are twenty-one, twenty-two, learn to stand up in the face of really intelligent mockery, the put-downs, and learn the power and the moral courage of doing it. . . . I see them coming out of law schools ready to assume real responsibilities. . . . It is just a sad sort of thing that ten people with think tanks, fifteen people in think tanks have more impact on the public policy process than all 12,000 members, or maybe 22,000 members, God knows, at the American Law School Association [sic]. . . .

The same senior lawyer expressed ambivalence about "rescu[ing]" law "from increasing marginalization." What would be good for law school faculties and American society, he argued, might be bad for the conservative movement:

> I can't quite figure out whether I want the law schools to change. . . . [O]n the one hand, I'd like for there to be more change. . . . Economics is kind of soulless; I like the moral content of law. I think law served America spectacularly well, as Tocqueville put it, as lawyers were the lubricant that stopped bone from rubbing on bone. In Europe it was an aristocracy, and in America it is a more democratic lawyer class. But that was when lawyers were engaged

in service. And I'd like to see that return. On the other hand, these idiot savants teaching in law schools are wonderful training tools for these wonderful young conservatives that I see coming out. When they finish taking on these really smart, radical, critical legal studies guys and learn to think for themselves, Hell, taking care of Washington politics is a piece of cake. And that's what's shaping this next generation of conservative lawyers. Thank you, Duncan Kennedy!

Conservatives also are challenging what they see as a liberal tilt of large-firm pro bono policies. In 2003, the Federalist Society published a report asserting that large law firms' pro bono programs were strongly biased in favor of left-leaning projects (Federalist Society 2003). But many conservative lawyers interviewed for this book pursued conservative pro bono work from large firms, and several claimed that firms are becoming increasingly receptive to such projects. One said it helped that firms feel pressure to meet pro bono targets set by the ABA's "Law Firm Pro Bono Challenge" and to improve their positions in the *American Lawyer* magazine's rankings, which take pro bono service records into account.[6] This lawyer claimed that conservatives are willing to perform pro bono work but require projects that fit their political commitments: "A lot of big firms . . . insist that their lawyers do pro bono work. . . . They're used to representing clients they don't agree with all the time. The last thing [they] want to do is do a pro bono project on a cause [they] don't agree with. So they're looking for opportunities." The Federalist Society's Pro Bono Center facilitates such matchmaking, linking conservative lawyers with "opportunities for pro bono service in the causes of individual liberty, traditional values, limited government, and the rule of law" (Federalist Society 2006e). Big-firm pro bono service to conservative causes has increased over the last twenty years, although the issues of greatest concern to religious conservatives—abortion and gay rights—remain anathema for many of the most profitable large firms (Chen 2007). Phyllis Schlafly's son, Andrew Schlafly, who was an associate at Wachtell, Lipton, Rosen and Katz for several years before becoming a solo practitioner, recently complained that "[l]arge firms never do work [on the conservative side] on homosexual or abortion issues" (Chen 2007).

Some conservatives also have targeted the use of international law as authority in the U.S. courts and the resort to international tribunals to influence domestic policy. Progressives have pursued these alternatives as their opportunities have narrowed under domestic law and in domestic courts; they have experimented with new forms of transnational advocacy and with efforts to "bring human rights home" (Cummings 2007b). Conservatives, in turn, have characterized these practices as extensions of American elites' left-wing agenda—part of a larger effort to override the will of majorities, to escape the limitations of the Rehnquist Court's federalism decisions, and to impose the international elite's political values. Robert Bork recently described "[i]nternational law and domestic constitutional law in the United States" as "two battlegrounds in the same ideological war within and among the nations of the west"—both involving elites who "employ non-democratic institutions to override the expressed desire of majorities" (Bork 2004). Edwin Meese claims that "perhaps nothing troubles [him] more" than "justices who invoke international law and the decisions of international tribunals in interpreting the Constitution" (Meese 2005a, 211). Justices O'Connor and Ginsburg generated a political firestorm among American conservatives by arguing that international law should inform the courts' interpretation of the U.S. Constitution (Liptak 2006; Lane 2006). Justice Kennedy's citation of a European Court of Human Rights decision in *Lawrence v. Texas* provoked similar outrage from social conservatives (Toobin 2005), and his opinion in *Roper v. Simmons,* which relied partly on international sources to find that the Constitution forbids the execution of juveniles, led Phyllis Schlafly and Michael Farris, chairman of the Home School Legal Defense Association, to call for Kennedy's impeachment (Toobin 2007, 198–99). The Alliance Defense Fund's (ADF) Web site proudly proclaims that ADF plays a leading role in "tak[ing] on the international law movement" (ADF 2007c).

But this issue, like so many others noted in chapters 3–5, has generated disagreement within the conservative alliance. The natural law views of many Christians and some libertarians, and their occasional embrace of international human rights rhetoric, fuels conflict with conservatives who emphasize national sovereignty and democratic accountability and take a dim view of transnational legal institutions and international law. Some Christian conservatives have welcomed opportunities to use international sources of law and international tribunals to defend religious expression abroad. The American Center for Law and Justice's sister organizations—the European Centre for Law and Justice, located in Strasbourg, and the Slavic Centre for Law and Justice, based in Moscow—have pursued international campaigns on issues relating to religious expression (including rights to proselytize and wear religious apparel) and association, gay rights, abortion, and homeschooling. Their arguments often rest on assertions of fundamental, inalienable, God-given rights protected by international law. The Becket Fund, for example, asserts that religious freedom is "a basic human right that no government may lawfully deny; it is not a gift of the state, but instead is rooted in the inherent dignity of the human person" (Becket Fund 2007). Some rights-based libertarians also have argued that property rights and free enterprise are fundamental principles that should help define international law, but they generally have been less active in the international arena than their Christian evangelical counterparts. Business interests, meanwhile, have been keen to use international agreements and institutions to broaden markets. Thus, tension between two positions—on the one hand, asserting rights based on international law and treaties and resorting to international and supranational tribunals, and, on the other hand, insisting on the primacy of national sovereignty and local accountability—divides lawyers of the conservative coalition.

Lawyers for conservative causes appear to be as committed as ever to transforming professional culture and shaping the conservative movement, but they face several significant challenges. Their largest problems are dwelled upon in this book: divisions within the alliance and professional stratification among the lawyers who serve it. Those differences threaten the common objective of lawyers associated with the movement: maintaining a winning coalition. During the years in which I conducted these interviews and wrote the book, conservatives dominated government and public debates and were able to maintain reasonable order within their ranks. For the most part, they avoided open conflict in the federal courts and Congress. But the conservative alliance today is more troubled than it was five years ago, and the alignments among the constituencies are fluid and changing in ways that threaten the GOP's ability to govern. Divisions among lawyers who serve the conservative coalition have become especially pronounced, and the combative style of many lawyers for conservative causes—their tendency to see themselves as under attack and to strike back aggressively—may make it difficult for them to forge new alliances as old ones fail.

Recent policy controversies have exposed deep fissures in the conservative alliance (Ponnuru 2005; Liasson 2005; Savage 2005). Immigration reform proposals and trade policy have separated social conservatives from business interests. Libertarians have rejected the Bush Administration's stands on civil liberties and presidential power in connection with the War on Terror and its creation of large new government programs, including the No Child Left Behind initiative and the Medicare prescription drug plan (Sager 2006). Libertarians have also resisted social conservatives' efforts to use federal government power to strengthen families, churches, and communities (Sager 2006, 134). Some leading libertarians talk openly of supporting Democrats in the next election just to impede the Republican agenda (Tierney 2006).[7] The business constituency has joined libertarians in resisting the Republican Party's positions on symbolic moral issues, such as the proposed constitutional amendment to ban gay marriage, a proposal to allow religious groups to use federal funds to proselytize while delivering social services, and an effort to increase broadcasting regulation to discourage obscenity.

The Iraq War has exacerbated the tensions highlighted in this book and exposed additional fault lines within the alliance—especially between neoconservatives, who seek to project American power abroad to spread Western values, and other constituencies that are more skeptical about foreign entanglements. The issue-events method used to select the organizations and lawyers examined here included only domestic policy issues, but national security has since become a more prominent and divisive concern within the GOP. The Bush Administration's handling of the Iraq war has triggered a substantial backlash among Republicans (Hulse 2007). The War on Terror, which might temporarily have played a role comparable to the Cold War in uniting the conservative coalition immediately after September 11, 2001, no longer accomplishes that end, as libertarians balk at encroachments on civil liberties and expansions of presidential power advanced in the name of winning that "war."

There is even some evidence of a splintering of support among religious conservatives, the most solid backers of the Republican Party in recent years. Leaders of the religious right have complained that the GOP has taken its support for granted, and they have threatened to retreat from politics if the party does not begin taking its concerns more seriously (Cavuto 2006; Kuo 2006a). Focus on the Family's James Dobson has warned that "values voters are not going to carry water for the Republican Party if it ignores their deeply held convictions" (Berkowitz 2006). Ken Connor, former president of the Family Research Council, has argued that conservative Christians have been sullied by their continued support for a party mired in ethics scandals and unprincipled policy making (Berkowitz 2006; Kuo 2006). And David Kuo, former deputy director of the White House Office of Faith-Based and Community Initiatives, has charged that White House personnel and other high-level Republican Party officials do not respect the religious right—"[S]ocial conservatives are viewed with eye-rolling . . . People don't like them. You know, they are—quote, unquote—'the nuts' or 'the goofballs.'" (Cavuto 2006). He claims that the GOP has cynically used evangelicals to maintain a winning coalition (Cavuto 2006).

Evangelicals are also internally divided, with a younger generation re-sisting the identification of evangelicals with the Republican Party (Good-stein 2006; Willis and Hardcastle 2005; cf. Dreher 2006). In what Rever-end Jim Wallis has called "a sea change in evangelical Christian politics" (Wallis 2006), young evangelicals have begun challenging the religious right's heavy emphasis on abortion and gay marriage and its inattention to environmental issues, HIV/AIDS, and global and domestic poverty (Luo and Goodstein 2007). Perhaps the most noticed of those initiatives, the "What Would Jesus Drive?" campaign, urges Christians to understand that pollution "has a major impact on human health and the rest of God's creation" and that "[o]beying Jesus in our transportation choices is one of the great Christian obligations and opportunities of the twenty-first century" (Evangelical Environmental Network 2007). The campaign was launched by several small evangelical groups in 2002 (McKibben 2006), but these trends are gaining force, as larger and more established groups sign on. In 2004, the National Association of Evangelicals issued a statement, "For the Health of the Nation: An Evangelical Call to Civil Responsibility," which urged Christians to attend to the environment and climate change by honoring the principle that "We labor to protect God's creation" (Wal-lis 2006). In early 2006, eighty-five prominent evangelical leaders signed a "call to action" on global warming (Tooley 2006). That position drew a counterstatement by leaders of the religious right asserting that global warming probably resulted from natural causes, that it was not a matter grave concern, and that imposing emissions controls would exacerbate global poverty (Tooley 2006). In early 2007, leaders of conservative Chris-tian groups urged the National Association of Evangelicals to require its policy director to refrain from speaking out about global warming and to focus instead on "the great moral issues of our time"—abortion, same-sex marriage, and sexual abstinence (Goodstein 2007). But the elders have not managed to curb the insurgency. Jim Wallis has described the results of the 2006 midterm elections as a "defeat for the religious right and the secular left" (Wallis 2006). He has argued that "moderate, and even some conservative, Christians—especially evangelicals and Catholics—want a moral agenda that is broader than only abortion and same-sex marriage" (Wallis 2006) and that the religious right's "monologue" about evangelical voters' priorities is "over" (Simon 2007).

Thus, the constituencies that have coalesced behind the Republican Party during the past few decades are less than happily married today. In the wake of the Republicans' defeat in the midterm elections, constituen-cies that previously agreed to table their differences appear to feel freer to

dissent (Hulse 2007). The benefits of cooperation and the costs of infighting have decreased, and the political networks that facilitated communication among conservatives have become less valuable. There is nothing
organic about the ties that link business interests and libertarians to social
conservatives. Although no major political realignment seems likely soon,
the fusionist formula that gave the GOP such a remarkable period of electoral success appears to be strained.

The alignments of advocacy organizations in Supreme Court litigation during the past few years reflect some of these divisions and tensions
among the constituencies and their lawyers. In most cases, organizations
and lawyers in each of the constituencies proceeded alone, without significant support or opposition from other elements of the conservative
alliance. Social conservatives pursued mostly symbolic moral issues of
primary concern to their base, while business interests proceeded independently on issues of trade, regulation, taxes, and liability under securities, employment, and tort law. Libertarian groups, which agree with
social conservatives on school choice and religious liberty and with business interests on many regulatory matters, occasionally sided with one or
the other of these constituencies.[8] For the most part, lawyers for the various
strands of the coalition avoided open conflict in the courts.[9] In fact, business and religious conservatives even worked together in two cases—
McConnell v. FEC (2003) and *FEC v. Wisconsin Right to Life, Inc.* (2007)—in
opposition to campaign finance reform.

But the constituencies also sometimes clashed in high-profile litigation,
demonstrating in a very public way that efforts to suppress conflict and
to promote cooperation within the conservative coalition do not always
succeed. Libertarian groups have fought business interests in several matters, including *Granholm v. Heald* (2005), in which the Institute for Justice
successfully challenged state laws that limit out-of-state wine sales, and
A.B. Coker Co., Inc. v. Charles C. Foti (2006), in which the Competitive Enterprise Institute challenged the settlement of massive tobacco litigation
by the states. The Cato Institute has taken issue with coalition partners
in case after case. In *Lawrence v. Texas* (2003), challenging the constitutionality of criminal prosecution of gay sex, Cato and the Institute for
Justice filed briefs in support of the plaintiffs and were opposed by more
than a dozen conservative advocacy groups. In *Hamdi v. Rumsfeld* (2004),
which held that citizens detained as enemy combatants in the War on Terror must have an opportunity to challenge their status and detention, Cato
sided with the ACLU and ABA and against the Washington Legal Foundation, the Claremont Institute, the American Center for Law and Justice,

several anti-immigration groups, and Citizens for the Common Defence, a new organization of lawyers dedicated to advancing an expansive view of executive power. Cato opposed religious conservatives in *Gonzales v. Oregon* (2006), which held that the U.S. attorney general's rule-making power under the Controlled Substances Act did not give him authority to issue a rule that would disrupt physician-assisted suicide under an Oregon statute. In *Hamdan v. Rumsfeld* (2006), in which the Supreme Court addressed the use of military commissions to try and punish "enemy combatants," Cato and the Rutherford Institute opposed the American Center for Law and Justice, Washington Legal Foundation, and Criminal Justice Legal Foundation. In *Gonzales v. Carhart* (2006), a challenge to the Partial-Birth Abortion Ban Act of 2003, Cato sided with Planned Parenthood, NARAL Pro-Choice America Foundation, and the ACLU against a host of social conservative groups.

Last term's *Morse v. Frederick* exposed rifts among social conservatives. The case involved a public high school senior who was suspended after he displayed a banner reading "Bong Hits 4 Jesus" across the street from his school in Juneau, Alaska. Kenneth Starr argued on behalf of the school district, arguing that the principal did not violate the First Amendment by restricting expression that he believed might promote illegal drug use. The U.S. solicitor general and other administration officials filed an amicus brief in support of that position, as did other groups that seek to curb the use of illegal drugs. But they were opposed by many religious conservative groups—such as the American Center for Law and Justice, Rutherford Institute, Christian Legal Society, Alliance Defense Fund, and Liberty Counsel—which argued against giving principals broad discretion to restrict religious expression. These organizations were joined by libertarian organizations such as the Center for Individual Rights and several liberal public interest law groups, including the Lambda Legal Defense and Education Fund.

Differences over professional values as well as policy priorities have appeared in other types of public battles. Such divisions were reflected in the infighting ignited by Harriet Miers's 2005 nomination for Justice Sandra Day O'Connor's seat on the U.S. Supreme Court. The nomination appeared at first glance to be well calculated to enlist the support of both of the primary constituencies. As a born-again Christian and abortion opponent, Miers might have drawn approval from social conservatives, who had long awaited the appointment of a Supreme Court justice who would shift the balance in the culture wars. Miers's three decades of experience in a large Dallas firm might have persuaded business advocates to rally to defend a prospective jurist drawn from their ranks. Her statement accepting President Bush's nomination asserted her commitment to "be true to the Founders' vision of the proper role of courts in our society . . . and to help ensure that the courts meet their obligations to strictly apply the laws and the Constitution" (Broder 2005)—language signaling her approval of the originalism around which lawyers for the various strands of the conservative coalition generally agree. But social conservatives and inside-the-Beltway conservatives quarreled over Miers's qualifications. Elites argued that Bush should have selected a candidate from the large pool of young conservatives educated at top law schools and carrying impeccable conservative establishment credentials. Robert Bork, for example, called her nomination "a slap in the face to the conservatives who've been building up a conservative legal movement for the last 20 years" (Cannon 2005). He argued that she had "no visible judicial philosophy" and "lack[ed] the basic skills of persuasive argument and clear writing" (Bork 2005). Social conservatives complained that such resistance reflected a familiar Eastern elitism, and they initially embraced her nomination (Scheiber 2005). But Christian activists later concluded that Miers had not taken sufficiently clear positions on abortion, gay rights, and religious expression in public life. Her professional identity, as a business lawyer with no record of activism on issues of concern to Christian evangelicals, generated questions about the depth of her devotion to their causes. Business leaders may have had their own doubts about her competence and commitment to the values and issues important to them, and they declined to defend the nomination (Liasson 2005). Some critics charged that Miers's primary loyalties were neither to the causes that social conservatives hold dear nor to the interests of corporations, but rather to President Bush and his campaign to expand executive power (Daniel and Waldmeir 2005). The White House withdrew Miers from consideration following a ferocious fight among conservative activists and particularly among lawyers of the conservative movement, without significant participation by Democrats (Weisman 2005).

Several other recent public controversies reflect differences among lawyers of the conservative coalition over the extent to which causes should prevail over professional values. When Charles Stimson, former deputy assistant secretary for detainee affairs, suggested in January 2007 that corporations should break their ties to the large law firms that represent Guantanamo detainees, elite conservative lawyers joined with liberals to criticize him. Harvard law professor, Charles Fried, for example, published a *Wall Street Journal* editorial condemning Stimson's "ignorance and malice," and Ted Olson, former solicitor general and member of the Federalist Society's board of visitors, coauthored a critical column with Georgetown law professor Neal Katyal.[10] Similarly, the controversy over the firing of U.S. attorneys and the reshaping of the Department of Justice staff dismayed the Republican establishment, which prizes credentials and other indicia of intellectual achievement and competence. Under former attorney general John Ashcroft, the department's system for hiring entry-level attorneys, known as the honors program, shifted authority from career officials to political appointees. While the former system emphasized elite law school credentials and clerkship experience, the revised system values commitment to the administration's new civil rights priorities. The change resulted in a substantial increase in the hiring and promotion of graduates from religiously affiliated law schools (Lewis 2007), and it heightened tensions between career attorneys and new attorneys, whom some career lawyers disparagingly call "holy hires" (Lewis 2007). In the controversy over the dismissals of federal prosecutors, Monica Goodling, former senior aide to Attorney General Alberto Gonzales, drew attention when it came to light that she had screened employees based on improper political considerations. The shared disapproval by elite liberal and conservative lawyers of Goodling's role focused not only on the impropriety of her questions but also on her own unconventional résumé. (She graduated from Messiah College and Regent University Law School rather than the top-ranked schools from which Department of Justice lawyers traditionally come.) Chief Justice John Roberts's easy confirmation process was partly attributable to the substantial support he drew from elite liberal lawyers who admired his sterling academic credentials and practice background. Thus, elites of the left and right sometimes agree on the importance of defending the profession's commitment to procedural ideals and merit as prerequisites for top government jobs. Bonds between conservative elites and their liberal counterparts sometimes trump ties between elites and the rank and file within the conservative coalition.

In addition to problems relating to divisions within the alliance, conservative lawyers also face potential challenges to their stature within the conservative movement. They have lost important Supreme Court battles—for example, on gay rights in *Lawrence v. Texas* (2003), affirmative action in *Grutter* (2003), government funding for religious programs in *Locke v. Davey* (2004), Internet pornography regulation in *Ashcroft v. ACLU* (2004), the use of eminent domain power in *Kelo v. City of New London* (2005), and the legality of the military commissions established by the Bush Administration to try Guantanamo Bay detainees. Those defeats may bolster lawyers' roles in the long term, as conservatives invest in challenging the decisions, but they have at least temporarily disappointed those who had hoped that conservative litigators could deliver immediate victories.[11] The Democratic Party's assumption of control over the Senate in 2006 reduced the Federalist Society's informal role in identifying conservative judicial candidates (Lewis 2006). That change has temporarily lessened the Society's allure as a proving ground for ambitious lawyers, and it may also have diminished the organization's standing within the movement. Some religious conservatives have even questioned the wisdom of evangelicals' engagement in law reform. The Rutherford Institute's John Whitehead, for example, recently targeted the movement's emphasis on "legalism" as a threat to social conservatives' spiritual agenda (Kuo 2006a).

But the infrastructure for conservative legal advocacy described in chapter 2 and the networks of conservative activists, patrons, and lawyers examined throughout the book have real staying power. They will not be reversed in one election cycle, and they will not be significantly undercut by setbacks for any particular organization within the support structure. The investments that conservatives have made during the past three decades in ideas, institutions, and networks will continue to yield dividends for decades to come. And lawyers are likely to remain among the most prominent leaders of the conservative coalition as long as the institutions that lawyers dominate—legislatures, courts, and advocacy organizations—remain essential arenas of contest over law and public policy.

Chapter 2 showed that the conservative law movement was primarily a response to a perceived threat from the Left—an attempt to replicate the institutional form, strategies, and "frames" of public interest law to build an infrastructure for conservative legal advocacy. Now the tables have turned. Progressive lawyers, their patrons, and their intellectual sponsors in the academy have suffered a stunning reversal at the hands of conservatives, and they are now scrambling to respond. This is not the place for a sustained analysis of lessons for the American political Left, but two obvious points deserve brief mention—both concerning the role of law, lawyers, and lawyer networks in social movements.

During the past few decades, as the conservative movement has embraced and elevated lawyers within its ranks, the Left has become much more ambivalent about lawyers' contributions. A large literature has attributed the Left's setbacks to its investment in law reform at the expense of political mobilization and extralegal activism (Lobel 2007). Much of the academic literature on progressive lawyers has focused on the limits of legal liberalism (e.g., Galanter 1974; Rosenberg 1991), the threat of lawyer domination (e.g., Bezdek 1992; Alfieri 1991a), and the benefits of ceding decision-making authority to clients (e.g., Lopez 1992; White 1990). This literature suggests more certainty about the failings of law and lawyers than about their potential contributions (Handler 1992; Bellow 1996; Cummings 2007a; Cummings and Eagly 2006).

But the account presented in this book suggests that at least part of the problem for the Left is that it has been outmaneuvered and, to some extent, even *outlawyered* by activists of the Right. The successes of lawyers for conservative and libertarian causes have coincided with a long string of defeats for lawyers associated with causes of the Left (McCann and Dudas 2006), and those trends are linked. The strategies that the Left used effectively in the 1970s became less successful in part because lawyers of the Right and their patrons mobilized to defeat them.

Of course, many of the difficulties encountered by progressives during the past two decades are attributable to forces having little to do with the efforts of the lawyers profiled in this book. The decline of the New Deal coalition that dominated American government from the late 1930s through the late 1960s removed important advantages enjoyed by progressive lawyers during that period: a receptive federal judiciary, sympathetic government bureaucracies, favorable legislation, and a generally hospitable political climate (McCann and Dudas 2006, 41). It is undoubtedly true that "the relatively favorable context for rights-based, legally oriented social movement activity in the United States in the middle part of the twentieth century gave way to an increasingly unsupportive, hostile context by the century's end" (McCann and Dudas 2006, 38). But that unfavorable context was partly the work of creative lawyers on the Right, who exploited connections among the arenas in which law is made and charted an ambitious and coordinated approach to challenging liberal legalism. Conservatives built a strategy focusing on larger macrolevel concerns—building organizations, coalitions, and networks, reframing public policy debates, replacing judges, and changing the institutional contexts in which policy makers operate. Lawyers participated in all of these strategies for radically shifting the dynamics of contemporary American politics.

For the most part, the conservative movement welcomed lawyers' participation. At least until very recently, there has been little grumbling within the conservative movement about the legal profession's inclination to domesticate radical elements and to side with the legal establishment.

Indeed, the very lawyer tendencies that have been decried by critics on the left—their propensity to channel energy into law-related strategies and to promote ties among elites at the expense of the rank and file—may actually have contributed to the conservative movement's success.

As discussed in chapter 6, the Federalist Society played an especially important role in the Right's ability to mobilize conservative and libertarian lawyers and to create a network based on shared political identity. Progressives acknowledged the significance of the Federalist Society's achievements in 2001, when they created the American Constitution Society (ACS), which is modeled directly on its competitor (Baldas 2004; Carter 2003). Just as the Federalist Society declared its mission to challenge the "orthodox liberal ideology" in law schools and the legal profession and to create a network of conservative and libertarian lawyers and law students (Federalist Society 2006a), ACS has committed itself to countering "the narrow conservative agenda" and establishing a network of moderate and progressive students, law professors, lawyers, and policy makers (ACS 2006b). Like the Federalist Society, ACS seeks to establish a presence throughout the country, and it now has 157 student and twenty-five lawyer chapters. Its national conventions employ the debate format of Federalist Society meetings, with panels dominated by left and moderate liberals but complemented by prominent conservative lawyers and judges, including some of the lawyers highlighted in this book. The organization has succeeded in attracting luminaries to speak at its events. Recent guests have included Senator Hillary Rodham Clinton, U.S. Supreme Court justices Stephen Breyer and Ruth Bader Ginsburg, dozens of federal judges, senators Joseph Biden, Russ Feingold, Tom Harkin, Edward Kennedy, Charles Schumer, and the late Paul Wellstone, former attorney general Janet Reno, and former vice president Al Gore.[12] Just as the Federalist Society identifies general themes upon which its members can agree—"that the state exists to preserve freedom, that the separation of governmental powers is central to our Constitution, and that it is emphatically the province and duty of the judiciary to say what the law is, not what it should be"—ACS seeks "to ensure that fundamental principles of human dignity, individual rights and liberties, genuine equality, and access to justice enjoy their rightful, central place in American law" (ACS 2006b). The Federalist Society's mission statement calls for "reordering priorities within the legal system to place a premium on individual liberty, traditional values, and the rule of law"—an agenda comparable in breadth to ACS's call for "synthesizing and promoting a progressive vision of the Constitution, law and policy" (ACS 2006c).

In many respects, then, ACS is the mirror image of the organization upon which it is patterned. It goes further than the Federalist Society in advancing a public policy agenda, however, and it does less than the Federalist Society to articulate a unifying set of themes around which to rally lawyers for the various constituencies it seeks to attract. The Federalist Society refrains from endorsing public policy positions beyond the very general ones in its mission statement but encourages its members to do so and facilitates their participation. ACS also formally declines to take specific policy positions but does so in effect through its efforts to "advance a progressive vision of the law on issues across the policy spectrum" (ACS 2006c). One of its major initiatives is the Constitution in the 21st Century, which seeks "to promote positive, much-needed change in our legal and policy landscape" by bringing together scholars and lawyers "to formulate and advance a progressive vision of our Constitution and laws that is intellectually sound, practically relevant and faithful to our constitutional values and heritage" (ACS 2006d). The "centerpiece" of the project is "a series of issue groups focused on discrete areas of law and policy, through which a wide range of members will develop, communicate and popularize progressive ideas through papers, conferences and media outreach" (ACS 2006d). Each of these issue groups endorses reasonably specific policy propositions. The Equality and Liberty issue group, for example, states its purpose as "combating inequality resulting from race, color, ethnicity, gender, sexual orientation, disability, age and other factors" and "explor[ing] ways of protecting reproductive freedom, privacy and end-of-life choices and of making work accessible and meaningful" (ACS 2006e).

ACS's more direct approach toward influencing public policy and the legal profession positions it to generate policy proposals for a Democratic president and Congress, but it is at odds with the Federalist Society's strategy for wielding influence—building a network by providing a space for conservative lawyers to gather and interact, while encouraging its members to use their brokerage positions in the network to shape policy toward conservative ends. The mission statement of ACS's Equality and Liberty issue group, for example, is not designed to promote debate about the content of those values. Nor is it pitched at a level of generality likely to attract Catholics—historically among the most reliable supporters of the Democratic Party—or the large block of moderate religious voters, many of them African American or Hispanic, who lean left on environmental and economic issues but have qualms about abortion and gay marriage (O'Donnell 2006). It may be worth noting that the Federalist Society quite self-consciously rejected proposals to define a conservative agenda beyond the very broad principles of its mission statement for fear of provoking fights among the constituencies it hoped to bring under its umbrella (Teles 2005). Gary Lawson, one of the organization's founders and still a board member, predicted that "[I]f you ever view this [the Federalist Society] as a device for organizing and galvanizing or anything else, it will blow up, and we all know that and we're not going to let that happen" (Teles 2008, 162). In order to attract participation from the varied types of lawyers interviewed for this research—for example, the libertarian who told me that he and all other lawyers in his organization favored legalizing marijuana, the pro-life advocate who said that he makes all important career decisions through prayer, and the business lawyer who described golf as his religion—the Federalist Society has declined to choose among the sometimes competing policy agendas of its constituencies.

The rise of the conservative law movement coincided with several trends that have divided the legal profession. This period has seen the death of confidence in the separation of law and politics—the idea that legal expertise gives lawyers a special vantage point that enables them to offer superior and politically neutral advice about the content of law. All of the arenas in which lawyers work—including not only courts, agencies, legislatures, and the media, but also bar associations and faculty appointments committees—are sites of struggle over political ideology and professional values. Moreover, the conservative law movement has unfolded during a period marked by a waning of the legal profession's claim to hold special obligations to protect the public (Brint 1994, 15; Gordon 2000). The term "public interest law" is commonly used to describe lawyers who receive little pay and serve causes full time, but there is no consensus among lawyers about what public policy goals this form of lawyer service should promote. Indeed, American lawyers cannot even agree about the core professional values to which they owe allegiance.[13] The profession has become more diverse, specialized, and stratified during this period, and lawyers are more deeply divided than ever before by practice areas, income, and types of clients served (Heinz et al. 2005).

This book has considered how lawyers have helped to link different constituencies of the conservative alliance and to build electoral, lobbying, and litigation coalitions among them. It suggests that lawyers have contributed to the Republican Party's success in harnessing a political movement and finding common ground among constituencies that are fundamentally divided by class, culture, and geography. The mediating roles served by lawyers in this account span divisions *within* the conservative movement, and the mediator organizations profiled here are essentially vehicles for organizing political support behind the GOP. But lawyers' capacity to promote consensus *could* apply across political lines as well. Lawyers have been credited with the potential to bridge divides even greater than the ones that plague the conservative coalition (cf. Tocqueville 1835, 283–90; Halliday 1987, 47).[14] This account focuses on the contest between activist lawyers of the Left and Right, but most American lawyers are not so clearly committed to either camp. Just as most citizens are neither red nor blue, but "purple" (O'Donnell 2006, 35; cf. Hacker and Pierson 2005), so are most lawyers (Heinz et al. 2005, 187–88). Perhaps, then, there is reason to hope that lawyers' generally moderate political leanings might predispose them to facilitate the structured public deliberation necessary to tackle some of this nation's most daunting and divisive problems. In theory, they might help rescue public policy from extreme elements and participate in organizing the "radical center"—citizens who want to achieve "reasonable, fair and just outcome[s]" (cf. Brown 2004). Such mediation would complement the highly partisan roles played by most of the conservative and libertarian lawyers considered in this book and the lawyers of the Left with whom they battle.[15]

Research Methods

This book draws primarily from data I gathered during interviews with seventy-two lawyers and two other conservative public figures in 2001 and 2002. The interviews grew out of a project I launched in 2000 with John Heinz and Anthony Paik, which is summarized at the beginning of chapter 3. To identify the set of organizations and lawyers for that analysis, we used complementary methods (Laumann, Marsden, and Prensky 1989; Knoke 1994). We first selected seventeen "issue events"—legislative controversies involving matters that were important to different conservative constituencies in the late 1990s. The events, all of which occurred in 1995–1998, included proposals regarding abortion, affirmative action, school prayer, tort reform, environmental policy, gay rights, civil rights, flag burning, funding for the National Endowment for the Arts, the minimum wage, compulsory union dues, property rights, gun control, criminal procedure, funding for the Legal Services Corporation, and cultural assimilation for immigrants.

We then searched online archives for articles about these legislative controversies in eighteen newspapers and magazines: the *Wall Street Journal, New York Times, Washington Post, Los Angeles Times, Chicago Tribune, Dallas Morning News, Atlanta Journal & Constitution, Time, Newsweek, U.S. News & World Report, National Journal, Washington Monthly, Roll Call, Washington Times, National Review, Weekly Standard, American Spectator,* and *Public Interest.* We identified all nongovernmental, nonprofit organizations that appeared in these articles on the conservative side of the issues. This method produced the names of eighty-one organizations. In 2000, we gathered data about each of the organizations' revenue and foundation funding. We also searched a variety of sources—including organization Web sites, board lists, litigation records, and a database of legislative testimony—to identify lawyers who worked for these organizations as officers, litigators, board members, lobbyists, and senior scholars. Seventy-one of the eighty-one organizations used lawyers in some capacity.

Every method for identifying organizations active in public policy formation has a systematic bias that tends to select certain types of groups and neglect others (Salisbury 1984; Salisbury et al. 1987, 1220). The issue-event method is more likely to identify organizations active in legislative and administrative work than groups focusing primarily on litigation and research. It also may tend to select organizations that seek publicity for their work and undercount groups that influence law and public policy without drawing media attention. To compensate for the method's possible bias against litigation and research organizations, we supplemented the list with five additional organizations that were particularly active in those policy arenas, using two directories: *The Conservative Directory*, published by RightGuide.com, and the Heritage Foundation's list of "U.S. Policy Organizations" (Wagner, Hilboldt, and Korsvall 2000, 681–789). The five organizations identified through this method were the Home School Legal Defense Association, Manhattan Institute for Policy Research, Washington Legal Foundation, Rutherford Institute, and Criminal Justice Legal Foundation. Four of the five groups appeared on both lists.

I then identified particularly prominent lawyers for the seventy-six organizations that used lawyers. I requested interviews with ninety-eight lawyers, and I interviewed seventy-two of them. The twenty-six lawyers I attempted to contact but did not interview included seven who did not respond and three who had moved to other jobs. Scheduling problems (theirs and mine) prevented me from interviewing sixteen lawyers who appeared willing to meet with me.

The seventy-two interviewed lawyers represented sixty-nine different conservative and libertarian nonprofit advocacy organizations. They worked for fifty-six of the seventy-six organizations identified through the methods described above. (Organizations identified through the issue-events method but not represented by the interviewed lawyers include six trade associations, three organizations that focused their efforts on only one state, two fraternal organizations, the National Association for the Advancement of White People, several groups that no longer exist, and an organization that engaged in "street theater.") In preparing for the interviews and during the interviews themselves, I learned that these lawyers worked for another thirteen conservative policy organizations listed in one or both of the published directories of conservative organizations noted above. The interviewed lawyers served all the major conservative constituencies, with some variation by age, gender, practice setting, and geographic location.

During semistructured interviews, I collected information about lawyers' demographic characteristics, social backgrounds, career histories, current practices, service to conservative and libertarian organizations, civic involvement, and communication with other conservative and libertarian lawyers. To learn about communication networks among lawyers of the conservative coalition, I asked the respondents to indicate how frequently they contacted each of fifty notable conservative and libertarian lawyers: "Please review this list of 50 lawyers. Of the ones you know, please indicate approximately how often you are contact with these people: daily or almost daily; 2 or 3 times per week, weekly, 2 or 3 times per month, monthly, 2 or 3 times per year, or less often." Because this question was not included in the initial interviews, we have these data for fifty-nine of the seventy-two respondents. The names on the list of notables were selected through extensive prior research on the conservative movement and through consultation with knowledgeable informants in the field. All of the notables were prominent lawyers who worked for one of the eighty-six organizations identified through the methods described here. The "notables" list included no more than one lawyer from each organization, with variation in constituency, practice setting, geographic location, and age.

Most of the interviews were taped and transcribed. They varied in length from forty-five minutes to almost four hours. I promised confidentiality to the lawyers I interviewed. Therefore, I have paraphrased and quoted generously from interviews but disguised the identities of the lawyers. All interview transcripts and notes were coded to help me identify patterns and analyze similarities and differences by personal characteristics, ideology, practice type, constituency served, and geographic location.

Notes

CHAPTER TWO

1. Section 501(c)(3) of the Internal Revenue Code, which allows for tax-deductible contributions, applied to litigating organizations only if their work was "in representation of a broad public interest rather than a private interest" (Rev. Proc. 71–39, § 3.01, 1971–2 C.B. 575, 576). The organization could not receive fees for its services from clients and could receive court-awarded fees only if the prospect of the award did not substantially influence the organization's case selection (see Rev. Proc. 75–13 § 3.02, 1975–1 C.B. 662; Rev. Rul. 75–76, 1975–1 C.B. 154, 155). The objective of the guidelines appeared to be "to reserve the exemption for representation of broad public interests that cannot command representation in the traditional marketplace for legal services. . . . " (Chisolm 1987–88, 214). The Internal Revenue Service has since modified these standards, primarily by establishing procedures under which public interest law firms may accept fees for their services (Rev. Proc. 92–59, 1992–2 C.B. 411).

2. The founders of the Pacific Legal Foundation, the first of the conservative public interest law groups, were primarily lawyers. Daniel Popeo, a lawyer who served in the Nixon Administration, established the Washington Legal Foundation (Stefancic and Delgado 1996, 47). Former Moral Majority activist Michael Farris founded the Home School Legal Defense Association (Stevens 2001, 98–99), and Yale Law graduate Pat Robertson established the National Legal Foundation (Papajohn 1985) and American Center for Law and Justice. Edwin Meese III, attorney general in the Reagan Administration and now Ronald Reagan Distinguished Fellow in Public Policy at the Heritage Foundation, participated in founding the Pacific Legal Foundation, Crime Victims' Legal Advocacy Institute (Harrington 1981), and the American Civil Rights Union (Koff 1998).

Other lawyer founders include Fred Inbau (Americans for Effective Law Enforcement), Manuel Klausner (Libertarian Law Council), Leonard Theberge (National Legal Center for the Public Interest and its affiliates), Sam Kazman (Competitive Enterprise Institute's Free-Market Legal Program), Jordan Lorence (Northstar Legal Center), John Whitehead (The Rutherford Institute), Thomas Patrick Monahan (Free Speech Advocates), Mathew Staver (Liberty Counsel), Roger Pilon (Cato Institute's Center for

Constitutional Studies), Michael McDonald (Center for Individual Rights), Jay Seku-
low (American Center for Law and Justice), Clint Bolick and Chip Mellor (Institute
for Justice), Alan Sears (Alliance Defense Fund; National Family Legal Foundation),
Robert Showers (National Law Center for Children and Families), William Bennett
(Empower America), Kevin Hasson (Becket Fund), David Llewellyn (Western Center
for Law and Religious Freedom), Joseph Morris (Lincoln Legal Foundation), Peter
Ferrara (American Civil Rights Union), Larry Klayman (Judicial Watch Inc.), Steven
Calabresi, Lee Liberman, and David McIntosh (Federalist Society), Nancie and Roger
Marzulla (Defenders of Property Rights), John Howard (Individual Rights Project),
John Eastman (Center for Constitutional Jurisprudence, Claremont Institute), Kelly
Shackelford (Liberty Legal Institute), and Allan Parker (Texas Justice Foundation).

3. Their reliance on corporate contributions also fueled suspicion that they should not
qualify for charitable status. Under the prevailing standard, public interest law groups
merited such advantageous tax treatment and the "white hat" status it conferred (Houck
1984, 1429–30) only if they provided representation on issues where the individuals or
groups involved lacked "a sufficient economic interest to warrant the utilization of private counsel" (Rev. Rul. 75–76, 1975–1 C.B. 154).

4. The divergence in geographic focus of conservative and liberal groups may have
narrowed since the 1970s. In her 1983–84 survey of mostly liberal public interest law
centers, Nan Aron found that 62 percent were headquartered in the Northeast, primarily
in Washington, D.C., and New York. The proportion of groups centered in Washington,
D.C., had fallen from 44 percent in 1975 to 29 percent in 1983–1984 (Aron 1989, 31). As
noted in the next chapter, thirty-four of seventy-two lawyers interviewed for this book
worked in D.C. or D.C. suburbs.

5. This prescription echoed themes that Irving Kristol had begun advancing several
years earlier in the *Public Interest* and the *Wall Street Journal*—that corporate philanthropy needed to invest in intellectual firepower if it hoped to influence public policy
(e.g., Kristol 1975, 1977). Indeed, the Horowitz report cited Kristol: "the public interest
phenomenon has had enormous impact on what Irving Kristol has called 'the war of
ideas and ideologies' by which American values and ideals are defined" (9).

6. In his view, this meant that conservatives should "go to constitutional litigation and
not fight over the niceties of the Clean Air Act."

7. The data from which these figures are compiled come from the Federal Judicial
Center Web site, http://www.fjc.gov/public/home.

8. Some founders of Reagan/Bush era conservative legal advocacy groups indicated
that they had studied and learned from the "traditional" public interest law movement.
A lawyer for a libertarian group said, "[W]e owe our success to the pioneering work that
was done by a variety of organizations, starting most notably and obviously, of course,
with the NAACP and the ACLU, through Ralph Nader. . . . " Another libertarian said that
his organization's practice of "having a blueprint and really thinking it through before
we do it and then sticking with that area of law over a long period of time" was "patterned after the NAACP Legal Defense Fund very, very consciously." Larry Klayman, the
founder, chief executive, and general counsel of Judicial Watch, said that he had "talked
with Nader's people" about how they were structured and tried to emulate Nader's tactics

(Keene 2001). The founder of a religious liberties group asserted that conservatives only recently had taken the offensive in proposing favorable constitutional doctrine, learning from "ACLU groups," which had done so for decades and "are much better at it." An abortion opponent said that he strongly believed in incrementalism in law reform litigation, a "view which we drew from desegregation" history.

9. In 1981, Michael Joyce and James Piereson (who joined Olin as a grants officer in 1981) wrote the Olin Foundation's trustees a memo asserting that "[l]arge grants to a few organizations appear to be a more effective use of the Foundation's resources than small grants to a large number of organizations" (Miller 2006, 115). Joyce also urged the foundation to take a more aggressive approach to grant making by identifying worthy projects from the start and participating in their creation. He likened this model of the foundation's role to the "'venture capitalist,' who seeks new and more productive investments for his funds" (Miller 2006, 116).

An informal group called the Grantmakers Roundtable, led by Leslie Lenkowsky of the Smith Richardson Foundation, began meeting in the 1970s to coordinate conservative foundation grants. The Philanthropy Roundtable, a more formal organization established in 1991, sought to enlist philanthropists in a coordinated effort to promote conservative goals. By 2005, it had more than five hundred affiliated foundations (Miller 2006, 132).

10. Steven Calabresi is the nephew of Guido Calabresi, who was on the faculty at Yale Law School at the time and served as dean from 1985 through 1994.

11. Speakers for the first Federalist Society Symposium included Robert Bork, United States Court of Appeals judge for the District of Columbia and now a fellow at the Hudson Institute; Harvard University law professor Charles Fried, who served as solicitor general of the United States, 1985–1989; Theodore Olson, then assistant attorney general, Office of Legal Counsel, Department of Justice, later U.S. solicitor general, 2001–2004, and now partner, Gibson, Dunn and Crutcher; Antonin Scalia, then University of Chicago law professor, later D.C. Circuit judge, and now U.S. Supreme Court justice; University of Texas Law Professor Lino Graglia; Richard Posner, Seventh Circuit Court of Appeals judge; Harvard University law professor Paul M. Bator, who served as deputy solicitor general, 1982–85; Berkeley law professor John T. Noonan, Jr., now Ninth Circuit Court of Appeals judge; Michael McConnell, then assistant general counsel for the Office of Management and Budget, later University of Chicago law professor, University of Utah law professor, and now Tenth Circuit Court of Appeals judge; Yale law professor Ralph Winter, now Second Circuit Court of Appeals judge (Preface 1982: iii–iv.); and Morton Blackwell, long-time Republican Party activist, founder of the Leadership Institute, and board member of the American Conservative Union.

12. The Competitive Enterprise Institute Free-Market Legal Program and the Cato Institute's Center for Constitutional Studies are programs within think tanks, not separate organizations.

13. The Alliance Defense Fund does not litigate cases but serves as a clearinghouse for grants to legal advocacy groups (Diamond 1994, 35–37).

14. Indeed, lawyers' accounts of their roles in creating conservative lawyer groups indicate that they *viewed* themselves as institutional entrepreneurs. A lawyer who es-

tablished one of the earliest conservative public interest law firms said that he and some other lawyers had decided that "what we need is a different type of public interest law firm, and it started a conversation" and they "took a fly at it." Another explained how he had vowed to create a new kind of advocacy group committed to libertarian principles: "There [was] a role for this, there is a vital niche for this, a desperate need, an important potential." A founder of another conservative public interest law firm reported that he and a colleague had identified a "market niche" and had concluded that "there's a better way to do this, and we should give that a shot at some point—build a better mousetrap." Another observed, "I thought there was a real need in the conservative legal community for a group that engaged in direct litigation, as opposed to amicus briefs, for individuals that were ignored by the traditional public interest groups like the ACLU and the NAACP." A lawyer who took a sabbatical from his private law practice to establish an organization that would help local enforcement officials prosecute pornography had believed it necessary to "pioneer some new tactics." A lawyer who founded a group using money from the Legal Services Corporation characterized his efforts as "entrepreneurial" and, describing his work to establish a new civil liberties group, said, "Conservatives who believe in free speech don't give to the ACLU, you know. . . . They needed a vehicle, and so I created one to help them."

15. The founders of the Center for Individual Rights, for example, had previously worked together at the Washington Legal Foundation (*National Law Journal* 2000). The creators of the Institute for Justice had served together at the Mountain States Legal Foundation (Holmes 1997). John Whitehead worked at the Christian Legal Society before founding the Rutherford Institute (Whitehead 1999, 147–49), and Michael Farris, the founder of the Home School Legal Defense Association, was formerly general counsel of Concerned Women for America Legal Defense Foundation (Clendinen 1986). Alan Sears, president and general counsel of the Alliance Defense Fund, previously ran Citizens for Decency through Law and later the National Family Legal Foundation (Lovett 1992, 46). Thomas Jipping, who headed the Judicial Selection Monitoring Project for the Free Congress Foundation, moved to Concerned Women for America to run their "campaign for judicial nominees" (Green 2004). The first general counsel of the American Family Association Center for Law and Policy had previously handled pornography prosecutions for Citizens for Decency through Law. The general counsel of the Competitive Enterprise Institute had worked as a staff attorney at the Pacific Legal Foundation (Ottaway and Brown 1997). The chief counsel of the American Center for Law and Justice previously worked for Christian Advocates Serving Evangelism (Foskett 1991), and the director of the National Legal Center for Children and Families was employed by Citizens for Decency through Law (O'Shaughnessy 1987). The Center for Equal Opportunity's general counsel came from the National Legal Center for the Public Interest (Moore 1994). Liberty Legal Institute was founded by a regional coordinator for the Rutherford Institute (Liberty Counsel 2004).

16. The charitable status of some of these organizations may be questionable under the "broad public interest" and commercial infeasibility criteria of the governing Internal Revenue Service guidelines. Most of the groups listed in Table 2.1, however, appear to meet these broad requirements, which have never been well defined and whose ap-

plication to groups representing consumers, women, and environmentalists long ago undercut any notion that only groups serving the poor or powerless should qualify. I do not attempt to assess whether the agendas of any particular groups described here serve the private interests of their patrons and thus disqualify them from 501(c)(3) status.

17. Other conservative and libertarian groups that describe themselves as public interest law firms, or as legal advocacy organizations engaged in public interest litigation, in their own promotional literature include the Atlantic Legal Foundation ("Atlantic Legal Foundation is a nonprofit, nonpartisan public interest law firm whose mission is to advance the rule of law by advocating limited, effective government, free enterprise, individual liberty and sound science"); Southeastern Legal Foundation (an "Atlanta-based public interest law firm which advocates limited government, individual economic freedom, and the free enterprise system in the courts of law and public opinion"); Landmark Legal Foundation (a public interest law firm dedicated to preserving "America's founding principles of individual liberty, free enterprise and limited government"); Mountain States Legal Foundation ("MSLF undertakes nationally significant public interest litigation" to "(1) . . . ensure that the law is applied in accordance with the requirements of the Constitution and the intent of Congress, that is, the rule of law; and (2) to change public attitudes regarding important matters of public policy."); New England Legal Foundation ("The New England Legal Foundation is a not-for-profit public interest foundation whose mission is promoting public discourse on the proper role of free enterprise in our society and advancing free enterprise principles in the courtroom."); Center for Individual Rights ("CIR marked an attempt to duplicate the success of liberal public interest law firms in the conservative public interest realm"); Community Defense Counsel ("CDC cooperates with both public and private entities in serving the public interest."); Center for Constitutional Jurisprudence, Claremont Institute ("Claremont Institute formed the Center for Constitutional Jurisprudence, a public interest law firm, in order to further its mission through strategic litigation"); National Federation of Independent Business Legal Foundation ("The NFIB Legal Foundation, a 501(c)(3), tax-exempt public-interest law firm, . . . protects the rights of America's small- and independent-business owners by ensuring that the voice of small business is heard in the nation's courts and by providing small businesses with important legal resources."); National Legal Foundation ("The National Legal Foundation is a Christian public interest law firm dedicated to the preservation of America's freedom and constitutional rights."); Thomas More Law Center ("The Thomas More Law Center is a not-for-profit public interest law firm dedicated to the defense and promotion of the religious freedom of Christians, time-honored family values, and the sanctity of human life."); and American Unity Legal Defense Fund ("a national, non-profit public interest law firm established in 2001 to defend human and civil rights, including the rights of American workers who are faced with displacement by illegal immigrant workers").

18. These organizations were the Advocates for Faith and Freedom, Alliance Defense Fund, American Center for Law and Justice, American Unity Legal Defense Fund, Americans United for Life, Atlantic Legal Foundation, Becket Fund for Religious Liberty, Center for Individual Rights, Claremont Institute Center for Constitutional Jurisprudence, Concerned Women for America, Defenders of Property Rights, European Centre

for Law and Justice, Family Research Council, Foundation for Moral Law, Institute for Justice, Judicial Watch, Landmark Legal Foundation, Mountain States Legal Foundation, National Law Center for Children and Families, National Federation of Independent Business Legal Foundation, National Legal Foundation, New England Legal Foundation, Northwest Legal Foundation, Oregonians in Action Legal Center, Pacific Legal Foundation, Southeastern Legal Foundation, Thomas More Law Center, Thomas More Society, Inc., and Washington Legal Foundation.

19. See, e.g., Institute for Justice, *Training Programs,* http://www.ij.org/students/body .html (indicating that "[s]ummer clerkships are highly competitive" and noting that while most students arrange their own funding, "some paid positions are available."); and Center for Individual Rights, http://www.cir-usa.org/intern.html (inviting applications for a limited number of paid summer clerkships for students with "first-rate legal academic credentials, a commitment to public interest work, and excellent writing skills.").

20. These are estimates to the nearest $0.1 million, based on income figures provided by the organizations' Internal Revenue Service Form 990s, which tax-exempt entities are required to file. The year 2005 was the most recent tax year for which comprehensive data were available.

21. These organizations included the American Center for Law and Justice, Liberty Counsel, Public Advocate of the United States, Conservative Legal Defense and Education Fund, Lincoln Institute for Research and Education, Traditional Values Coalition, Traditional Values Education and Legal Institute, Concerned Women for America, Family Research Council, Focus on the Family, Center for the Original Intent of the Constitution, and United Families International. Two libertarian organizations, the Cato Institute and the Institute for Justice, filed briefs in support of petitioners.

22. These opponents included the Claremont Institute Center for Constitutional Jurisprudence, Center for Individual Freedom, Focus on the Family, Family Research Council, Alliance Defense Fund, American Legion, Christian Legal Society, Concerned Women for America, Wallbuilders, Inc., Catholic League for Religious and Civil Rights, Thomas More Law Center, Liberty Counsel, Pacific Research Institute, Pacific Legal Foundation, and Rutherford Institute.

23. In the seventies, Kenney Hegland predicted that the goals of various liberal public interest advocates might sometimes conflict: "Insistence on strict conservation measures will raise the costs of low cost housing; curtailment of pollution causing power generation will mean that many poor families will go without heat" (Hegland 1971, 809). Today, the number and variety of conflicts among public interest law groups and their representatives are much greater. As Judge Patricia Wald recently noted, "across the legal landscape we see environmentalists opposing Native Americans; labor unionists vying with racial and ethnic minorities and women's advocates; pro-choicers pitted against right-to-lifers, all perceiving themselves as public interest lawyers" (Wald 1995, 6).

24. Edwin Meese III, who helped found the Pacific Legal Foundation and the Crime Victims' Legal Advocacy Institute, served as U.S. attorney general in the Reagan Administration and was one of President Reagan's most important advisors. Michael Horowitz, author of the "Horowitz Report," served as general counsel for the Office of Management and Budget from 1981 to 1985. Alan Sears, president and general counsel of the Alliance

Defense Fund, served as executive director of the Attorney General's Commission on Pornography (Kowet 1991). Michael Carvin, a founding board member of the Center for Individual Rights, was special assistant to the deputy assistant attorney general and deputy assistant attorney general, Civil Rights Division in 1983–87, and deputy assistant attorney general, Office of Legal Counsel in 1987–88 (*Martindale-Hubbell* 2004). Joseph Morris, founder of Lincoln Legal Foundation, served as general counsel of the United States Office of Personnel Management (formerly the U.S. Civil Service Commission) and later as chief of staff and general counsel of the United States Information Agency and assistant attorney general of the United States in charge of the Office of Liaison Services (*Chicago Sun-Times* 1994). Clint Bolick, founder of the Institute for Justice, was assistant to Assistant Attorney General William Bradford Reynolds in 1987–88 and special assistant to Equal Employment Opportunity Commission commissioner Ricky Silberman (wife of D.C. Circuit judge Lawrence Silberman) 1985–86 (*Who's Who* 2007–2008). William Mellor, cofounder of the Institute for Justice, served in the Reagan Administration as deputy general counsel for legislation and regulations in the Department of Energy. Roger and Nancie Marzulla, founders of Defenders of Property Rights, both served in the Reagan Justice Department; he as assistant attorney general for the Land and Natural Resources Division and she in the Civil Rights Division (Moore 1992; *Real Estate/Environmental Liability News* 1997). Robert Showers, Jr., founder of the National Law Center for Children and Families, served as special assistant to Attorney General Edwin Meese in 1986 and acting deputy assistant attorney general in 1988 (*Who's Who* 2007–2008). C. Boyden Gray, founder of the Committee for Justice, served as counsel to the president in 1989–1993 and counsel to the vice president in 1981–89 (*Who's Who in American Law* 2007–2008). William Bennett served as head of the National Endowment for the Humanities and Secretary of Education in the Reagan Administration and as "drug czar" in the first Bush Administration (Colford 1998). Kevin (Seamus) Hasson, founder of the Becket Fund, served as attorney-advisor for the U.S. Department of Justice's Office of Legal Counsel, where his responsibilities included advising the Reagan Administration on church/state issues. Steven Calabresi, cofounder of the Federalist Society, served as special assistant to Attorney General Edwin Meese after clerking for Judge Ralph Winter and Justice Anton Scalia (Bossert 1997). Two other founders of the Federalist Society, Lee Liberman Otis, and David McIntosh, also worked for Ed Meese in the Reagan Justice Department, and Otis served in the White House under President G. W. Bush, assisting C. Boyden Gray in screening judicial nominees (Bossert 1997).

CHAPTER THREE

1. In their analyses of national policy making in the mid-twentieth century, Horsky (1952, 10–11) and Mills (1956, 288–89) characterized lawyers as professional mediators among major private and governmental institutions. But the ties between corporate lawyers "from the great law factories" and other elites in national politics (Mills 1956, 289) fifty years ago may not exist among lawyers for the larger set of interests that make up today's conservative coalition. In addition to the economic concerns analyzed in Mills's *The Power Elite*, American politics today revolves around moral and symbolic

issues such as abortion, school prayer, and affirmative action, and each of those controversies draws lawyers into the fray. In his afterword in a recent edition of *The Power Elite,* Alan Wolfe observed,

> In his emphasis on politics and economics, Mills underestimated the important role that symbolic and moral crusades have had in American life, including McCarthy's witch-hunt after communist influence. Had he paid more attention to McCarthyism, Mills would have been more likely to predict such events as the 1998–99 effort by Republicans to impeach President Clinton, the role played by divisive issues such as abortion, immigration, and affirmative action in American politics, and the continued importance of negative campaigning. (377)

2. Examples of mediator organizations include the American Conservative Union, Hudson Institute, Federalist Society for Law and Public Policy Studies, Heritage Foundation, Ethics and Public Policy Center, American Enterprise Institute, Committee for Justice, and Claremont Institute.

Omitted from the analysis were six organizations that could not be clearly assigned, each of which was active on only one issue.

3. In Table 3.1, the characteristics of a lawyer who represented organizations in more than one category were counted in all of the categories in which those lawyers appeared. To the extent that lawyers served across organizational categories, therefore, differences among the categories would be reduced.

4. The "elite" category included schools ranked in the top 7 in the 2000 *U.S. News & World Report* rankings, and the "prestige" category included those ranked from 8 to 20. The "regional" category included those ranked from 21 to 50 (*U.S. News & World Report* 2000).

5. This analysis reflected total foundation grants for the period from 1996 through 1998.

6. This analysis assumes some ideological affinity among lawyers if they worked for the same organizations (Breiger 1974; Feld 1981). But lawyers employed by the same organizations might not always share an ideology or issue agenda; some may represent organizations for hire without identifying with the groups' goals. As demonstrated in chapter 4, this is more likely for lawyers who represent business associations than for those who represent expressive groups such as the American Center for Law and Justice or the Cato Institute.

7. We constructed a matrix in which each lawyer was recorded as either active or inactive in each organization. This method did not assess the degree of lawyers' involvement.

Most lawyers were *not* involved in most of the organizations. Therefore, in analyzing the matrix, we used the Jaccard measure, which ignores similarity between lawyers that is attributable solely to their joint inactivity.

8. Since there are fifty-four lawyers, there are 2862 pairs. The challenge was to describe accurately the distance (i.e., similarity) between lawyer A and lawyer B while also accurately depicting the distance between A and C, B and C, A and D, and 2858 other pairs. Such a representation can be achieved perfectly in a solution with one dimension fewer than the number of cases analyzed. We could have perfectly represented all

the relationships among fifty-four lawyers in a solution with fifty-three dimensions, but such a space would have been difficult to comprehend. If the structure of relationships among the lawyers' constituencies were highly systematic—perhaps principally determined by two or three major variables that separate them into categories—it would be possible to produce a satisfactory representation in only two or three dimensions, or possibly even one. The number of dimensions required to depict the relationships within an acceptable limit of stress is an indication of the complexity of the structure of relationships.

The solution presented in figure 3.1 has a very low level of stress in two dimensions (.04). In fact, a solution with only one dimension would fit the data quite well (.08 stress). These relationships appear then to be highly structured by some organizing principle. Figure 3.1 presents the two-dimensional solution because the additional dimension adds interesting nuance.

Twenty-eight of the eighty-one organizations had no representative among these most active lawyers. Therefore, the analysis was based on affiliations with a total of fifty-three organizations.

9. McConnell was affiliated with the American Insurance Association as well as Christian and family values organizations, and Dyer served the American Insurance Association, Associated General Contractors of America, and U.S. English. There was otherwise no overlap in the lawyers working with the two broad constituencies.

10. These five lawyers are Charles Cooper, Theodore Olson, William Bennett, Edwin Meese III, and Edward Warren. In the Reagan Administration, Meese served as U.S. attorney general and was one of President Reagan's most trusted advisors. Bennett served as Reagan's chair of the National Endowment for Humanities (1981–85) and Secretary of Education (1985–88) and as President Bush I's "drug czar." Olson served as solicitor general from 2001 through 2004, although in the period reflected in Figure 3.1, he was in private practice with Gibson, Dunn and Crutcher. Cooper served as assistant attorney general, Office of Legal Counsel (1985–88), and as deputy assistant attorney general, Civil Rights Division (1982–85). Warren was a prominent member of a large law firm, Kirkland and Ellis.

11. All of the lawyers in the core of the figures (as well as McConnell, who is also close to the center of the space) were affiliated with the Ethics and Public Policy Center, which was established in 1976 "to clarify and reinforce the bond between the Judeo-Christian moral tradition and the public debate over domestic and foreign policy issues" and "to foster a wiser moral and political debate across ideological barricades." Meese serves as Ronald Reagan Distinguished Fellow in Public Policy and Chairman of the Center for Legal and Judicial Studies at the Heritage Foundation, whose mission is "to formulate and promote conservative public policies based on the principles of free enterprise, limited government, individual freedom, traditional American values, and a strong national defense." In that capacity, Meese convenes regular meetings of lawyers representing organizations that pursue the agendas of the various constituencies of the coalition. Four lawyers in the core of Figure 3.1—Meese, Cooper, Warren, and Olson—also were active in the Federalist Society, whose mission statement claims that it "has created a conservative and libertarian intellectual network that extends to all levels of the legal community." Olson and Meese served on the Board of Visitors, Cooper served as chair of the Civil

Rights Practice Group, and Warren chaired the Administrative Law and Regulation Practice Group.

12. Although there are no comprehensive data on lawyers for liberal causes, piecemeal data suggest that women are much better represented among such lawyers than they are among lawyers for conservative causes. The American Bar Foundation's *Lawyer Statistical Report* found that women were overrepresented in legal aid and public defender positions; they made up 44 percent of all such lawyers (Carson 2004, 9–10). The *After the JD* study, an ambitious project on lawyer careers, found in a large sample of law graduates admitted to the bar in 2000 that 77 percent of lawyers in the public interest field were women (Sterling, Garth, and Dinovitzer 2007). However, the absence of comprehensive data on public interest lawyers makes detailed comparisons between public interest lawyers of the Left and Right difficult.

13. The same lawyer remembered "very distinctly driving home at noon from law school on January 22, 1973, when I was a senior in law school and hearing the radio reports [on *Roe v. Wade*]. . . . I didn't think that it would turn out that way. . . . "

14. Two of the three Catholics were affirmative action opponents. The only Catholic libertarian described himself as a "lapsed Catholic," but he noted that "Catholicism and libertarianism share a number of things in common, because they stress the importance of the individual."

15. The set of organizations represented by the interviewed lawyers overlaps with the set analyzed in the previous research, but it is not the same. As described in more detail in the appendix, the interviewed lawyers worked for fifty-six of the seventy-six organizations identified through two complementary methods. They also represented thirteen additional organizations that appeared on one or both of two published directories of conservative organizations: *The Conservative Directory*, published by RightGuide.com, and the Heritage Foundation's list of "U.S. Policy Organizations" (Wagner, Hilboldt, and Korsvall 2000, 681–789).

16. The abortion category includes only organizations whose primary focus is opposing abortion. But many of the religious conservative groups also were active abortion opponents. One of the organizations served by an interviewed lawyer no longer exists and was therefore excluded from this analysis.

17. Their son, Erik Prince, is the founder and owner of Blackwater, USA, the controversial private contractor that has provided security services for the United States in Iraq and Afghanistan (Dreazen 2007).

18. It is one of the largest of a relatively new type of "faith-based community foundations" to have emerged during the past few years (Heinen 2004).

19. The Bradley Foundation then hired Michael Joyce from the Olin Foundation to raise the foundation's profile (Howell 1995), and he served there until 2001, when he turned over control of the foundation to Michael Grebe (Miller and Ponnuru 2001). According to Grebe, the foundation has distributed more than $500 million since its founding (Miller and Ponnuru 2001). It is known for picking grantees and then funding them annually without requiring much additional evaluation (O'Keefe 2003).

20. The Smith Richardson Foundation, which is based on the Vicks VapoRub fortune, was the sixth largest contributor to the anti-affirmative action and mediator categories. The Olin Foundation, which in the previous research had appeared among the

top five funders in three categories—mediators, libertarians, and business—did not appear at all in table 3.3. It closed its doors in 2005 in accordance with the wishes of its founder, John M. Olin, president of Olin Industries chemical and munitions manufacturing businesses.

21. Except where otherwise noted, the quotations come from the foundations' Web sites.

22. Edward Noble, a trustee of the Noble Foundation, was head of the Synthetic Fuels Corporation, a federal agency, which was on the verge of being abolished in the 1980s when the Heritage Foundation, typically critical of government spending, issued a paper on "salvaging the Synthetic Fuels Corporation" (Easterbrook 1986).

23. Kovner attended Harvard College and later pursued (but did not finish) a Ph.D. at Harvard, where he studied with Edward C. Banfield, a prominent conservative scholar. The Kovner Foundation's other major grant recipients included the Julliard School ($2.5 million in 2002–2003), the Dalton School ($2.25 million in 2002–2003), and the Bronx Preparatory Charter School ($1 million in 2002).

24. Organizations to which Bradley made grants of $100,000 or more in the 2003–2005 period included Americans for Tax Reform, Cato Institute, Center for Education Reform, Competitive Enterprise Institute, Institute for Justice, National Center for Policy Analysis, National Right to Work Legal Defense Foundation, Free Congress Foundation, Washington Legal Foundation, Center for Individual Rights, Center for Equal Opportunity, American Enterprise Institute, Claremont Institute, Ethics and Public Policy Center, Hudson Institute, Heritage Foundation, and Federalist Society.

CHAPTER FOUR

1. Murray Schwartz (1978, 671) and David Luban (1988, 20) have argued that the hired-gun model is the "standard conception of the lawyer's role"—that moral unaccountability is a basic element of the predominant professional ideology (Schwartz 1978, 671–73; Luban 1988, xx). Other commentators have agreed with this assessment (e.g., William H. Simon 1978, 36; Wolfram 1986, 580; Abel 1989, 247; Wasserstrom 1975, 4). However, the empirical foundation for that claim is weak. Although there is substantial evidence that lawyers in large corporate firms do not independently evaluate the social and political consequences of their clients' goals (Kagan and Rosen 1985; Nelson 1985, 436) and rarely decline work on the ground that it conflicts with their personal values (Heinz et al. 2005; Nelson 1988, 254–56), lawyers in other practice types exercise more autonomy in selecting clients (Heinz et al. 2005). Moreover, lawyers' political values generally are closely aligned with their clients' interests (Heinz et al. 2005). It is unclear whether this correlation reflects lawyer self-selection, firms' selective recruitment of lawyers, power relationships between lawyers and clients, or "mutually-reinforcing processes" (Heinz et al. 2005). But if lawyers agree with the positions they take on behalf of clients, they are not hired guns in the sense in which that term ordinarily is used.

2. What I have described as the "quintessential cause lawyer" is a much narrower category than the group who have been called cause lawyers in a large literature on the subject. But scholars have had difficulty agreeing about the boundaries of the "cause lawyer"

concept—the extent to which lawyers must depart from conventional understandings of professional role in order to qualify. They also have disagreed about what types of causes count (see Sarat and Scheingold 1998, 13; Menkel-Meadow 1998, 37) and whether and to what extent professional and financial sacrifice are required (e.g., Menkel-Meadow 1998, 34; Scheingold and Sarat 2004, 96). I take no position on how one should define the term.

3. Several business lawyers participated in pro bono work for conservative causes in addition to pursuing paid work for business clients. One said that he had "carved out a profile as . . . one of a number of articulate, committed, conservative lawyers" and that his mentor at the firm had recognized that his participation in these high-profile controversies would help him build his practice. Regarding a matter he undertook on a contingency basis where there was a good chance he would lose, he said, "My firm counts that as pro bono although we ended up, thank goodness, getting a half-million dollar check because we won the case."

4. Lawyers for causes of the Left have drawn criticism for using clients to pursue causes. See, for example, Hegland (1971), arguing that public interest lawyers sometimes use clients as "tickets" to litigate and that lawyers become unaccountable when they represent interests rather than clients; see also Bell (1976), arguing that NAACP Legal Defense and Education Fund attorneys failed to represent the interests of African-American parents who were dissatisfied with the results of integration; cf. *NAACP v. Button* (Harlan, J., dissenting), warning about ideological conflicts between civil rights lawyers and their clients.

5. This lawyer did not elaborate on what ethical restrictions constrained his conduct, but might have been referring to rules governing conflicts of interest, confidentiality, and relationships with clients—for example, ABA Model Rules 1.7, 1.6, and 1.2.

6. This term was coined by Marc Galanter (1974, 97) to describe actors who "have only occasional recourse to the courts."

7. This religious liberties advocate was one of several who referred to themselves as civil rights lawyers.

8. He professed to "read every word" of the *New York Review of Books* even though it routinely "gores [his] oxes" because it is "powerful and wonderfully written": "I just love it, and I am shaped and changed and rethink on the basis of it."

CHAPTER FIVE

1. Martin (1994) included those who were twenty-three to thirty-five in 1975; Delli Carpini (1986) included those aged twenty-five to thirty-six in 1975; and Davis (1980) defined this generation as those aged twenty-one to thirty-six in 1975.

2. He recalled, "Communists on the student council were always ready to up the ante so we never could succeed; it was a self-fulfilling notion for them. Whatever efforts we made would always fail. And my notion was, America is a place where things are possible. Social justice is possible if you work hard enough."

3. Of seventy-four pieces of testimony before the House and Senate Judiciary Committees by nonprofit advocacy organizations represented by the interviewed lawyers

from 2003 through 2007, there was no overlap in the hearings in which business and social conservative groups participated.

4. He singled out for particular criticism *Wallace v. Joffree,* which struck down a statute allowing prayer in public schools, and *City of Grand Rapids v. Ball* and *Aguilar v. Felton,* which prohibited public school teachers from teaching in parochial schools.

5. The speech drew a strong response from Justice Brennan, who asserted that Meese's position reflected "little more than arrogance cloaked as humility" (Kamen 1985). Brennan noted that determining what the framers meant by constitutional provisions such as prohibitions on "unreasonable searches and seizures," "cruel and unusual punishment," and equal protection was highly problematic and that the Court should not be "captive to the anachronistic views of long-gone generations" (Kamen 1985). Similarly, Justice Stevens asserted that Meese's criticism of the Supreme Court was based on a "somewhat incomplete" understanding of legal history (*Christian Science Monitor* 1985). Legal historians generally took the same view, arguing that "originalism was probably not the original understanding, and that, in any event, the surviving record was too fragmentary to permit definitive conclusions about the Founders' intent" (Kalman 1996, 134).

6. Judge Douglas Ginsburg, chief judge of the U.S. Court of Appeals for the District of Columbia Circuit, an advocate for reinstituting what he calls "the Constitution in Exile," has conceded that this approach would dramatically alter the landscape of constitutional law. It would, he has suggested, require courts to reverse decisions finding a right of privacy (beginning with *Griswold v. Connecticut,* which struck down a statute prohibiting married people from using contraceptives), upholding gun control laws, and limiting capital punishment. It would reverse Supreme Court decisions finding that the Commerce Clause gave Congress broad powers to regulate labor/management relations and to address crime, the environment, civil rights, and workplace conditions (Sunstein 2005, 4).

7. Both Earl Warren and Warren Burger were appointed by Republican presidents. Dwight D. Eisenhower appointed Warren as chief justice in 1953, and Richard Nixon appointed Burger in 1969.

8. Federal Election Commission, Transaction Query by Individual Contributor, http://www.fec.gov/finance/disclosure/norindsea.shtml.

9. One of these lawyers had contributed $1500 to a Democratic candidate, but the amount of that contribution was dwarfed by his contributions ($27,065) to Republican candidates and organizations during the same period.

10. This lawyer's mother's advice notwithstanding, John F. Kennedy was not a lawyer.

11. See, e.g., 42 U.S.C. 2996(a)(7)(1994) (forbidding legal assistance attorneys from participating in political activities such as voter registration); 2996(b)(5) (forbidding legal assistance attorneys from participating in or encouraging public demonstrations, picketing, boycotts, or strikes); 2996(f)(a)(5) (forbidding LSC funds from being used to influence executive orders, administrative regulations, or legislation unless necessary to represent a client); 29963(d)(5) (prohibiting LSC grantees from using non-LSC funds for class action lawsuits).

12. Omnibus Consolidated Rescissions and Appropriation Act 504(a)(17).

13. "NIMBY" is an acronym for "not in my backyard." The term refers to a person who resists development in his own neighborhood.

14. These criticisms are similar to ones voiced by well-known lawyers in the press. Recently, for example, Edward Whelan, president of the Ethics and Public Policy Center, accused the chair of the ABA's judicial evaluations committee of lying, and he explained her behavior as possibly attributable to "the ideological partisanship, intellectual mediocrity, and institutionalized mendacity of the ABA—the ABA's culture, so to speak—[which] tend to degrade those who rise within its ranks" (Whelan 2007).

CHAPTER SIX

1. Gray, Sekulow, Leo, and Meese dubbed themselves "the four horsemen" (Edsall and Milbank 2005, A4).

2. The Jay and Betty Van Andel Foundation was founded by Jay Van Andel, cofounder of Amway Corporation. Van Andel served on the Heritage Foundation's board from 1985 until 2004, the year he died. *Forbes Magazine* estimated his worth to be over $1 billion.

3. The first of these exchanges was between Louisiana State University law professor John Baker, Jr., and the Cato Institute's Timothy Lynch. Participants in the second debate were Roger Pilon, vice president for legal affairs at Cato; Ed Whelan, president of the Ethics and Public Policy Center; Jonathan Adler, Case Western Reserve University law professor; and Curt Levey, general counsel of the Committee for Justice (Federalist Society 2007a).

4. In his remarks, Bryant assured the audience that, despite his suspect association with the trial lawyers' bar, he was a long-time member of the Federalist Society, "not to be some spy in your midst . . . [but] because I actually believe in federalism . . . " (Bryant 2001).

5. Bryant further argued that corporations seek to federalize tort law because they expect to fare better in federal courts than in state courts. He claimed that the effort to eliminate state jurisdiction over tort claims was an affront to "what federalism principles are all about" (Bryant 2001).

6. Practice group chairs in 2007 included Columbia law professor Thomas Merrill as chairman of the Administrative Law Practice Group; University of San Diego School of Law professor Gail Heriot as chairman of the Civil Rights Practice Group; Linklaters' Edward Fleischman as chairman of the Corporations, Securities and Antitrust Practice Group; Kent Scheidegger, director of the Criminal Justice Legal Foundation, as chairman of the Criminal Law Practice Group; James Burling, principal attorney at the Pacific Legal Foundation, as chairman of the Environmental Law and Property Rights Practice Group; Chapman University dean John Eastman, who also runs the Claremont Institute's Center for Constitutional Jurisprudence, as chairman of the Federalism and Separation of Powers Practice Group; Julius Loeser, chief regulatory and compliance counsel, Comerica Bank, as chairman of the Financial Services and Electronic Commerce Practice Group; Ronald Cass, dean emeritus of Boston University Law School, as chairman of the International and National Security Law Practice Group; Eugene Scalia, former labor secretary in the Bush Administration and now partner at Gibson, Dunn

and Crutcher (and son of U.S. Supreme Court justice Antonin Scalia), as chairman of the Labor and Employment Practice Group; and Raymond Gifford, president of the Progress and Freedom Foundation, as chairman of the Telecommunications and Electronic Media Practice Group. Practice committee chairmen elect included Kevin Hasson, director of the Becket Fund (Religious Liberties Practice Group), and Kenneth Starr, dean of Pepperdine University School of Law (Litigation Practice Group).

7. Olin closed its doors in 2005, in accordance with John Olin's wish that the foundation should not outlive him by more than a generation. This condition reflected Olin's fear that "the enemies of free enterprise might gain control of it and undermine its goals" (Edwards 2005).

8. Cribb served as assistant to the president for domestic affairs in the Reagan Administration and now is president of the Intercollegiate Studies Institute.

9. The names on the list were selected through extensive prior research on the conservative movement (see Heinz, Paik, and Southworth 2003) and through consultation with knowledgeable informants in the field. All of the lawyers on the list worked for one of the eighty-six organizations identified through the methods described in chapter 1.

10. The arrows show the connections. Some of the arrows have a point at one end but not the other because not all of the reported ties are reciprocated.

The locations of the notables were computed with a "spring embedding" algorithm (Eades 1984; Kamada and Kawai 1991; for a review, see Freeman 2005 and Moody, McFarland, and Bender-deMoll 2005).

11. One business lawyer expressed doubts about whether the Federalist Society really embraced him and his clients' interests: "Certainly I think federal preemption of state tort law is important, and for [Federalist Society members] that's a struggle. To the extent that they represent businesses in their private law practices, preemption is something that they have to advance, and yet I don't think it's consistent with the underpinnings of the organization. I've never had anything to do with the Federalist Society itself." Another lawyer had briefly served as a practice group chair but said that he had been "just kind of a figurehead" and had served "only because they requested that I do it." Another business lawyer reported that she "deal[s] very little with the Federalist Society."

12. This finding is consistent with previous research demonstrating that religious conservative groups used fewer lawyers than business and libertarian groups (Heinz, Paik, and Southworth 2003).

13. Records of testimony submitted to federal committees by the organizations represented by the interviewed lawyers from January 2003 through August 2007 are consistent with this conclusion. Mediator organizations testified in hearings with organizations representing each of the major constituencies: in fifteen sets of hearings with libertarian groups, seven with business organizations, and three with social conservative groups. Thus, mediator organizations provided support to each of the major constituencies, but they more reliably took up the legislative priorities of libertarian and business interests than those of social conservatives.

CHAPTER SEVEN

1. Scheingold wrote,

> The political approach . . . prompts us to approach rights as skeptics. Instead of thinking of judicially asserted rights as accomplished social facts or as moral imperatives, they must be thought of, on the one hand, as authoritatively articulated goals of public policy and, on the other, as political resources of unknown value in the hands of those who want to alter the course of public policy. The direct linking of rights, remedies, and change that characterizes the *myth of rights* must, in sum, be exchanged for a more complex framework, the *politics of rights,* which takes into account the contingent character of rights in the American system. (6–7)

2. At first glance, Scheingold's "politics of rights" seems an inapposite frame for analyzing conservative and libertarian lawyers' understanding of the relationship among rights, law, and politics. Scheingold defines the concept in terms of movements to improve prospects for "oppressed" people (2004, 132), and his preface to the second edition of *The Politics of Rights* suggests that studying causes of the Right is useful primarily for understanding "how the politics of rights can go wrong" (Scheingold 2004, xxxiii). He further argues that "[g]enerally speaking, . . . right-wing cause lawyers, with the exception of Christian evangelicals, do not need and/or do not believe in the politics of rights" (Scheingold 2004, xl), because they serve clients who are sufficiently powerful to achieve their ends through conventional political processes and through courts that they control. Among right-wing activists, Scheingold suggests, only the Christian Right, who believe that they are in a losing battle with a dominant secular culture, have any use for the politics of rights and its capacity to assist in political mobilization. But if the term "politics of rights" refers to how rights rhetoric is used in the various arenas in which law and policy are negotiated and, even more broadly, as Scheingold suggests elsewhere in the book, as "the interplay between ideology and action in American politics" (83), there is much to investigate here.

3. These sources may not have captured some lawyers who served as outside advisors and/or patrons.

4. The retirement of Justice Sandra Day O'Connor, the appointments of Justices Alito and Roberts, and the Supreme Court's holding in *Gonzales v. Carhart* are likely to spur more litigation by abortion opponents.

5. For purposes of analyzing patterns of conflict and cooperation in Supreme Court litigation, I searched for briefs filed from January 1, 2003, through July 1, 2007.

6. I included as a "split" any instance in which at least one organization in a category opposed at least one organization in another category.

7. A religious liberties advocate, for example, said that his work included "writing and researching, education, constituent service, work done with Congress and the administration, [and] filing briefs in the Supreme Court and other courts. . . . " A lawyer in another Christian organization said that he was responsible for all litigation and policy work for his office, including briefs, position papers, legislation, and rule making. A por-

nography opponent asserted that there were "three power buttons: judicial, legislative, and administrative" and that he and his colleagues "like to push all three." A religious liberties advocate stated, "We litigate. We do amicus briefs. We do legislative advocacy, and we do what I'll call public education or public information." A business lawyer said that he files briefs, writes law review articles, testifies before legislatures, litigates, and counsels clients. Another business advocate said when his clients came to him with a problem, "I'd figure out a way or almost die trying, of putting a coalition together, of getting the right people, raising money, having a public relations segment there, having a political segment there." A libertarian described himself as "a full-service guy" for a libertarian group; his work for them included writing briefs, consulting, and public speaking. Another libertarian emphasized that "public interest law involves the strategic use of litigation and all appropriate related means to achieve the aims of the client and the cause. . . . "

8. I did not ask lawyers about the allocation of decision-making authority between themselves and their clients, but several lawyers commented on the issue. One, who represented many individual clients, said that he typically involved clients in basic questions about "whether a case [is] filed, what claims you're gonna make, are you gonna appeal or not, whether you settle or not." A lawyer who handled large impact work said, "The clients are really not in my cases consulted in strategic decisions. It would be like having a scientist asking me what I think about physics. A lot of our clients are low income and really have no familiarity with the law." These comments are consistent with Heinz and Laumann's conclusion that differences in professional autonomy among lawyers are attributable primarily to differences in the market power and sophistication of their clients (1982, 108–9, 336–37). For a discussion of the relationship between client control, professional power, and practice setting in civil rights and poverty practice, see Southworth (1996) and sources cited therein.

9. This lawyer noted that he had the same background as the think tank's leaders and therefore that "our thinking on these things is almost unstated."

10. Several lawyers also said that they worked to maintain some independence from their financial supporters. One libertarian said, "It is very important that in your fundraising strategy you convince people to buy into your mission, not you buying into their hot buttons." The founder of another litigation group recalled that he and his cofounder were determined to avoid "a situation where the fund-raising drives case selection" and where they would be driven to "write letters to scare your traditional blue-haired old lady into giving money. Wild-eyed radicals are at the door, and unless you give us money . . . we're not going to be able to stop them from converting your kids into Marxist animals, and things like that." Another emphasized that it was critical to him that "principles would dictate funding."

CHAPTER EIGHT

1. As of October 2007, 694 of the 1275 judges on the federal bench (54 percent) were appointed by presidents Reagan, George H. W. Bush, or George W. Bush, and another eighty-two (6 percent) were appointed by presidents Nixon and Ford. These statistics

were compiled from data posted on the Web site for the Federal Judicial Center: http://www.fjc.gov/public/home.nsf/isigbar_standalone!OpenPage.

2. Many of them view the other Republican appointees, especially Justice Kennedy, as irredeemable activists. Kennedy wrote the now infamous opinion in *Lawrence v. Texas*, which earned the disdain of conservatives not only for its conclusion that homosexual conduct is constitutionally protected but also for its citation of international law. He drew the wrath of social conservatives again in *Roper v. Simmons* by stating that it "is proper [to] . . . acknowledge the overwhelming weight of international opinion against the juvenile death penalty . . . " (543 U.S. 551, 578).

3. The National Right to Life Committee's Web site states that, like *Dred Scott*, which "denied citizenship to an entire class of people based on race," *Roe v. Wade* "[d]enied personhood to an entire class of people based on development." Just as *Dred Scott* found that "[p]roperty rights of slaveholder trump the interests of the slave, who has no rights," *Roe v. Wade* similarly held that "[p]rivacy rights of mother trump the interests of the unborn child, who has no rights" (National Right to Life Committee 2006).

4. In the late 1990s, when Tulane Law School's environmental law clinic represented a community group in its attempt to stop the building of a large chemical plant, business groups, members of the Louisiana bar, and the governor pressured Tulane to rein in its clinic and amend student practice rules to prevent such work in the future (Kuehn 2000). More recently, a suit filed by an international human rights clinic at St. Mary's University School of Law on behalf of more than fifty religious, human rights, and labor groups— alleging that the Mexican government had failed to comply with occupational health and safety laws—generated a similar reaction (Kuehn and Joy 2003).

5. One prominent conservative described some tension between the goals of increasing the representation of conservatives on law faculties and remaking the federal judiciary because conservatives have "left law schools and gone onto the bench as quickly as we could appoint them."

6. The ABA's Law Firm Pro Bono Challenge calls on firms to commit 3–5 percent of their billable hours to pro bono (Cummings 2004, 40–41).

7. Tierney quotes Nick Gillespie, the editor of *Reason*: "We're the long-suffering, battered spouse in a dysfunctional political marriage of convenience. . . . Most of the libertarians I know have given up on the G.O.P. The odds that we'll stick around for the midterm election are about as good as the odds that Rick Santorum will join the Village People" (Tierney 2006).

8. Some libertarian groups side with business interests more frequently than others. The Washington Legal Foundation is an especially reliable business ally.

9. Libertarian groups occasionally came to the aid of social conservatives on education and First Amendment issues. In *Zelman v. Simmons-Harris* (2002), for example, advocates for religious conservative and libertarian legal advocacy organizations filed briefs in support of Cleveland's school choice program, which would allow parents to use government funds to attend religious schools. In *U.S. v. American Library Association* (2003), the American Civil Rights Union took religious conservatives' side in a First Amendment challenge to the filtering provisions of the Children's Internet Protection Act, and in *Elk Grove v. Newdow* (2004), the Pacific Legal Foundation and Pacific Research Institute argued against the claim that the Pledge of Allegiance violated the Estab-

lishment and Free Exercise Clauses of the First Amendment. In *Locke v. Davey* (2004), the Institute for Justice, Center for Education Reform, and Cato Institute supported social conservative groups in challenging a restriction that prevented a student from using state scholarship funds to pursue a degree in theology. In *Scheidler v. NOW* (2006), the Center for Individual Rights supported social conservative groups sued for protesting at abortion clinics. And in *Rumsfeld v. Forum for Academic and Institutional Rights* (2006), various Christian groups and the Center for Individual Rights opposed a claim by law schools and law faculties that the Solomon Amendment, which ties federal funding to universities to giving military recruiters equal access, infringed on its members' First Amendment freedoms of speech and association.

Libertarian groups also frequently teamed up with business organizations on regulatory matters. In *Rapanos v. Army Corp of Engineers* (2006), for example, the Pacific Legal Foundation, Mountain States Legal Foundation, and Cato Institute joined dozens of industry groups in challenging the jurisdiction of the U.S. Army Corps of Engineers to regulate wetlands under the Clean Water Act. In *Pacificare Health Systems v. Book*, 538 U.S. 401 (2002), the Pacific Legal Foundation sided with the National Association of Manufacturers and the U.S. Chamber of Commerce on the enforceability of arbitration agreements.

10. Stimson has since joined the Heritage Foundation's Center for Legal and Judicial Studies as a senior legal fellow (Heritage Foundation 2007).

11. Kevin den Dulk has suggested that a string of litigation defeats for Protestant evangelicals could begin a cycle of disengagement from politics and legal advocacy (den Dulk 2001, 6).

12. ACS executive director Lisa Brown served as counsel to Vice President Gore during the Clinton Administration.

13. Some continue to champion the idea that lawyers are obliged to uphold the integrity of the processes in which they participate and to contribute toward improving them, but the dominant view appears to be that lawyers are little different from other high-status occupational groups. According to this conception, lawyers are essentially agents for their clients, with few public obligations beyond obeying unambiguous commands of law (Gordon 2000).

14. Tocqueville claimed that lawyers made government more responsive to populist elements while curbing democracy's excesses (Tocqueville 1835, 283–90), and Halliday has suggested that lawyers' shared professional interests, distinctive ideology, and culture of professionalism might enable them to find common ground among people of diverse backgrounds and values (1987, 47).

15. It also would require creating an infrastructure of a different sort than the one described in chapter 2—a set of institutions devoted to promoting reasoned debate and accommodation across a larger portion of the political spectrum.

References

CASE REFERENCES

Aguilar v. Felton, 473 U.S. 402 (1985).

Ashcroft v. ACLU, 542 U.S. 656 (2004).

City of Grand Rapids v. Ball, 473 U.S. 373 (1985).

United States v. Carolene Products Co., 304 U.S. 144 (1938).

A.B. Coker Co., Inc. v. Charles C. Foti, 2006 U.S. Dist. LEXIS 82537 (W.D. La.)

Cruzan v. Director, Mo. Dept. of Health, 497 U.S. 261 (1990).

Dred Scott v. Sandford, 60 U.S. (19 How.) 393 (1857).

Elk Grove Unified School District v. Newdow, 542 U.S. 1 (2004).

Employment Division v. Smith, 494 U.S. 872 (1990).

FEC v. Wisconsin Right to Life, Inc., 127 S. Ct. 2652 (2007).

Goldberg v. Kelly, 397 U.S. 254 (1970).

Gonzales v. Carhart, 127 S. Ct. 1610 (2007).

Gonzales v. Oregon, 546 U.S. 243 (2006).

Good News Club v. Milford Central School, 533 U.S. 98 (2001).

Granholm v. Heald, 544 U.S. 460 (2005).

Gratz v. Bollinger, 539 U.S. 244 (2003).

Griswold v. Connecticut, 381 U.S. 479 (1965).

Grutter v. Bollinger, 539 U.S. 306 (2003).

Hamdan v. Rumsfeld, 548 U.S. 557 (2006).

Hamdi v. Rumsfeld, 542 U.S. 507 (2004).

Hill v. Colorado, 530 U.S. 703 (2000).

Keller v. State Bar of California, 496 U.S. 1 (1990).

Kelo v. City of New London, 546 U.S. 807 (2005).

Lamb's Chapel v. Center Moriches Union Free School District, 508 U.S. 384 (1993).

Lawrence v. Texas, 539 U.S. 558 (2003).

Locke v. Davey, 540 U.S. 712 (2004).

McConnell v. FEC, 540 U.S. 93 (2003).

Miller v. California, 413 U.S. 15 (1973).

Miranda v. Arizona, 384 U.S. 436 (1966).

Morse v. Frederick, 127 S. Ct. 2618 (2007).

NAACP v. Button, 371 U.S. 415 (1963).

Pacificare Health Systems v. Book, 538 U.S. 401 (2002).

Planned Parenthood of Southeastern Pennsylvania v. Casey, 505 U.S. 833 (1992).

Plessy v. Ferguson, 163 U.S. 537 (1896).

Rapanos v. Army Corps of Engineers, 547 U.S. 715 (2006).

Regents of the University of California v. Bakke, 438 U.S. 265 (1978).

Roe v. Wade, 410 U.S. 113 (1973).

Roper v. Simmons, 543 U.S. 551 (2005).

Rosenberger v. Rector, 515 U.S. 819 (1995).

Rumsfeld v. Forum for Academic and Institutional Rights, Inc., 547 U.S. 47 (2006).

Scheidler v. NOW, 547 U.S. 9 (2006).

Slaughterhouse Cases, 83 U.S. (16 Wall.) 36 (1873).

Sole v. Wyner, 127 S. Ct. 2188 (2007).

United States v. American Library Association, 539 U.S. 194 (2003).

United States v. Lopez, 514 U.S. 549 (1994).

Wallace v. Jaffree, 472 U.S. 38 (1985).

Wisconsin Right to Life, Inc. v. Federal Election Commission, 127 S. Ct. 2652 (2007).

Zelman v. Simmons-Harris, 536 U.S. 639 (2002).

STATUTES

Religious Land Use and Institutionalized Persons Act of 2000, 42 U.S.C. 2000 et seq.

Religious Freedom Restoration Act, 42 U.S.C. 2000bb et seq.

GENERAL REFERENCES

Abel, Richard L. 1985. "Lawyers and the Power to Change." *Law and Policy Quarterly* 7: 5.

———. 1989. *American Lawyers.* Oxford: Oxford University Press.

Abramson, Jill. 1986. "Right Place at the Right Time." *American Lawyer* June: 99–100.

Acknowledgements. 1982. *Harvard Journal of Law and Public Policy* 6: vii.

Alfieri, Anthony V. 1991a. "Reconstructive Poverty Law Practice: Learning Lessons of Client Narrative." *Yale Law Journal* 100: 2107–47.

———. 1991b. "Speaking out of Turn: The Story of Josephine V." *Georgetown Journal of Legal Ethics* 4: 619–53.

Allen, Michael Patrick. 1992. "Elite Social Movement Organizations and the State: The Rise of the Conservative Policy-Planning Network." In *Research in Politics and Society: The Political Consequences of Social Networks,* edited by Gwen Moore and J. Allen Whitt, 87–109. Greenwich, CT: JAI Press.

Alliance Defense Fund. 2006. "About Our Founders." http://www.alliancedefensefund.org/about/founder/index.php.

———. 2007a. "Molding Today's Litigators into Tomorrow's Leaders: The Power of the Alliance." http://www.alliancedefensefund.org/whatwedo/litigation/Default.aspx.

———. 2007b. "National Litigation Academy." http://www.alliancedefensefund.org/whatwedo/training/nla.aspx?cid=3151.

———. 2007c. "International Law." http://www.alliancedefensefund.org/issues/Religious-Freedom/InternationalLaw.aspx.

American Center for Law and Justice. 2006. "About the A.C.L.J." http://www.aclj.org/about/aboutm.asp.

———. 2008. "About Chief Counsel." http://www.aclj.org/About/Default.aspx?Section=11.

American Conservative Union. 2005. Brief of Amici Curiae the American Conservative Union and the National Taxpayers Union in Support of Affirmance, Metro-Goldwyn-Mayer Studios, Inc. v. Grokster, 2005 U.S.S.Ct. Briefs LEXIS 240, March 1.

American Constitution Society. 2006a. "Recent ASC Issue Briefs." http://www.acslaw.org/.

———. 2006b. "About the American Constitution Society." http://www.acslaw.org/about/.

———. 2006c. "About the American Constitution Society." http://www.acslaw.org/node/1001.

———. 2006d. "Constitution in the 21st Century." http://www.acslaw.org/c21.

———. 2006e. "Equality and Liberty." http://www.acslaw.org/c21/equalityliberty.

Americans for Effective Law Enforcement. 2004. "About AELE." http://www.aele.org/About.html.

American Enterprise Institute. n.d. "About the American Enterprise Institute." http://www.aei.org/aboutaei.htm.

Archibald, George. 1991. "Mellowing in the Warmth of Establishment Respect." *Washington Times,* December 2, A1.

Aron, Nan. 1989. *Liberty and Justice for All: Public Interest Law in the 1980s and Beyond.* Boulder, CO: Westview Press.

Auerbach, Jerold. 1976. *Unequal Justice: Lawyers and Social Change in Modern America.* New York: Oxford University Press.

Bach, Amy. 2001. "Movin' on Up with the Federalist Society: How the Right Rears Its Young Lawyers." *The Nation,* October 1, 11.

Baldas, Tresa. 2004. "Law School Turf War Ignites: The Federalist Society Vies with Emerging ACS." *National Law Journal* 26: 1.

Barone, Michael. 1984. "Back in Law Enforcement." *Washington Post,* January 24, A13.

Becket Fund. 2007. "About Us." http://www.becketfund.org/index.php/article/82.html.

Bell, Derrick A. 1976. "Serving Two Masters: Integration Ideals and Client Interests in School Desegregation Litigation." *Yale Law Journal* 85: 470–516.

———. 1986. "The Supreme Court 1984 Term Foreword: The Civil Rights Chronicles." *Harvard Law Review* 99: 4–83.

Bellow, Gary. 1977. "Turning Solutions into Problems." *NLADA Briefcase* 34: 106, 108.

———. 1996. "Steady Work: A Practitioner's Reflections on Political Lawyering." *Harvard Civil Rights–Civil Liberties Law Review* 31:297–309.

Berkowitz, Bill. 2006. "Politics-U.S.: Evangelicals Lost Some Clout in Mid-Term Election." *IPS-Inter Press Service,* December 3.

Bezdek, Barbara. 1992. "Silence in the Court: Participation and Subordination of Poor Tenants' Voices in Legal Process." *Hofstra Law Review* 20: 533–608.

Birnbaum, Jeffrey H. 2005. "A Moving Force in Fight for Bush's Judicial Nominees." *Washington Post,* May 24, A15.

Bisharat, George. 1998a. "Right Lawyers for the Right Time." Unpublished manuscript, on file with author.

———.1998b. "Attorneys for the People, Attorneys for the Land." In *Cause Lawyering: Political Commitments and Professional Responsibilities,* edited by Austin Sarat and Stuart Scheingold, 453–86. Oxford: Oxford University Press.

Blanchard, Dallas A. 1994. *The Anti-Abortion Movement and the Rise of the Religious Right: From Polite to Fiery Protest.* New York: MacMillan Publishing Company.

Blodgett, Nancy. 1984. "The Ralph Naders of the Right." *American Bar Association Journal,* May, 71.

Blumenthal, Sidney. 1986. *The Rise of the Counter-Establishment: From Conservative Ideology to Political Power.* New York: Times Books.

Bolick, Clint. 2004. "School Choice: Triumph for Freedom." In *Bringing Justice to the People,* edited by Lee Edwards, 55–84. Washington, DC: Heritage Books.

Bolthouse Foundation. 2006. www.thebolthousefoundation.org.

Bolton, Alexander. 2006. "White House Renews Push for Nominees." *The Hill,* June 7, 1.

Bork, Robert. 1990. *The Tempting of America: The Political Seduction of the Law.* New York: Simon & Schuster, Inc.

———. 2000. "There's No Choice: Dismember Microsoft." *Wall Street Journal,* May 1, A34.

———. 2004. *Address to Rome Conference on "International Law, Democratic Accountability, and Moral Diversity,"* June 13.

———. 2005. "Slouching towards Miers." *Wall Street Journal,* October 19, A12.

Borosage, Robert, et al. 1970. "The New Public Interest Lawyers." *Yale Law Journal* 49: 1069–148.

Bossert, Rex. 1997. "Conservative Forum Is a Quiet Power: ABA Watchdog." *National Law Journal,* September 8, A1.

Bourdieu, Pierre. 1990. *The Logic of Practice.* Stanford, CA: Stanford University Press.

Bradley Foundation. 2006. "The Bradley Foundation's Mission." http://www.bradleyfdn.org/foundations_mission.asp.

Braungart, Richard G., and Margaret M. Braungart. 1986. "Life-Course and Generational Politics." *Annual Review of Sociology* 12: 205–31.

Breiger, Ronald L. 1974. "The Duality of Persons and Groups." *Social Forces* 53: 81–190.

Brint, Steven. 1994. *In an Age of Experts: The Changing Role of Professionals in Politics and Public Life.* Princeton, NJ: Princeton University Press.

Broder, David S. 2005. "From Miers, Telling Words." *Washington Post,* October 6, A27.

Brookhiser, Richard. 1983. "Another Round, Legal Services Corp." *National Review,* 3: 36.

Brown, Jennifer Gerarda. 2004. "Lawyers' Roles in Deliberative Democracy." *Nevada Law Journal* 5: 370–78.

Brown, Steven P. 2002. *Trumping Religion: The New Christian Right, The Free Speech Clause, and the Courts.* Tuscaloosa, AL: University of Alabama Press.

Bryant, Arthur. 2001. "The Conflict between Federalism and Corporate Interests." *Seton Hall Law Review* 31: 734–38.

Buckhorn, Robert F. 1972. *Nader: The People's Lawyer.* Englewood Cliffs, NJ: Prentice-Hall, Inc.

Buckley, William F. 1951. *God and Man at Yale: The Superstitions of "Academic Freedom."* Chicago: Regnery Publishing, Inc.

Bumiller, Elisabeth. 2005. "War Rooms (and Chests) Ready for Court Vacancy." *New York Times,* June 20, A13.

Burke, Thomas F. 2001. "The Rights Revolution Continues: Why New Rights Are Born (and Old Rights Rarely Die)." *Connecticut Law Review* 33: 1259–74.

———. *Lawyers, Lawsuits, and Legal Rights.* Berkeley, CA: University California Press.

Burt, Dan M. 1982. *Abuse of Trust: A Report on Ralph Nader's Network.* Chicago: Regnery Gateway.

Burt, Ronald S. 1992. *Structural Holes: The Social Structure of Competition.* Harvard: Harvard University Press.

Byrnes, Timothy A., and Mary C. Segers, eds. 1992. *The Catholic Church and the Politics of Abortion: A View from the States.* Boulder, CO: Westview Press.

Cahn, Edgar S., and Jean Camper Cahn. 1970. "Power to the People or the Profession?—The Public Interest in Public Interest Law." *Yale Law Journal* 79: 1005–48.

Caldeira, Gregory A., and Samuel C. Patterson. 1987. "Political Friendship in the Legislature." *Journal of Politics* 4: 953–75.

Calmes, Jackie. 2006. "Evangelicals Fire Up the Faithful." *Wall Street Journal,* October 18, A1.

Canellos, Peter S. 2003. "A Call to Order Sounds for Liberals on Message." *Boston Globe,* August 5, 2003, A3.

Cannon, Carl M. 2005. "What Was It about Miers and the Intellectuals?" *National Journal,* November 12, 2005.

Carle, Susan D. 2001. "Historical Perspectives on Pro Bono Lawyering: Re-Envisioning Models for Pro Bono Lawyering: Some Historical Reflections." *American University Journal of Gender Social Policy and Law* 9: 81–96.

Carson, Clara N. 2004. *The Lawyer Statistical Report: The U.S. Legal Profession in 2000.* Chicago: American Bar Foundation.

Carter, Terry. 2003. "A New but Growing Group Seeks to Counter the Influence of the Conservative Federalist Society." *American Bar Association Journal* 39: 50.

Cassidy, John. 2005. "The Ringleader: How Grover Norquist Keeps the Conservative Movement Together." *New Yorker,* August 1, 42.

Cavuto, Neil. 2006. "Interview with Former Deputy Director of the Office of Faith-Based and Community Initiatives." *Global News Wire,* November 17.

Center for Individual Rights. 2000. "Mission Statement." http://www.cirusa.org/mission_new.html.

Chaddock, Gail Russell. 2005. "A Judicial Think Tanks—or a Plot?" *Christian Science Monitor,* August 4, A1.

Chayes, Abram. 1976. "The Role of the Judge in Public Law Litigation." *Harvard Law Review* 89: 1281–311.

Chen, Vivia. 2007. "Shhh! Pro Bono's Not Just for Liberals Anymore." *American Lawyer,* July 9.

Chicago Sun-Times. 1994. "Candidate File." October 23, A25.

Chisolm, Laura B. 1987–88. "Exempt Organization Advocacy: Matching the Rules to the Rationales." *Indiana Law Journal* 63: 201–98.

Christian Science Monitor. 1985. "Supreme Court Justice Rebuts Charges of 'Judicial Activism.'" October 28, 2.

Christianity Today. 1979. "Beyond Personal Piety." November 16, 13.

———. 1981. "Contemporary Civil Climate Threatens Religious Freedoms." February 6, 14, 16.

Chronicle of Philanthropy. 2006. "Awards." May 4, 50.

Cillizza, Chris. 2006. "Conservatives Backing Nominee Look at Graham." *Washington Post,* June 4, A5.

Claremont Institute for the Study of Statesmenship and Political Philosophy. 2007. "Center for Constitutional Jurisprudence." http://www.claremont.org/projects/projectid.31/project_detail.asp.

Clegg, Roger. 2004. "Equality under the Law." In *Bringing Justice to the People,* edited by Lee Edwards, 97126. Washington, DC: Heritage Books.

Clemens, Elisabeth. 1993. "Organizational Repertoires and Institutional Change: Women's Groups and the Transformation of U.S. Politics, 1890–1920." *American Journal of Sociology* 98: 755–98.

Clemetson, Lynette. 2005. "Meese's Influence Looms in Today's Judicial Wars." *New York Times,* August 17, 2005, A1.

Clendinen, Dudley. 1986. "Conservative Christians Again Take Issue of Religion in Schools to Courts." *New York Times,* February 28, A19.

Colford, Paul D. 1998. "Impatience Proves a Virtue for 'Czar' William Bennett." *L.A. Times,* September 3, E7.

Committee for Justice. 2006. "Promoting Constitutionalist Judicial Nominees." http://www.committeeforjustice.org/.

"Constitutional Law for Enlightened Citizens." 2008. http://conlaw.hs/da.org/cms/.

Council for Public Interest Law. 1976. *Balancing the Scales of Justice: Financing Public Interest Law in America.* Washington, DC: The Council.

Coutin, Susan Bibler. 2001. "Cause Lawyering in the Shadow of the State: A U.S. Immigration Example." In *Cause Lawyering and the State in a Global Era,* edited by Austin Sarat and Stuart Scheingold, 117–40. New York: Oxford University Press.

CQ Press and Foundation for Public Affairs. 2005. *Public Interest Group Profiles 2004–2005.*

Crampton, Thomas. 2004. "Using the Courts to Wage a War on Gay Marriage." *New York Times,* May 9, A12.

Crawford, Alan. 1980. *Thunder on the Right: The "New Right" and the Politics of Resentment.* New York: Pantheon Books.

Crenshaw, Kimberle W. 1988. "Race, Reform, and Retrenchment: Transformation and Legitimation in Antidiscrimination Law." *Harvard Law Review* 101: 1331–87.

Culhane, R. McGreggor. 1994. *Federal Land, Western Anger: The Sagebrush Rebellion and Environmental Politics.* Lawrence: University of Kansas Press.

Cummings, Scott L. 2001. "Economic Development as Progressive Politics: Toward a Grassroots Movement for Economic Justice." *Stanford Law Review* 54: 399–493.

———. 2004. "The Politics of Pro Bono." *UCLA Law Review* 52:1–149.

———. 2005. "Mobilization Lawyering: Community Economic Development in the Figueroa Corridor." In *Cause Lawyers and Social Movements,* edited by Austin Sarat and Stuart Scheingold, 302–35. Stanford, CA: Stanford University Press.

———. 2007a. "Critical Legal Consciousness in Action." Unpublished manuscript.

———. 2007b. "The Internationalization of Public Interest Law." *Duke Law Journal* (forthcoming).

Cummings, Scott L., and Ingrid V. Eagly. 2001. "Á Critical Reflection on Law and Organizing." *UCLA Law Review* 48: 443–517.

———. 2006. "After Public Interest Law." *Northwestern University Law Review* 100: 1251–93.

Cunningham, Clark D. 1992. "The Lawyer as Translator, Representation as Text: Towards an Ethnography of Legal Discourse." *Cornell Law Review* 77: 1298–387.

Daniel, Caroline, and Patti Waldmeir. 2005. "Miers Expected to Be President's Terror Ally: Bush Court Nominee Is More Likely to Make Her Mark on the War on Terror Than on Abortion." *Financial Times,* October 15, 7.

Davis, James A. 1980. "Conservative Weather in a Liberalizing Climate: Changes in Selected NORC General Social Survey Items, 1972–1978." *Social Forces* 58: 1129–56.

Delli Carpini, Michael X. 1986. "Stability and Change in American Politics: The Coming of Age of the Generation of the 1960s." New York: New York University Press.

Demerath, Nicholas. 1965. *Social Class in American Protestantism.* Chicago: Rand McNally.

DeMoss, Nancy Leigh. 1986. *The Rebirth of America.* DeMoss Foundation: U.S.

den Dulk, Kevin. 2001. *Prophets in Caesar's Courts: The Role of Ideas in Catholic and Evangelical Rights Advocacy.* Doctoral dissertation. Madison: University of Wisconsin.

———. 2006. "In Legal Culture, but Not of It." In *Cause Lawyers and Social Movements,* edited by Austin Sarat and Stuart Scheingold. Stanford, CA: Stanford University Press.

DeParle, Jason. 2005. "Debating the Subtle Sway of the Federalist Society." *New York Times,* August 1, A12.

Dezalay, Yves, and Bryant Garth. 2001. "Constructing Law out of Power: Investing in Human Rights as an Alternative Political Strategy." In *Cause Lawyering and the State in a Global Era,* edited by Austin Sarat and Stuart Scheingold, 354–81. New York: Oxford University Press.

———. 2002. *The Internationalization of the Palace Wars: Lawyers, Economists, and the Contest to Transform Latin American States.* Chicago: University of Chicago Press.

Diamond, Sara. 1989. *Spiritual Warfare: The Politics of the Christian Right.* Boston, MA: South End Press.

———. 1994. "Watch on the Right: The Religious Right Goes to Court." *Humanist,* May, 35–37.

———. 1995. *Roads to Dominion: Right-Wing Movements and Political Power in the United States.* New York: Guildford Press.

DiMaggio, Paul J., and Walter W. Powell. 1983. "The Iron Cage Revisited: Institutional Isomorphism and Collective Rationality in Organizational Fields." *American Sociology Review* 48: 147–60.

———. 1988. "Interest and Agency in Institutional Theory." In *Institutional Patterns and Organizations: Culture and Environment,* edited by Lynne G. Zucker. Cambridge, MA: Ballinger Publishing Co.

DiMaggio, Paul J., and Walter W. Powell. 1991. Introduction to *The New Institutionalism in Organizational Analysis,* edited by Walter W. Powell and Paul J. DiMaggio, 1–38. Chicago: University of Chicago Press.

Domhoff, G. William. 1983. *Who Rules America Now? A View from the '80s.* Englewood Cliffs, NJ: Prentice-Hall.

Dreher, Rod. 2006. *Crunchy Cons: The New Conservative Counterculture and Its Return to Roots.* New York: Crown Forum.

Dreazen, Yochi. 2007. "Politics and Economics: New Scrutiny for Iraq Contractors— Killing by Blackwater Worker Poses Dilemma for U.S. Authorities." *Wall Street Journal,* May 14, A4.

Drury, John, and Steve Reicher. 2000. "Collective Action and Psychological Change: The Emergence of New Social Identities." *British Journal of Social Psychology* 39: 579–604.

Duxbury, Neil. 1995. *Patterns of American Jurisprudence.* Oxford: Oxford Press.

Eades, Peter. 1984. "A Heuristic for Graph Drawing." *Congressus Numerantium* 42: 149–160.

Eagle Forum. n.d. "Mission." http://www.eagleforum.org/misc/descript.html.

Easterbrook, Gregg. 1986. "Ideas Move Nations." *Atlantic Monthly,* January, 66.

Edsall, Thomas B. 2001. "Federalist Society Becomes a Force in Washington: Conservative Group's Members Take Key Roles in Bush White House and Help Shape Policy and Judicial Appointments." *Washington Post,* April 18, A4.

———. 2005. "Rich Liberals Vow to Fund Think Tanks: Aim Is to Compete with Conservatives." *Washington Post,* August 7, A1.

———. 2006. "White-Guy Rebellion." *National Journal,* November 11.

Edsall, Thomas B., and Chris Cillizza. 2005. "California Groups Steps into Vacuum on the Left." *Washington Post,* October 23, A5.

Edsall, Thomas B., and Dana Milbank. 2005. "The Right's Moment, Years in the Making." *Washington Post,* July 3, A1.

Edwards, Lee. 2004. *Bringing Justice to the People: A Story of the Freedom-Based Public Interest Law Movement.* Washington, DC: Heritage Books.

———. 2005. "Mother's Milk—a Gift of Freedom: How the John M. Olin Foundation Changed America, by John Miller." *National Review,* December 31.

Ellemers, Naomi, Russell Spears, and Bertjan Doosje. 1999. *Social Identity: Context, Commitment, Content.* Oxford: Blackwell.

Empower America. n.d. "About Empower America." http://www.empoweramerica.org/eaAbout/about.jsp.

Engel, David M., and Frank W. Munger. 1996. "Rights, Remembrance, and the Reconciliation of Difference." *Law and Society Review* 30: 7–54.

Epp, Charles. 1998. *The Rights Revolution: Lawyers, Activists, and Supreme Courts in Comparative Perspective.* Chicago: University of Chicago Press.

Epstein, Lee. 1985. *Conservatives In Court*. Knoxville, TN: University of Tennessee Press.

Epstein, Richard. 1988. "The Political Economy of Product Liability Reform." *American Economic Review* 78: 311–15.

———. 1995. *Simple Rules for a Complex World*. Cambridge, MA: Harvard University Press.

Equivel, David R. 1996. "The Identity Crisis in Public Interest Law." *Duke Law Journal* 46: 327–51.

Erlanger, Howard, and Douglas Klegon. 1978. "Socialization Effects of Professional School: The Law School Experience and Student Orientations to Public Interest Careers." *Law and Society Review* 13: 1135.

Evangelical Environment Network. 2007. "What Would Jesus Drive?" http://whatwouldjesusdrive.org/intro.php.

Federalist Society. 1994. *The ABA in Law and Social Policy: What Role?* Washington, DC: Federalist Society for Law and Public Policy.

———. 1996. "ABA Watch: August 1996: From the Editors." August.

———. 2003. "Pro Bono Activity at the AmLaw 100." http://www.fed-soc.org/Publications/Pro%20Bono/probonosurvey.htm.

———. 2004a. "Form 990. Return of Organization Exempt from Income Tax."

———. 2004b. "Our Background." http://www.fed-soc.org/ourbackground.htm (visited May 24, 2004).

———. 2004c. "News: Pro Bono Center Launch." https://www.probonocenter.org/News.aspx?newsid=3 (visited May 24, 2004).

———. 2005. "Why Join?" http://www.fed-soc.org/whytojoin.htm.

———. 2006a. "Our Purpose." http://www.fed-soc.org/ourpurpose.htm.

———. 2006b. "Frequently Asked Questions." http://www.fed-soc.org/Press/FAQs.htm.

———. 2006c. "Participants and Speakers." http://www.fed-soc.org/Press/participants-speakers.htm.

———. 2006d. "Five Questions Debate on *Hamdan v. Rumsfeld*. http://www.fed-soc.org/pdf/hamdan.pdf.

———. 2006e. "News: Pro Bono Center Launch." https://www.probonocenter.org/News.aspx?newsid=3.

———. 2006f. "Five Questions Debate: Immigration Reform." http://www.fed-soc.org/pdf/immigrationreform4.pdf.

———. 2007a. "The Federalist Society Online Debate Series." http://www.fed-soc.org/debates.

———. 2007b. "Why Join." http://www.fed-soc.org/membership/.

———. 2007c. "About Us." http://www.fed-soc.org/aboutus/.

———. 2007d. "Executive Power in Wartime—Event Audio." http://www.fed-soc.org/publications/pubID.205/pub_detail.asp.

Feeley, Malcolm. 1976. "The Concept of Laws in Social Science: A Critique and Notes on an Expanded View." *Law and Society Review* 10: 497–523.

———. 1993. "Hollow Hopes, Flypaper, and Metaphors." *Law and Social Inquiry* 1993: 745–60.

Feld, Scott L. 1981. "The Focused Organization of Social Ties." *American Journal of Sociology* 86: 1015–35.

Ferguson, Thomas, and Joel Rogers. 1986. *Right Turn: The Decline of the Democrats and the Future of American Politics.* New York: Hill & Wang.

Fisher, Marc. 1997. "Unlikely Crusaders: Jay Sekulow, 'Messianic Jew' of the Christian Right." *Washington Post,* October 21, D1.

Fiss, Owen M. 1979. "The Supreme Court 1978 Term—Foreword: The Forms of Justice." *Harvard Law Review* 93:1–58.

Flaherty, Francis J. 1983. "Briefs Swamp Courts, Amicus: A Friend or a Foe?" *National Law Journal,* November 14, 1.

Fletcher, Michael A. 2005. "What the Federalist Society Stands For: Group Is Haven for Conservative Thought." *Washington Post,* July 29, A21.

Florida Times Union. 2002. "Jacksonville Journal." September 25, B3.

Focus on the Family. n.d. "Mission Statement." http://www.family.org/welcome/aboutfof/a0005554.html.

Forbes. 1980. "Defender of the Right." January 21, 86.

Foskett, Ken. 1991. "Religion to the Rescue: Lawyer Rides Fundamentalist Tide from Ruin to Riches." *Atlanta Journal and Constitution,* November 5, D1.

Foundation Center. 2000. *Foundation Grants Index.* New York: Columbia University Press.

Foundation Directory. 2006. New York: Columbia University Press.

Frank, Thomas. 2004. *What's the Matter with Kansas? How Conservatives Won the Heart of America.* New York: Henry Holt & Co.

Freeman, Linton. 1979. "Centrality in Social Networks: Conceptual Clarifications." *Social Networks* 1: 125–39.

———. 2005. "Graphic Techniques for Exploring Social Network Data." In *Models and Methods in Social Network Analysis,* edited by Peter J. Carrington, John Scott, and Stanley Wasserman, 248–69. Cambridge: Cambridge University Press.

Freidson, Eliot F. 1986. *Professional Powers: A Study of the Institutionalization of Formal Knowledge.* Chicago: University of Chicago Press.

Galanter, Marc. 1974. "Why the 'Haves' Come Out Ahead: Speculations on the Limits of Legal Change." *Law and Society Review,* Fall, 95–160.

———. 1983. "Reading the Landscape of Disputes: What We Know and Don't Know (and Think We Know) about Our Allegedly Contentious and Litigious Society." *UCLA Law Review* 31: 4–71.

———. 2002. "The Turn against Law: The Recoil against Expanding Accountability." *Texas Law Review* 81: 285–304.

Garth, Bryant G. 2004. "Noblesse Oblige as an Alternative Career Strategy." *Houston Law Review* 41: 93–111.

Gerber, Paul C. 1981. "The Pacific Legal Foundation: Its Goal is Deregulation." *California Lawyer,* November, 26.

Gilroy, Leonard. 2006. "Taking 'Takings' to the Voters: The California, Idaho, Arizona, and Washington Initiatives." *Weekly Standard,* October 30.

Ginsburg, Douglas H. 2002. "Reflections on the Twenty-Fifth Anniversary of the *Harvard Journal of Law and Public Policy.*" *Harvard Journal of Law and Public Policy* 25:835–38.

Glazer, Nathan. 1975. "Towards and Imperial Judiciary?" *The Public Interest* 41:104–23.

Glendon, Mary Ann. 1991. *Rights Talk: The Impoverishment of Political Discourse.* New York: Free Press.

Goldman, Sheldon. 1997. *Picking Federal Judges: Lower Court Selection From Roosevelt Through Reagan.* New Haven, CT: Yale University Press.

Goldthorpe, John H. and Keith Hope. 1972. "Occupational Grading and Occupation Prestige," in Keith Hope, ed., *The Analysis of Social Mobility: Methods and Approaches.* Oxford: Clarendon Press.

Goodstein, Laurie. 2006. "Disowning Conservative Politics, Evangelical Pastor Rattles Flock." *New York Times.* July 20, A1.

———. 2007. "Evangelical's Focus on Climate Draws Fire of Christian Right." *New York Times.* March 3, A9.

Gordon, Jennifer. 2005. *Suburban Sweatshops: The Fight for Immigrant Rights.* Cambridge, MA: Harvard University Press.

Gordon, Robert W. 1988. "The Independence of Lawyers." *Boston University Law Review* 1: 23–24.

———. 1990. "Corporate Law Practice as Public Calling." *Maryland Law Review* 49: 255–92.

———. 2000. "Why Lawyers Can't Just Be Hired Guns." In *Ethics in Practice*, edited by Deborah Rhode. New York: Oxford University Press.

Gottfried, Paul. 1993. *The Conservative Movement.* New York: MacMillan.

Granfield, Robert. 1992. *Making Elite Lawyers: Visions of Law at Harvard and Beyond.* New York: Routledge.

Green, Tanya L. 2004. "Democrats Continue Killing Bush's Judicial Nominations." http://www.cwfa.org/articledisplay.asp?id=1818&department=legal&categoryid=misc.

Greenhouse, Linda. 2007. "In Steps Big and Small, Supreme Court Moved Right." *New York Times,* July 1, A1.

Hacker, Hans J. 2005. *The Culture of Conservative Christian Litigation.* Lanham, MD: Rowman & Littlefield.

Hacker, Jacob S., and Paul Pierson. 2005. Off Center: The Republican Revolution and the Erosion of American Democracy. New Haven: Yale University Press.

Halliday, Terence D. 1987. *Beyond Monopoly: Lawyers, State Crises, and Professional Empowerment.* Chicago: University of Chicago Press.

———. 1999. "Lawyers and Politics and Civic Professionalism: Legal Elites and Cause Lawyers." *Law and Social Inquiry* 24: 1013–60.

Halpern, Charles R., and John M. Cunningham. 1971. "Reflections on the New Public Interest Law: Theory and Practice at the Center for Law and Social Policy." *Georgetown Law Journal* 59: 1095–126.

Halvorssen, Thor L. 2004. "Freedom of Speech for All." In *Bringing Justice to the People: The Story of the Freedom-Based Public Interest Law Movement.* Washington, DC: Heritage Books.

Haltom, William, and Michael McCann. 2004. *Distorting the Law: Politics, Media, and the Litigation Crisis.* Chicago: University of Chicago Press.

Hamburger, Tom, and Peter Wallsten. 2005. "Business Lobby to Get Behind Judicial Bids: An Industry Group's Plan to Spend Millions Promoting Conservative Nominees

Brings a New Dimension to the Divisive Confirmation Battles." *Los Angeles Times,* January 6, A1.

Hamilton, Marci. 2005. "The First Amendment, Lost and Found: The Establishment Clause during the 2004 Term: Big Cases, Little Movement." *Cato Supreme Court Review,* 159–85.

Handler, Joel F. 1978. *Social Movements and the Legal System: A Theory of Law Reform and Social Change.* New York: Academic Press.

———. 1992. "Postmodernism, Protest, and the New Social Movements." *Law and Society Review* 26: 697–731.

Handler, Joel, et al. 1978a. *Lawyers and the Pursuit of Legal Rights.* New York: Academic Press.

———. 1978b. "The Public Interest Law Industry." In *Public Interest Law: An Economic and Institutional Analysis,* edited by Burton A. Weisbrod, et al., 42–101. Berkeley, CA: University of California Press.

Hansen, Susan. 2006. "Our Lady of Discord: A Schism over Giving away a Pizza Fortune." *New York Times,* July 30, B1.

Harrington, Richard. 1981. "Connie Francis' Crusade." *Washington Post,* December 16, C1.

Harris, Elizabeth. 2006. "The Policy Revolutionaries." *Worth,* May 1. http://www.worth. com/Editorial/Money-Meaning/Philanthropy-The Policy-Revolutionaries-Print.asp.

Hart, Jeffrey. 2005. *The Making of the American Conservative Mind: National Review and Its Times.* Wilmington, DE: ISI Books.

Hassler, Gregory L., and Karen O'Connor. 1985–1986. "Woodsy Witchdoctors versus Judicial Guerrillas: The Role and Impact of Competing Interest Groups in Environmental Litigation." *Boston College Environmental Affairs Law Review* 13: 487–520.

Hatcher, Laura. 2005. "Economic Libertarians, Property, and Institutions: Linking Activism, Ideas, and Identities among Property Rights Advocates." In *The Worlds Cause Lawyers Make: Structure and Agency in Legal Practice,* edited by Austin Sarat and Stuart Scheingold, 112–46. Stanford, CA: Stanford University Press.

Hayek, F.A. 1994. *The Road to Serfdom.* Chicago: University of Chicago Press.

Hegland, Kenny. 1971. "Beyond Enthusiasm and Commitment." *Arizona Law Review* 13: 805–17.

Heineman, Benjamin W., Jr. 1974. "In Pursuit of the Public Interest." *Yale Law Journal* 84: 182–98.

Heinen, Tom. 2004. "Christian Foundation Has Become a Model for Stewardship." *Milwaukee Journal Sentinel,* September 4, 5B.

Heinz, John, Anthony Paik, and Ann Southworth. 2003. "Lawyers for Conservative Causes: Clients, Ideology and Social Distance." *Law and Society Review* 37: 5–50.

Heinz, John P., and Edward O. Laumann. 1982. *Chicago Lawyers: The Social Structure of the Bar.* New York: Russell Sage Foundation.

Heinz, John P., Edward O. Laumann, Robert L. Nelson, and Robert H. Salisbury. 1993. *The Hollow Core: Private Interests in National Policymaking.* Cambridge, MA: Harvard University Press.

Heinz, John P., Robert L. Nelson, Rebecca Sandefur, and Edward O. Laumann. 2005. *Urban Lawyers: The New Social Structure of the Bar.* Chicago: University of Chicago Press.

Heinz, John P., with Monique R. Payne. 2005. "Divided Opinions." In *Urban Lawyers: The New Social Structure of the Bar,* edited by J. Heinz, et al. Chicago: University of Chicago Press.

Heritage Foundation. 2004a. http://www.heritage.org/About/Staff/.

———. 2004b. "Form 990: Return of Organization Exempt from Income Tax."

———. 2005. *The Heritage Foundation 2005 Annual Report.*

———. 2006a. "Our Mission." http://www.heritage.org/about/.

———. 2006b. "About the Heritage Foundation." http://www.heritage.org/About/Departments/coalitionrelations.cfm.

———. 2006c. "Where We Stand: Our Principles on Restoring the Proper Role of the Courts." http://www.heritage.org/research/features/mandate/205/topic.cfm?topic=10.

———. 2006d. *The Heritage Foundation 2006 Annual Report.*

———. 2007a. "The DeVos Center for Religion and Civil Society." http://www.heritage.org/about/departments/devos.cfm.

———. 2007b. "Issues." http://www.heritage.org/research/legalissues/index.cfm.

Hicks, George W. 2006. "The Conservative Influence of the Federalist Society on the Harvard Law School Student Body." *Harvard Journal of Law and Public Policy* 29: 623–718.

Himmelstein, Jerome L. 1990. *To the Right: The Transformation of American Conservatism.* Berkeley: University of California Press.

Hodgson, Godfrey. 1996. *The World Turned Right Side Up: A History of the Conservative Ascendancy in America.* New York: Houghton Mifflin Co.

Holmes, Steven A. 1997. "Political Right's Point Man on Race." *New York Times,* November 16, A24.

Hoover, Dennis R., and Kevin R. den Dulk. 2004."Christian Conservatives Go to Court: Religion and Legal Mobilization in the United States and Canada." *International Political Science Review* 25: 9–34.

Horan, Dennis J., et al, "Editors' Introduction." In *Abortion and the Constitution: Reversing Roe v. Wade through the Courts,* edited by Dennis J. Horan, et al, xi. Washington, DC: Georgetown University Press.

Horowitz, Donald L. 1977. *The Courts and Social Policy.* Washington, DC: Brookings Institution.

Horowitz, Michael. 1980. "The Public Interest Law Movement: An Analysis with Special Reference to the Role and Practices of Conservative Public Interest Law Firms" (unpublished manuscript on file with author).

Hosticka, Carl J. 1979. "We Don't Care What Happened, We Only Care about What Is Going to Happen: Lawyer-Client Negotiations of Reality." *Social Problems* 26: 599–610.

Horsky, Charles A. 1952. *The Washington Lawyer.* Boston: Little, Brown.

Houck, Oliver. 1984. "With Charity for All." *Yale Law Journal* 93: 1415–563.

Howd, Aimee. 1999. "Law Schools vs. Dissenting Views." *Insight in the News,* December 20, 16.

Howell, Leon. 1995. "Funding the War of Ideas." *Christian Century* 112: 701.

Hueter, Ernest. 1986. "Public Interest Law." In *Public Interest Profiles,* 61–65. Washington, DC: Foundation for Public Affairs.

Hulse, Carl. 2006. "Senate Emphasis on Ideology Has Some in G.O.P. Anxious: Appeals for Conservatives Are Seen as Misguided." *New York Times,* June 7, A1.

———. 2007. "Newly in the Minority, G.O.P. Shows Signs of Division on Iraq and Domestic Policies." *New York Times,* January 14, A19.

Hunt, Albert R. 1997. "Politics and People: Daschle Charts Common Ground on Abortion." *Wall Street Journal,* May 22, A15.

Hunt, Scott A., and Robert D. Benford. 1994. "Identity Talk in the Peace and Justice Movement." *Journal Contemporary Ethnography* 22: 488–517.

Institute for Justice. 2006a. "Institute Profile: Who We Are." http://www.ij.org/profile/index.html.

———. 2006b. "IJ's Merry Band of Litigators." http://www.ij.org/merry_band/index.html.

Ivers, Gregg. 1998. "Please God, Save This Honorable Court: The Emergence of the Conservative Religious Bar." In *The Interest Group Connection: Electioneering, Lobbying, and Policymaking in Washington,* edited by Paul S. Herrnson, Ronald G. Shaiko, and Clyde Wilcox, 289–301. Chatham, NJ: Chatham House Publishers, Inc.

Jacobson, Jennifer. 2004. "On Left-Leaning Campuses around the Country, Professors on the Right Feel Disenfranchised." *Chronicle of Higher Education,* September 24, A8.

Jeffries, John C., and James E. Ryan. 2001. "A Political History of the Establishment Clause." *Michigan Law Review* 100: 279–370.

Jenkins, J. Craig. 1987. "Nonprofit Organizations and Policy Advocacy." In *The Nonprofit Sector: A Research Handbook,* edited by Walter Powell, 289–318. New Haven, CT: Yale University Press.

Johnson, Earl. 1974. *Justice and Reform: The Formative Years of the OEO Legal Services Program.* New York: Russell Sage Foundation.

Johnston, David, and Eric Lipton. 2007. "E-Mail Identified G.O.P. Candidates for Justice Jobs." *New York Times,* April 14, A1.

Joy, Peter, and Charles D. Weisselberg. 1998. "Access to Justice, Academic Freedom, and Political Interference: A Clinical Program Under Seige." *Clinical Law Review* 4: 531–37.

Kabaservice, Geoffrey. 2004. *The Guardians: Kingman Brewster, His Circle, and the Rise of the Liberal Establishment.* New York: Henry Holt and Company L.L.C.

Kagan, Robert A., and Robert E. Rosen. 1985. "On the Social Significance of Large Law Firm Practice." *Stanford Law Review* 37: 399–443.

Kalman, Laura. 1996. *The Strange Career of Legal Liberalism.* New Haven: Yale University Press.

Kamada, Tomihisa, and Satoru Kawai. 1991. "A General Framework for Visualizing Abstract Objects and Relations." *ACM Transaction on Graphics* 10: 1–29.

Kamen, Al. 1985. "High Court Is Defended by Brennan; Senses 'Arrogance' in Recent Attacks." *Washington Post,* October 13, A8.

Katz, Jay. 1982. *Poor People's Lawyers in Transition.* New Brunswick, NJ: Rutgers University Press.

Keck, Thomas M. 2004. *The Most Activist Supreme Court in History: The Road to Modern Judicial Conservatism.* Chicago: University of Chicago Press.

———. 2006. "From Bakke to Grutter: The Rise of Rights-Based Conservatism." In *The Supreme Court and American Political Development,* edited by Ronald Kahn and Ken I. Kersch, 414–42. Lawrence, KS: University Press of Kansas.

Keene, David. 2001. "Clinton-Basher Klayman Targets Bush." *The Hill,* April 18.

Kelly, Michael J. 1994. *The Lives of Lawyers: Journeys in the Organization of Practice.* Ann Arbor: University of Michigan Press.

Kennedy, Duncan. 1997. *A Critique of Adjudication.* Cambridge, MA: Harvard University Press.

Kerwin, Kathleen. 2003. "Fists Are Flying over Online Booze." *Business Week,* November 24, 16.

Key, V. O., Jr. 1964. *Politics, Parties and Pressure Groups.* New York: Thomas Crowell.

Kirkpatrick, David D. 2005a. "Despite Recent Gains, Conservative Group Is Wary on Direction of Court." *New York Times,* November 11, A20.

———. 2005b. "Ruling on Property Seizures Rallies Christian Groups." *New York Times,* July 11, A13.

———. 2006a. "Christian Groups Warn G.O.P. That Inaction Could Be Costly." *New York Times,* May 15, A1.

———. 2006b. "Conservatives See Court Shift as Culmination." *New York Times,* January 30, A1.

———. 2006c. "In Alito, G.O.P. Reaps Harvest Planted in '82." *New York Times,* January 30, A1.

———. 2006d. "Two Legal Careers that Diverged May Intertwine Again." *New York Times,* January 9, A16.

———. 2006e. "Republican Woes Lead to Feuding by Conservatives." *New York Times,* October 20, A1.

Klatch, Rebecca E. 1987. *Women of the New Right.* Philadelphia: Temple University.

———. 1999. *A Generation Divided: The New Left, the New Right, and the 1960s.* Berkeley, CA: University of California Press.

Knoke, David. 1990. *Political Networks: The Structural Perspective.* New York: Cambridge University Press.

———. 1993. "Networks as Political Glue: Explaining Public Policy Making. In *Sociology and the Public Agenda,* edited by William J. Wilson, 164–83. Newbury Park, CA: Sage.

———. 1994. "Networks of Elite Structure and Decision Making." In *Advances in Social Network Analysis: Research in the Social and Behavioral Sciences,* edited by Stanley A. Wasserman and Joseph Galaskiewicz, 274–94. Thousand Oaks, CA: Sage.

Koff, Stephen. 1998. "Conservatives Propose Group to Counter ACLU." *Plain Dealer,* October 14, A12.

Komesar, Neil K., and Burton A. Weisbrod. 1978. "The Public Interest Law Firm: A Behavioral Analysis." In *Public Interest Law: An Economic and Institutional Analysis,* edited by Burton A. Weisbrod et al., 80–101. Berkeley, CA: University of California Press.

Kowet, Don. 1991. "PBS Referees a Fine Brawl over Politics of Fig Leaves." *Washington Times,* July 3, E1.

Krishnan, Jayanth K., and Kevin R. den Dulk. 2002. "So Help Me God: A Comparative Study of Religious Interest Group Litigation." *Georgia Journal of International Comparative Law* 30: 233–79.

Kristol, Irving. 1975. "Business and 'The New Class.'" *Wall Street Journal,* May 19, A8.

———. 1977. "On Corporate Philanthropy." *Wall Street Journal,* March 21, A18.

Kronman, Anthony T. 2000. "The Law as a Profession." In *Ethics in Practice: Lawyers' Roles, Responsibilities, and Regulation,* edited by Deborah Rhode, 29–41. New York: Oxford University Press.

Kuehn, Robert R. 2000. "Denying Access to Legal Representation: The Attack on the Tulane Environmental Law Clinic." *Washington University Journal of Law and Policy* 4: 33–147.

Kuehn, Robert R., and Peter Joy, "An Ethics Critique of Interference in Law School Clinics." *Fordham Law Review* 71: 1971–2050.

Kuo, David. 2006a. "Putting Faith before Politics." *New York Times,* November 1, A35.

———. 2006b. *Tempting Faith: An Inside Story of Political Seduction.* New York: Free Press.

Labaton, Stephen. 2001. "High-Stakes Appeal Could Be Last Court Date for Microsoft." *New York Times,* February 26, 2001, C1.

Labor Policy Association. 2001. "About LPA." http://www.lpa.org/lpapublic/insideLPA/AboutLPA_index.htm.

Lampman, Jane. 2005. "Property Rights: Not a Given for Churches." *Christian Science Monitor.* February 16, A15.

Lane, Charles. 2006. "Ginsburg Faults GOP Critics, Cites a Threat from 'Fringe.'" *Washington Post,* March 17.

Lasswell, Harold D. 1936. *Politics: Who Gets What, When, and How.* New York: McGraw-Hill.

———. 1960. *Psychopathology and Politics.* New York: Viking Press.

Lasswell, Harold D., and Abraham Kaplan. 1950. *Power and Society: A Framework for Political Inquiry.* New Haven: Yale University Press.

Laumann, Edward O., Peter V. Marsden, and David Prensky. 1989. "The Boundary Specification Problem in Network Analysis. In *Research Methods in Social Network Analysis,* edited by Linton C Freeman and Douglas R. White, 61–87. Fairfax, VA: George Mason University Press.

Laumann, Edward O., and Franz U. Pappi. 1976. *Networks of Collective Action: A Perspective on Community Influence Systems.* New York: Academic Press.

Levin, Mark R. 2005. *Men in Black: How the Supreme Court Is Destroying America.* Washington, DC: Regnery Publishing.

Levinson, Sanford. 1993. "Identifying the Jewish Lawyer: Reflections on the Construction of Professional Identity." *Cardozo Law Review* 14: 1577–612.

Levitsky, Sandra. 2006. "To Lead with Law: Reassessing the Influence of Legal Advocacy Organizations in Social Movements." In *Cause Lawyers and Social Movements,* edited by Austin Sarat and Stuart Scheingold, 145–63. Stanford, CA: Stanford University Press.

Lewin, Tamar. 2001. "3 Conservative Foundations Are in the Throes of Change." *New York Times,* May 20, A30.

Lewis, Neil. 2006. "A Somber Annual Meeting for Conservative Lawyers." *New York Times,* November 19, A26.

———. 2007. "Justice Department Reshapes Its Civil Rights Mission." *New York Times,* June 14, A1.

Liasson, Mara. 2005. "Miers Nomination Divides Conservatives." *Morning Edition,* October 21.

Liebman, Robert C., and Robert Wuthnow, eds. 1983. *The New Christian Right: Mobilization and Legitimation.* New York: Aldine Publishing Co.

Lindgren, James. 2005. "Assessing Peter Schuck's Diversity in America: Keeping Government at a Safe Distance: Conceptualizing Diversity in Empirical Terms." *Yale Law and Policy Review* 23: 5–13.

Lipset, Seymour Martin. 1986. "The Sources of Public Interest Activism: An Introduction." In *Public Interest Profiles,* 1–8. 5th ed. Washington, DC: Foundation for Public Affairs.

Liptak, Adam. 2006. "Public Comments by Justices Veer toward the Political." *New York Times,* March 19, A22.

Lobel, Orly. 2004. "The Renew Deal: The Fall of Regulation and the Rise of Governance in Contemporary Legal Thought." *Minnesota Law Review* 89: 342–470.

———. 2007. "The Paradox of Extralegal Activism: Critical Legal Consciousness and Transformative Politics." *Harvard Law Review* 120: 937–88.

Lopez, Gerald P. 1992. *Rebellious Lawyering: One Chicano's Vision of Progressive Law Practice.* Boulder, CO: Westview Press.

Lovett, Anthony R. 1992. "Naked Brunch: Bad Vibes and Ugly Food at an Antiporn Seminar." *Playboy,* June, 46.

Luban, David. 1988. *Lawyers and Justice: An Ethical Study.* Princeton, NJ: Princeton University Press.

———. 1990. "Partisanship, Betrayal, and Autonomy in the Lawyer-Client Relationship: A Reply to Stephen Ellmann." *Columbia Law Review* 90: 1004–43.

Luo, Michael, and Laurie Goodstein. 2007. "Emphasis Shifts for New Breed of Evangelicals." *New York Times,* May 21, A1.

MacDonald, Heather. 2006. "This Is the Legal Mainstream? Law Schools Are Stuck in the Sixties." *City Journal,* winter. http://www.city-journal.org/printable.php?id=1926.

Mack, Kenneth. 2005. "Rethinking Civil Rights Lawyering and Politics in the Era Before Brown." *Yale Law Journal* 115: 256–354.

Madden, Dan. 2004. "Big-hearted Butcher Doesn't Hog Wealth. *Tower Topics,* summer. http://www.conceptionabbey.org/TowerTopics/TTSummer04/ochylski.htm.

Mannheim, Karl. 1952. "The Problem of Generations." In *Essays on the Sociology of Knowledge,* edited by Paul Kecskemeti, 276–322. London: Routledge.

Marks, F. Raymond, et al. 1972. *The Lawyer, The Public, and Professional Responsibility.* Chicago: American Bar Foundation.

Martin, Bill. 1994. "Continuity and Discontinuity in the Politics of the Sixties Generation: A Reassessment." *Sociological Forum* 9: 403–430.

Martindale-Hubbell Law Directory. 2004. Summit, NJ: Martindale-Hubbell, Inc.

Mather, Lynn. 1998. "Theorizing about Trial Courts." *Law and Social Inquiry* 23: 897–922.

Mather, Lynn, Craig A. McEwen, and Richard Maiman. 2001. *Divorce Lawyers at Work: Varieties of Professionalism in Practice.* New York: Oxford University Press.

Mattei, Franco, and Richard G. Niemi. 1991. "Unrealized Partisans, Realized Independents, and the Intergenerational Transmission of Partisan Identification." *Journal of
Politics* 53: 161–74,

McAdam, Doug. 1989. "The Biographical Consequences of Activism." *American Society
Review* 54: 744–60.

McCann, Michael W. 1986. *Taking Reform Seriously: Perspectives on Public Interest Liberalism.* Ithaca, NY: Cornell University Press.

———. 1994. *Rights at Work: Pay Equity Reform and the Politics of Legal Mobilization.* Chicago: University of Chicago Press.

McCann, Michael, and Jeffrey Dudas. 2006. "Retrenchment . . . and Resurgence? Mapping
the Changing Context of Movement Lawyering in the United States." In *Cause Lawyers and Social Movements,* edited by Austin Sarat and Stuart A. Scheingold, 37–59.
Stanford, CA: Stanford University Press.

McCann, Michael W., and William Haltom. 2004. "Framing the Food Fights: How Mass
Media Construct and Constrict Public Interest Litigation." Paper presented in the
Center for the Study of Law and Society Bag Lunch Series. University of California,
Berkeley.

McCann, Michael W., and Helena Silverstein. 1998. "Rethinking Law's 'Allurements': A
Relational Analysis of Social Movement Lawyers in the United States." In *Cause Lawyering: Political Commitments and Professional Responsibilities,* edited by Austin Sarat
and Stuart Scheingold, 261–92. New York: Oxford University Press.

McGinnis, John O. 2004. "Federalist Society Colloquium on Democratic Accountability
in International and Supranational Fora." Rome, Italy.

McGinnis, John O., Matthew A. Schwartz, and Benjamin Tisdell. 2005. "The Patterns and
Implications of Political Contributions by Elite Law School Faculty." *Georgetown Law
Journal* 93: 1167–212.

McGirr, Lisa. 2001. *Suburban Warriors: The Origins of the New American Right.* Princeton, NJ: Princeton University Press.

McGough, Michael. 2003. "Sect or Seminar? The Federalist Society Is Both but Sets a
Standard for Legal Debate." *Pittsburgh Post-Gazette,* November 17, A15.

———. 2005. "Legal Societies Hold Divergent Views; Newer American Constitution
Society Modeled on More Conservative Federalist Society." *Pittsburgh Post-Gazette,*
August 14, A12.

McGuire, Kevin T. 1993. "Lawyers and the U.S. Supreme Court: The Washington Community and Legal Elites." *American Journal of Political Science* 37: 365–90.

McKibben, Bill. 2006. "Hot and Bothered: Facing Up to Global Warming. *Christian
Century,* July 11, 28.

Medeiros, Andrew. 2006. "Philanthropic Group to Mark 75th Anniversary." *Daily Record,*
February 4.

Meese, Edwin III. 1992. *With Reagan: The Inside Story.* Washington, DC: Regnery
Gateway.

———. 2004. "Foreword." In *Bringing Justice to the People,* edited by Lee Edwards, i–vi.
Washington, DC: Heritage Books.

———. 2005a. Afterword to *Men in Black: How the Supreme Court Is Destroying America,*
by Mark Levin. Washington, DC: Regnery Publishing.

————. 2005b. *Heritage Guide to the Constitution.* Washington, DC: Regnery Publishing.

Mellor, William H. 2004. "Economic Liberty and Judicial Activism." In *Bringing Justice to the People: The Story of the Freedom-Based Public Interest Law Movement,* edited by Lee Edwards, 85–95. Washington DC: Heritage Books.

Mellor, William H., and Clint Bolick. 1991. "Heritage Lecture 342: The Quest for Justice: Natural Rights and the Future of Public Interest Law." September 10. http://www. ij.org/profile/speech.shtml.

Melton, R.H. 1987. "Meese Sees Religious Freedom War: 'Political Power' Urged at Liberty University." *Washington Post,* May 4, B5.

Mengler, Thomas M. 2003. "Leadership in Legal Education Symposium IV: What's Faith Got to Do with It? (With Apologies to Tina Turner)." *University of Toledo Law Review* 35: 145–52.

Menkel-Meadow, Carrie. 1998. "The Causes of Cause Lawyering: Toward an Understanding of the Motivation and Commitment of Social Justice Lawyers." In *Cause Lawyering: Political Commitments and Professional Responsibilities,* edited by Austin Sarat and Stuart Scheingold, 31–68. New York: Oxford University Press.

Meyer, Eugene. 2004. "The Federalist Society." *In Bringing Justice to the People,* edited by Lee Edwards, 198–200. Washington, DC: Heritage Books.

Meyer, Frank. 1964. *What Is Conservatism?* New York: Holt, Rinehart and Winston.

Miller, Gary, and Norman Schofield. 2003. "Activists and Partisan Realignment in the United States." *American Political Science Review* 97: 245–60.

Miller, John J. 2006. *A Gift of Freedom: How the John M. Olin Foundation Changed America.* San Francisco, CA: Encounter Books.

Miller, John J., and Ramesh Ponnuru. 2001. "Kingsolver Strikes Again." *National Review Online,* November 26.

Miller, Mark. 1995. *The High Priests of American Politics: The Role of Lawyers in American Political Institutions.* Knoxville, TN: University of Tennessee Press.

Mills, C. Wright. 1956. *The Power Elite.* New York: Oxford University Press.

Milner, Neal. 1986. "Dilemmas of Legal Mobilization: Ideologies and Strategies of Mental Patient Liberation Groups." *Law and Policy* 8: 105–29.

Minda, Gary. 1995. *Postmodern Legal Movements: Law and Jurisprudence at Century's End.* New York: New York University Press.

Minow, Martha. 1996. "Political Lawyering: An Introduction." *Harvard Civil Rights-Civil Liberties Law Review* 31: 287–96.

Mnookin, Robert. 1985. *In the Interests of Children: Advocacy, Law Reform, and Public Policy.* New York: W.H. Freeman.

Moody, James, Daniel McFarland, and Skye Bender-deMoll. 2005. "Dynamic Network Visualization. *American Journal of Sociology* 110: 1206–41.

Moore, Stephen. 2000. "'Tax, Spend, and Elect': A Fiscal Free-for-all Congress." *National Review,* November 6, 21.

Moore, W. John. 1992. "Taking on 'Takings.'" *National Journal* 24: 582.

————. 1994. "Collision Course." *National Journal* 26: 2830.

Morgan, Don. 1981. "Conservatives: A Well-Financed Network." *Washington Post,* January 4, A1.

Nader, Ralph. 1969a. "Law Schools and Law Firms." *Beverly Hills Bar Association Journal,* December 8.

———. 1969b. "Crumbling of the Old Order: Law Schools and Law Firms." *The New Republic,* October 11, 20.

———. 1978. "Introduction." In *The Other Government: The Unseen Power of Washington Lawyers,* by Mark J. Green. New York: W.W. Norton & Company, Inc.

Nagel, Robert F. 2001. "Judicial Power and the Restoration of Federalism." *Annals of the American Academy of Political and Social Science* 574: 52–65.

Nagourney, Adam, and David D. Kirkpatrick. 2006. "Conservatives Unsettled about Movement's Future." *New York Times,* February 10, A18.

Nash, George H. 1998. *The Conservative Intellectual Movement in America.* Wilmington, DE: Intercollegiate Studies Institute.

National Law Journal. 2000. "Beachhead for Conservatism." January 3, A11.

———. 2004. "Christian Soldiers." December 4, vol. 36, no. 49.

National Public Radio. 2005. "Business Groups Silent on Miers," *All Things Considered,* October 20.

National Right to Life Committee. 2006. "Mission Statement." http://www.nrlc.org/ Missionstatement.htm.

Nelson, Robert L. 1985. "Ideology, Practice, and Professional Autonomy: Social Values and Client-Relationships in the Large Law Firm." *Stanford Law Review* 37: 503–51.

———. 1988. *Partners with Power: The Social Transformation of the Large Law Firm.* Berkeley: University of California Press.

Nelson, Robert L., and David M. Trubek. 1992. "Arenas of Professionalism: The Professional Ideologies of Lawyers in Context." In *Lawyers' Ideals/Lawyers' Practices: Transformations in the American Legal Profession,* edited by Robert L. Nelson, David M. Trubek, and Rayman L. Solomon, 177–214. Ithaca, NY: Cornell University Press.

Neuhaus, Richard John. 1984. *The Naked Public Square.* Grand Rapids, MI: William B. Eerdmans Publishing Company.

———. 1987. "What the Fundamentalists Want." In *Piety and Politics: Evangelicals and Fundamentalists Confront the World,* edited by Richard J. Neuhaus and Michael Cromartie, 5–18. Washington, DC: Ethics and Public Policy Center.

Niebuhr, Gustav. 1995. "Conservatives' New Frontier: Religious Liberty Law Firms." *New York Times,* July 8, A1.

———. 2006. "Empirical Studies of the Legal Profession: What Do We Know about Lawyers' Lives? The Organization of Public Interest Practice: 1975–2004." *North Carolina Law Review* 84: 1591–621.

Niemi, Richard, and M. Kent Jennings. 1991. "Issues and Inheritance in the Formation of Party Identification." *American Journal of Political Science* 35: 970–88.

Noonan, John T., Jr. 1982. "The Hatch Amendment and the New Federalism." *Harvard Journal of Law and Public Policy* 6: 93–102.

Nownes, Anthony J., and Grant Neeley. 1996. "Public Interest Group Entrepreneurship and Theories of Group Mobilization." *Political Research Quarterly* 49: 119–46.

O'Connor, Karen, and Lee Epstein. 1983. "The Rise of Conservative Interest Group Litigation." *Journal of Politics* 45: 478–89.

———. 1989. *Public Interest Law Groups: Institutional Profiles.* Westport, CT: Greenwood Press.

O'Donnell, Erin. 2006. "Twigs Bent Left or Right: Understanding How Liberals and Conservative Differ, from Conception On." *Harvard Magazine,* January-February, 34.

O'Keefe, Mark. 2003. "Bradley Group Fueling Conservative Agenda." *Christian Century.* November 15, 14.

Olson, Mancur. 1965. *The Logic of Collective Action: Public Goods and the Theory of Groups.* Cambridge: Harvard University Press.

Olson, Susan M. 1984. *Clients and Lawyers: Securing the Rights of Disabled Persons.* Westport, CT: Greenwood Press.

Omang, Joanne. 1980. *Washington Post,* November 16, A6.

O'Shaughnessy, Lynn. 1987. "Boycott Aimed at Stores with X-Rated Films." *Los Angeles Times,* July 12, 1.

Ottaway, David B., and Warren Brown. 1997. "From Life Saver to Fatal Threat: How the U.S. Automakers and a Safety Device Failed." *Washington Post,* June 1, A1.

Pacific Legal Foundation. 2006. "Cases." http://www.pacificlegal.org/list_PLFCases.asp.

Padgett, John F., and Christopher K. Ansell. 1993. "Robust Action and the Rise of the Medici, 1400–1434." *American Journal of Sociology* 98: 1259–319.

Paik, Anthony, Ann Southworth, and John P. Heinz. 2007. "Lawyers of the Right: Networks and Organization." *Law and Social Inquiry* 32: 883–917.

Papajohn, George. 1985. "Town to Bear Cross in Court." *Chicago Tribune,* December 27, C1.

Ponnuru, Remesh. 2005. "Why Conservatives Are Divided." *New York Times,* October 17, A19.

Popeo, Daniel J. 1981. "Public Interest Law in the 80's." *Barron's,* March 2, 27–28.

Posner, Richard. 1972. *Economic Analysis of Law.* Boston: Little, Brown.

———. 1975. "Economic Approach to Law." *Texas Law Review* 53: 757–82.

Postman, David. 2006. "Seattle's Discovery Institute Scrambling to Rebound after Intelligent-Design Ruling." *Seattle Times,* April 26, A1.

Povich, Elain S. 1998. "Memo Details Conspiracy Theory." *Newsday,* January 30, A39.

Powell, Lewis. 1971. "Confidential Memorandum: Attack on American Free Enterprise System." In *Washington Report Supplement,* August 23, 2.

"Preface." 1982. *Harvard Journal of Law and Public* Policy 6: iii–iv.

Provine, Doris Marie. 1986. *Judging Credentials: Nonlawyer Judges and the Politics of Professionalism.* Chicago: University of Chicago Press.

Rabin, Robert. 1976. "Lawyers for Social Change: Perspectives on Public Interest Law." *Stanford Law Review* 28: 207–61.

———. 1986. "Federal Regulation in Historical Perspective." *Stanford Law Review* 38: 1189–253.

Rabkin, Jeremy. 1985. "Public Interest Law: Is It Law in the 'Public Interest'?" 8 *Harvard Journal of Law and Public Policy* 8: 342–47.

Randolph, A. Raymond. 2006. "Before Roe v. Wade: Judge Friendly's Draft Abortion Opinion." *Harvard Journal of Law and Public Policy* 29: 1035–62.

Rand, Ayn. 1968. *The Fountainhead.* New York: Scribner.

Rao, Hayagreeva. 1998. "Caveat Emptor: The Construction of Nonprofit Consumer Watchdog Organizations." *American Journal of Sociology* 103: 912–61.

Rao, Hayagreeva, et al. 2000. "Power Plays: How Social Movements and Collective Action Create New Organizational Forms." *Research in Organizational Behavior* 22: 237–82.

Real Estate/Environmental Liability News. 1997. "Constitutionally Protected Rights and the Government's Power to Acquire Land." May 2.

Regent Law. 2008. "About Regent Law." http://www.regent.edu/acad/schlaw/admissions/abouthome.cfm.

Reinhold, Robert. 1969. "New Lawyers Bypass Wall St." *New York Times,* November 19, A37.

Rhode, Deborah L. 1981. "Why the ABA Bothers: A Functional Perspective on Professional Codes." *Texas Law Review* 59: 689–721.

Ricci, David M. 1993. *The Transformation of American Politics: The New Washington and the Rise of Think Tanks.* New Haven, CT: Yale University Press.

Riley, David P. 1970. "The Challenge of the New Lawyers: Public Interest and Private Clients." *George Washington University Law Review* 38: 547–87.

Risen, James. 2007. "Blackwater Chief at Nexus of Military and Business." *New York Times,* October 8, A6.

Roosevelt, Kermit, III. 2006. *The Myth of Judicial Activism: Making Sense of Supreme Court Decisions.* New Haven, CT: Yale University Press.

Rosenbaum, David E., and Lynette Clemetson. 2005. "In Fight to Confirm New Justice, Two Field Generals Rally Their Troops Again." *New York Times,* July 3, A19.

Rosenberg, Gerald N. 1991. *The Hollow Hope: Can Courts Bring about Social Change?* Chicago: University of Chicago Press.

Rowley, Charles K. 1992. *The Right to Justice: The Political Economy of Legal Services in the United States.* Brookfield, VT: E. Elgar Publishing.

Rozell, Mark J., and Clyde Wilcox. 1996. "Second Coming: The Strategies of the New Christian Right." *Political Science Quarterly* 111: 271–94.

Sabel, Charles F., and William H. Simon. 2004. "Destabilization Rights: How Public Law Litigation Succeeds." *Harvard Law Review* 117: 1015–101.

Sager, Ryan. 2006. The Elephant in the Room: Evangelicals, Libertarians, and the Battle to Control the Republican Party. Hoboken, NJ: John Wiley & Sons.

Salisbury, Robert. 1969. "An Exchange Theory of Interest Groups." *Midwest Journal of Political Science* 13: 1–32.

———. 1984. "Interest Representation: The Dominance of Institutions." *American Political Science Review* 78: 64–76.

Salisbury, Robert H., John P. Heinz, Edward O. Laumann, and Robert L. Nelson. 1987. "Who Works with Whom? Interest Group Alliances and Opposition." *American Political Science Review* 4: 1217–34.

Sarat, Austin, and Stuart Scheingold. 1998. *Cause Lawyering Political Commitments and Professional Responsibilities.* Oxford: Oxford University Press.

———. 2001. *Cause Lawyering and the State in a Global Era.* Oxford: Oxford University Press.

———. 2005. *The Worlds Cause Lawyers Make: Structure and Agency in Legal Practice.* Stanford, CA: Stanford Press.

Sarna, Jonathan D. 2004. "The Battle for the Jewish Vote: A Constituency Up for Grabs." *Boston Globe,* October 10, D12.

Savage, David G. 2005. "The Nation; Engaged in a Very Civil War: The Federalist Society Has Reshaped the Legal System without Ever Going to Court." *New York Times,* November 11, A1.

Schaeffer, Francis A. 1981. *A Christian Manifesto.* Westchester, IL: Crossway Books.

Scheiber, Noam. 2005. "Merit Scholars." *New Republic,* October 17.

Scheingold, Stuart A. 1974. *The Politics of Rights: Lawyers, Public Policy, and Political Change.* Ann Arbor: University of Michigan Press.

———. 2004. *The Politics of Rights.* 2d ed. Ann Arbor, MI: University of Michigan Press.

Scheingold, Stuart A., and Anne Bloom. 1998. "Transgressive Cause Lawyering: Practice Sites and the Politicization of the Professional." *International Journal of the Legal Profession* 5: 209–53.

Scheingold, Stuart A., and Austin Sarat. 2004. *Something to Believe In: Politics, Professionalism, and Cause Lawyering.* Stanford, CA: Stanford University Press.

Schlafly, Phyllis. 2004. *The Supremacists: The Tyranny of Judges and How to Stop It.* Dallas, TX: Spence Publishing Company.

———. 2006. "Conservatives on the March for Private Property." *Copley News Service,* September 29.

Schlesinger, Robert. 2001. "An Energy Chief Fueled by Intellect." *Boston Globe,* May 17, A21.

Schlozman, Kay L., and John T. Tierney. 1986. *Organized Interests and American Democracy.* New York: Harper & Row.

Schneyer, Theodore. 1984. "Moral Philosophy's Standard Misconception of Legal Ethics." *Wisconsin Law Review* 1984: 1529.

———. 1992. "Professionalism as Politics: The Making of a Modern Legal Ethics Code." In *Lawyers' Ideals/Lawyers' Practices: Transformations in the American Legal Profession,* edited by Robert L. Nelson, David M. Trubek, and Rayman L. Solomon, 95–143. Ithaca, NY: Cornell University Press.

Schuck, Peter H. 1993. "Book Review: Public Law Litigation and Social Reform." *Yale Law Journal* 102: 1763–86.

———. 2005. "Leftward Leaning." *American Lawyer,* December 1, 2005.

Schwartz, Murray. 1978. "The Professionalism and Accountability of Lawyers." *California Law Review* 66: 669–97.

Scott, Marvin B., and Stanford M. Lyman. 1968. "Accounts." *American Sociological Review* 33: 46–62.

Sears, Alan E. 2004. "Defending Religious Liberty." In *Bringing Justice to the People: The Story of the Freedom-Based Public Interest Law Movement,* edited by Lee Edwards. Washington, DC: Heritage Books.

Serwer, Andy. 2004. "The Waltons/Inside America's Richest Family." *Time,* November 15, 86.

Shabecoff, Alexa. Telephone conversation with the Assistant Dean for Public Interest Advising, Harvard Law School (November 12, 2004).

Shamir, Ronen, and Sara Chinsky. 1998. "Destruction of Houses and Construction of a Cause: Lawyers and Bedouins in the Israeli Courts." In *Cause Lawyering: Political*

Commitments and Professional Responsibilities, edited by Austin Sarat and Stuart Scheingold, 227–93. New York: Oxford University Press.

Siegel, Reva B. 2004. "Equality Talk: Antisubordination and Anticlassification Values in Constitutional Struggles over Brown." *Harvard Law Review* 117: 1470–547.

Silas, Faye A. 1985. "Meese Rips Court: Charges Unclear Direction." *American Bar Association Journal* 71: 17.

Silk, Leonard, and David Vogel. 1976. *Ethics and Profits: The Crisis of Confidence in American Business.* New York: Simon & Schuster.

Silva, Mark. 2006. "President Calls for Balance on Border; Seeks More Security, Guest-Worker Program." *Chicago Tribune,* May 16, C1.

Silverstein, Helena. 1996. *Unleashing Rights: Law, Meaning, and the Animal Rights Movement.* Ann Arbor: University of Michigan Press.

Simon, Stephanie. 2007. "Evangelical Agenda Fight Is Heating Up." *Los Angeles Times,* March 10, A1.

Simon, William E. 1978. *A Time for Truth.* New York: Readers Digest Press.

Simon, William H. 1978. "The Ideology of Advocacy: Procedural Justice and Professional Ethics." *Wisconsin Law Review* 1978: 29–144.

———. 2001. *The Community Economic Development Movement: Law, Business, and the New Social Policy.* Durham, NC: Duke University Press.

Singer, James W. 1979. "Liberal Public Interest Law Firms Face Budgetary, Ideological Challenges." *National Law Journal* 11: 2052–56.

Singer, Paul, and Lisa Caruso. 2005. "The Battle Is Joined." *National Law Journal,* July 9.

Smigel, Erwin O. 1964. *The Wall Street Lawyer: Professional Organization Man?* New York: Free Press of Glencoe.

Smith, Art. 1971. *Pro Bono Report to the ABA Section of Individual Rights and Responsibilities*

Smith, James A. 1991. *The Idea Brokers: Think Tanks and the Rise of the New Policy Elite.* New York: Free Press.

Snow, David A., and Richard Machalek. 1984. "The Sociology of Conversion." *Annual Review Sociology* 10: 367–80.

Soper, J. Christopher. 1994. *Evangelical Christianity in the United States and Great Britain: Religious Beliefs, Political Choices.* New York: New York University Press.

Sorauf, Frank J. 1976. *The Wall of Separation: The Constitutional Politics of Church and State.* Princeton, NJ: Princeton University Press.

Southworth, Ann. 1996. "Lawyer-Client Decisionmaking in Civil Rights and Poverty Practice: An Empirical Study of Lawyers' Norms." *Georgetown Journal of Legal Ethics* 9: 1101–55.

———. 1999. "Lawyers and the 'Myth of Rights' in Civil Rights and Poverty Practice." *Boston University Public Interest Law Journal* 8: 469–517.

———. 2000. "The Rights Revolution and Support Structures for Rights Advocacy." *Law and Society Review* 34: 1203–20.

———. 2005a. "Conservative Lawyers and the Contest over the Meaning of 'Public Interest Law.'" *UCLA Law Review* 52:1223–78.

———. 2005b. "Professional Identity and Political Commitment among Lawyers for Conservative Causes." In *The Worlds Cause Lawyers Make: Structure and Agency in Legal*

Practice, edited by Austin Sarat and Stuart Scheingold, 83–111. Stanford: Stanford University Press.

Spangler, Eve. 1986. *Lawyers for Hire: Salaried Professionals at Work.* New Haven: Yale University Press.

Spann, Girardeau A. 1993. *Race against the Court: The Supreme Court and Minorities in Contemporary America.* New York: New York University Press.

Sterling, Joyce, Bryant Garth, and Ronit Dinovitzer. 2007. "A Contemporary Picture of the Practice of Law: Views from the Inside." Paper presented at the annual meeting of the Law and Society Association, Berlin, July 25.

Spaulding, Norman. 2003. "Reinterpreting Professional Identity." *University of Colorado Law Review* 74: 1–104.

Stefancic, Jean, and Richard Delgado. 1996. *No Mercy: How Conservative Think Tanks and Foundations Changed America's Social Agenda.* Philadelphia, PA: Temple University Press.

Stevens, Mitchell L. 2001. *Kingdom of Children: Culture and Controversy in the Home-schooling Movement.* Princeton: Princeton University Press.

Stevens, Robert. 1983. *Law School: Legal Education in America from 1859 to the 1980s.* Chapel Hill: University of North Carolina Press.

Stewart, Richard B. 1975. "The Reformation of American Administrative Law." *Harvard Law Review* 88: 1669–813.

Stone, Alan. 1971. "Legal Education on the Couch." *Harvard Law Review* 85: 392–441.

Stover, Robert. 1989. *Making It and Breaking It: The Fate of Public Interest Commitment During Law School,* edited by Howard Erlanger. Urbana: University of Illinois.

Stryker, Robin. 1994. "Rules, Resources, and Legitimacy Processes: Some Implications for Social Conflict, Order and Change." *American Journal of Sociology* 1994: 847–910.

Sunstein, Cass R. 2005. *Radicals in Robes: Why Extreme Right-Wing Courts Are Wrong for America.* New York: Basic Books.

Teles, Steven. 2008. *The Rise of the Conservative Law Movement: The Battle for the Control of the Law.* Princeton, NJ: Princeton University Press.

Thomas, Dana L. 1976. "On the Right Side: The Pacific Legal Foundation Is Doing Yeoman Work." *Barron's,* February 2, 7.

Thomas, Landon. 2004. "Jay Van Andel, a Co-Founder of Amway, Dies at 80." *New York Times,* December 8, A29.

Tierney, John. 2006. "South Park Refugees." *New York Times,* August 29, A21.

Time. 2002. "A License to Revisit the Word 'Is,' That Will Be the Result if Clinton Keeps His Right to Practice Law." June 5, 47.

Tocqueville, de, Alexis. 1835. *Democracy in America.* Translated by Henry Reeve. Edited by Phillips Bradley. Revised by Francis Bowen. 1st ed. New York: Vintage Books. Reprint 1973.

Toner, Robin. 2001. "Conservatives Savor Their Role as Insiders at the White House." *New York Times,* Mar. 19, A1.

———. 2003. "For G.O.P., It's a Moment: Abortion Opponents' Strategy Is to Turn Tide of Opinion on Roe v. Wade, a Ripple at a Time." *New York Times,* November 6, A1.

———. 2006. "Optimistic, Democrats Debate the Party's Vision: Seeking Big Goals and a Clear Alternative to Conservatism." *New York Times,* May 9, A1.

Toobin, Jeffrey. 2005. "Swing Shift: How Anthony Kennedy's Passion for Foreign Law Could Change the Supreme Court." *New Yorker,* September 12, 42.

———. 2007. *The Nine: Inside the Secret World of the Supreme Court.* New York: Doubleday.

Tooley, Mark. 2006. "Nothing New under the Sun." *American Spectator,* July 31.

Tuohy, Lynne. 2002. "A Landmark Case on Land Rights." *Hartford Courant Company,* December 3, A1.

Trubek, Louise, and Elizabeth Kransberger. 1998. "Critical Lawyers: Social Justice and the Structures of Private Practice." In *Cause Lawyering: Political Commitments and Professional Responsibilities,* edited by Austin Sarat and Stuart Scheingold, 201–26. New York: Oxford University Press.

Turner, John. 1999. "Some Current Issues in Research on Social Identity and Self-categorization Theories." In *Social Identity: Context, Commitment, Content,* edited by Naomi Ellemers et al., 6–34. Oxford: Blackwell.

Tushnet, Mark V. 1984. "An Essay on Rights." *Texas Law Review* 62: 1363–403.

———. 1987. *The NAACP's Legal Strategy against Segregated Education, 1925–1950.* Chapel Hill, NC: University of North Carolina Press.

U.S. News & World Report. 2000. "Top Law Schools." http://www.usnews.com/usnews/edu/beyond/gradrank/law/gdlaw1.htm.

Van Biema, David. 1999. "Who Are Those Guys? The Secretive DeMoss Foundation Is Behind Those Power for Living Ads, and a Lot More." *Time Magazine,* August 9, 52.

Vogel, David. 1978. "Why Businessmen Distrust Their State: The Political Consciousness of American Corporate Executives." *British Journal of Political Science* 8: 45–78.

Vose, Clement E. 1959. *Caucasians Only: The Supreme Court, the NAACP, and the Restrictive Covenant Cases.* Berkeley, CA: University of California Press.

Wagner, Bridgett G., John E. Hilboldt, and Eric T. Korsvall. 2000. *Policy Experts 2000: A Guide to Public Policy Experts and Organizations.* Washington, DC: Heritage Foundation.

Wald, Patricia. 1995. "Frank M. Coffin Lecture on Law and Public Service: Whose Public Interest Is It Anyway? Advice for Altruistic Young Lawyers." *Maine Law Review* 47: 3–33.

Walker, Jack L. 1983. "The Origins and Maintenance of Interest Groups in America." *American Political Science Review* 77: 390–407.

Walker, Samuel. 1990. *In Defense of American Liberties: A History of the ACLU.* Carbondale: Southern Illinois University Press.

Wall Street Journal. 1981. "The Horowitz Report." March 19, A26.

Wallis, Jim. 2006. "A Defeat for the Religious Right and the Secular Left." *God's Politics,* November 9. http://belief.net/blogs/godspolitics/2006/11/jim-wallis-defeat-for-religious-right.html.

Wasby, Stephen L. 1995. *Race Relations Litigation in an Age of Complexity.* Charlottesville, VA: University Press of Virginia.

Wasserstrom, Richard. 1975. "Lawyers as Professionals: Some Moral Issues." *Human Rights* 5: 1.

Washington Legal Foundation. 2006. "Resources: WLF Mission." http://www.wlf.org/Resources/WLFMission/.

Weinstein, Henry. 1975. "Defending What? The Corporation's Public Interest." *Juris Doctor,* June, 39.

Weisbrod, Burton A., Joel F. Handler, and Neil K. Komesar. 1978. *Public Interest Law: An Economic and Institutional Analysis.* Berkeley, CA: University of California Press.

Weisman, Jonathan. 2005. "The Rift's Repercussions Could Last Rest of Term." *Washington Post,* October 28, A8.

Wexler, Stephen. 1970. "Practicing Law for Poor People." *Yale Law Journal* 79: 1049–67.

Whelan, Edward. 2007. "Not Credible 'Whatsoever.'" *National Review Online,* January 10.

White, Lucie E. 1988. "To Learn and Teach: Lessons from Driefontein on Lawyering and Power." *Wisconsin Law Review* 1988: 699–769.

———. 1990. "Subordination, Rhetorical Survival Skills, and Sunday Shoes: Notes on the Hearing of Mrs. G." *Buffalo Law Review* 38: 1–58.

———. 2001. "Symposium: Panel IIII: Creating Models for Progressive Lawyering in the 21st Century." *Journal of Law and Policy* 9: 297–334.

White, Michelle J. 1992. "Legal Complexity and Lawyers' Benefit from Litigation." *International Review of Law and Economics* 381–95.

Whitehead, John W. 1999. *Slaying Dragons: The Truth behind the Man Who Defended Paula Jones.* Nashville, TN: Thomas Nelson Publishers.

Whitman, Christine Todd. 2005. *It's My Party Too: The Battle for the Heart of the GOP and the Future of America.* New York: Penguin Press.

Who's Who In American Law. 2007–8. Chicago: Marquis Who's Who.

Wilkins, David B. 2000. "Beyond 'Bleached Out' Professionalism: Defining Professional Responsibility for Real Professionals." In *Ethics in Practice,* edited by Deborah Rhode, 207–39. New York: Oxford.

———. 2004a. "From 'Separate Is Inherently Unequal' to 'Diversity Is Good for Business': The Rise of Market-Based Diversity Arguments and the Fate of the Black Corporate Bar." *Harvard Law Review* 117: 1548–615.

———. 2004b. "Doing Well by Doing Good? The Role of Public Service in the Careers of Black Corporate Lawyers." *Houston Law Review* 41: 1–91.

Willis, Clint, and Nate Hardcastle. 2005. *Jesus Is Not a Republican: The Religious Right's War on America.* New York: Thunder's Mouth Press.

Wolfe, Alan. 1999. "Afterword." In *The Power Elite,* by C. Wright Mills. 2d ed. New York: Oxford University Press.

Wolfram, Charles. 1986. *Modern Legal Ethics.* Eagan, MN: West Group.

Zemans, F. K., and Victor Rosenblum. 1981. *The Making of a Public Profession.* Chicago: American Bar Foundation.

Ziv, Neta. 2001. "Lawyers, Clients, and the State: Congress as a Forum for Cause Lawyering during the Enactment of the Americans with Disabilities Act." In *Cause Lawyering and the State in a Global Era,* edited by Austin Sarat and Stuart Scheingold, 211–43. New York: Oxford University Press.

Zumbrun, Ronald. 2004. "Life, Liberty, and Property Rights." In *Bringing Justice to the People: The Story of the Freedom-Based Public Interest Law Movement,* edited by Lee Edwards, 41–53. Washington, DC: Heritage Books.

Index

Made in the USA
San Bernardino, CA
24 May 2019